THE
BOOK
OF
PINTXOS

MARTI
BUCKLEY

FOREWORD BY
JUAN MARI AND ELENA ARZAK

PHOTOGRAPHS BY
SIMON BAJADA

THE BOOK OF PINTXOS

DISCOVER THE LEGENDARY
SMALL BITES OF BASQUE COUNTRY

ARTISAN

ARTISAN • NEW YORK

Library of Congress Cataloging-in-Publication Data
Names: Buckley, Marti, author. | Arzak, Juan Mari, writer of foreword. |
Arzak, Elena, writer of foreword. | Bajada, Simon, photographer.
Title: The book of pintxos : discover the legendary small
bites of Basque country / Marti Buckley ; foreword by Juan Mari
and Elena Arzak ; photographs by Simon Bajada.
Description: New York : Artisan, [2023] | Includes index.
Identifiers: LCCN 2023032072 | ISBN 9781579659875 (hardback)
Subjects: LCSH: Tapas. | Cooking, Basque. | LCGFT: Cookbooks.
Classification: LCC TX740 .B753 2023 | DDC 641.81/2—dc23/eng/20230728
LC record available at https://lccn.loc.gov/2023032072

Design by Evi-O.Studio | Susan Le

Artisan books may be purchased in bulk for business, educational, or
promotional use. For information, please contact your local bookseller or the
Hachette Book Group Special Markets Department at special.markets@hbgusa.com.

The publisher is not responsible for websites (or their content)
that are not owned by the publisher.

Published by Artisan,
an imprint of Workman Publishing,
a division of Hachette Book Group, Inc.
1290 Avenue of the Americas
New York, NY 10104
artisanbooks.com

The Artisan name and logo are registered trademarks of Hachette Book Group, Inc.

Printed in China on responsibly sourced paper
First printing, March 2024

1 3 5 7 9 10 8 6 4 2

FOR THE

HARDWORKING PEOPLE

OF

BASQUE COUNTRY'S
PINTXO BARS

CHAPTER ONE

TOOTHPICK PINTXOS

35

CHAPTER TWO

BREAD PINTXOS

57

CHAPTER THREE

ENSALADILLA PINTXOS

103

Foreword

BY

Juan Mari and Elena Arzak

THE PINTXO. This small bite is so integral to our way of life in San Sebastián. Our family has made a life's work cooking here in the kitchen at Arzak, but we have spent a life's worth of time off in the bars of our city, whether we're grabbing a pastel de merluza after going for produce at La Bretxa or taking a night off to spend with friends, hopping from one pintxo bar to the next.

Pintxos are not just food. They are a way of life. Through the act of *poteo*, we share time with friends, we laugh, we enjoy— so much so that the history of this exquisite way of eating has remained a local secret, passed down in the form of gossip and local newspaper articles. Now, in *The Book of Pintxos*, we are so pleased to see the bars, the pintxos, and the people we know and love featured, along with their stories. Marti has taken these stories and presented them alongside their recipes with authenticity and rigor, unveiling the pintxo in dozens of our favorite recipes.

We are living in a time of rapid change, especially in the world of pintxos—older generations passing the torch, visitors to the city increasing every year, and the influx of new ideas greater than ever. That's why we feel this book is so important. It captures the recipes and stories that we know, that we have lived, but that don't always get written down.

Part of what makes a pintxo a pintxo is the context, the place, and the people, and that is what Marti shows us in this book. Her love for San Sebastián, Basque Country, and its food shines through her work, and we are proud to call her a *donostiarra*. Her book is a wonderful glimpse into the past, present, and future of the pintxo across Basque Country. Enjoy the cuisine of our city.

HIGOS
CON MOUSSE
DE QUESO
Y ANCHOAS
IRRINTZI

ABOVE Bar Irrintzi, Bilbao

Preface

PINTXOS ARE THE LIFEBLOOD of my adopted hometown, San Sebastián—they bring people together, serve as the raw material for urban legends, and are a source of pride for the locals.

I started writing this book after living in San Sebastián for nine years, enough time to have settled into a proverbial rut when it came to pintxos—from the bars I frequented to the pintxos I ate. I think it's part human nature, part physics; settling into a stasis where things are stable and unchanging. And it had happened to me.

Writing this book, however, demanded that I reopen my eyes—and my palate. It asked me to go to bars I had long since left off my route, not because they weren't worth a stop, but perhaps because I hadn't known their full context or tried their best pintxos. It allowed me to be curious again, like a child or a vacationer. It gave me the excuse to sit with the people who started the world of pintxos, the ones who revolutionized it, and the ones who still really, really care about it. I became obsessed with capturing their stories, which were disappearing quietly through changes, retirements, and then the COVID-19 pandemic.

The history of the pintxo, until now, has been more lived than cataloged, with few exceptions. The cities of San Sebastián, Bilbao, Pamplona, and Vitoria have evolved incredibly over the past century, but their culinary traces have faded along with the collective memory. Had this been a more navel-gazing area of the world, with a smoother twentieth-century history, perhaps that would not have been the case. So I set off gleefully to document the dishes and stories that connect the region's food and way of life.

Working on this book has given me hope for San Sebastián's food culture and traditions. While from the outside it may seem that things have changed, there are still plenty of bars and kitchens where things are the same as they've always been.

Writing the book also spurred me to ask myself, why are pintxos so good? That question has proved to have more than one answer: It's the superior raw materials of a land nestled between cold sea and fertile hills. It's the lifestyle, one lived in the street, that created an unwavering demand. It's a Nueva Cocina movement that lent legitimacy to cooking, trained chefs for the wider workforce, and adopted new techniques. It's the controversial yet important competitions and the institutional support from associations and local governments. But I think, above all, it's the joy the Basques derive from sharing food with each other. And my hope is that with this book, you can partake of both their history and their delicious pintxos. *On egin!*

Introduction

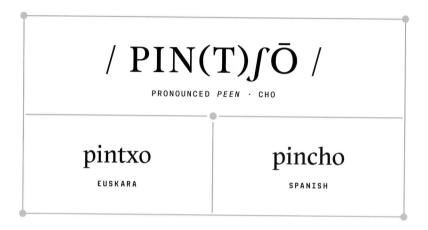

/ PIN(T)ʃŌ /

PRONOUNCED *PEEN* · CHO

pintxo

EUSKARA

pincho

SPANISH

DEFINITION ACCORDING TO THE REAL ACADEMIA ESPAÑOLA, or the Royal Spanish Academy: *porción de comida tomada como aperitivo, que a veces se atraviesa con un palillo.*

A pintxo is, as this arbiter of the Spanish language says, "a portion of food taken as an appetizer, which is sometimes pierced with a toothpick." Easy enough to understand and clear as day. If, however, the truth were as cut and dried as the dictionary would have you believe, you probably wouldn't be holding this book in your hands.

Pintxos are small bites of food, yes, and sometimes they indeed sport a toothpick skewered through their center. But the truth is, pintxos are a way of life, specific to a very small corner of the world, the Spanish side of Basque Country. A pintxo without a bar is not a pintxo. A pintxo without a drink

and a friend or barman to talk to is like the proverbial tree falling in the forest with no one to hear it—is it real? Pintxos are not only a "what," they are where you eat them and what you are doing while you eat them—they are inextricable from their cultural context.

Pintxos were born in San Sebastián in the early 1900s and have slowly evolved into the marvelous tiny pieces of culinary art they are today. It's high time they have a definition for the twenty-first century:

PIN · TXO / **PIN(T)ʃŌ** / *N.*: a small portion of food that can be consumed in two or three bites, served in a bar in the Basque region of northern Spain. Pintxos were traditionally served on a toothpick or bread, meant to be eaten with one's hands, but the name now also includes avant-garde miniature dishes eaten with a fork, spoon, and/or knife.

ABOVE Bodegón Sarria, Pamplona

ABOVE Gandarias, San Sebastián

ABOVE Bar Toloño, Vitoria

ABOVE Bar Gaucho, Pamplona

PINTXOS VERSUS TAPAS

Is the word *pintxo* just a Basque-flavored synonym for *tapa*? The short answer is a resounding no. So, what is the difference between a pintxo and a tapa? The Real Academia Española (Royal Spanish Academy) isn't much help when it comes to answering this question, defining them this way: tapas are small and always eaten with drinks, while pintxos are pointedly eaten before a meal and sometimes feature items skewered with a toothpick. The question of the difference between the two is a classic one, but the answer is wide-ranging. It becomes an even stickier situation when one considers the evolution of pintxos and of tapas and the blurring of lines between small plates and haute cuisine dishes. Many claim that if the bite must be eaten with a fork, spoon, and/or knife or is served on a plate, it is a tapa, but that is frankly not the reality in Basque Country today. In recent years, the points of contrast between the pintxo and the tapa have shifted. Here are some of the basic differences; note, though, that while they are accurate, they are also generalizations, so there are always exceptions.

1

The cost

While this practice is less and less common, tapas are sometimes served free with drinks. That is unheard of in pintxo bars; pintxos are always paid for.

2

The composition

Traditionally tapas are a single-food item, served in small-plate portions, while pintxos tend to be more elaborate combinations of ingredients or dishes, ranging from humble to avant-garde.

3

The size

Pintxos are often made in smaller portions than tapas.

4

The moment

Until very recently, unlike tapas, pintxos would never be eaten as a meal. They were always to be eaten before a meal as an appetizer.

5

The situation

While there is some deviation nowadays, traditionally pintxos have been eaten standing up, while tapas are generally eaten sitting down at a table.

6

The where

Pintxos are most often found in Basque Country and the surrounding provinces; the word *tapa* is more common in the rest of Spain.

About This Book

WHEN I SET OUT TO WRITE the definitive book on pintxos, I had a single mission: to capture the pintxo scene from its birth to the current day. Because of the sheer quantity of pintxos you can find on the region's bar counters, I wasn't able to include all the best bites in Basque Country, but I've included many of the most well-known favorites.

This book is designed for home cooks, wherever they may be. The recipes it offers are unavailable anywhere else in such detail—many of them have until now lived only in the heads of cooks working day in and day out in the tiny kitchens of Basque Country. The book includes step-by-step recipes in eight chapters, organized by type of pintxo. The chapters loosely trace the evolution of the pintxo starting with its first iteration, served on toothpicks (page 35), and changing drastically as ingredients found newer vehicles for presentation, from bread (page 57) to puff pastry (page 203) to fancy dishware. The creative revolution begins to show its face in the Bar Pintxos chapter (page 161), and the story continues to develop as pintxos are served hot from the kitchen (page 229) and even as desserts (page 285).

Within each chapter, the recipes are generally presented in chronological order according to when they first appeared on the scene. The recipes are accompanied by their origin stories along with the history of the bar where they were first served. Traditionally these bars have been run by families that work nonstop and have never had time to commit their stories and recipes to paper. This is the first time they have been gathered in one place, giving you both context and detailed instructions on how to re-create them. At the start of each recipe, I've listed when and where the pintxo was created and what the bar owners themselves recommend you drink with it. Along the way, you'll also find ingredient tips, glimpses into pintxo culture, and instructions on how to best enjoy each pintxo.

Amounts are given both in volume measures—the cups and tablespoons (and sometimes ounces) that are familiar to American cooks—and in metric measures, grams and milliliters, the measurements of choice in the Basque region. I've included a Resources guide (page 302) for the more hard-to-find ingredients.

Pintxos, first and foremost, are about fun. My hope is that with this book in hand, you'll not only be able to re-create some of Basque Country's best pintxos, you'll also have the information and tools you need to riff on them and make them your own. And that someday you'll come to enjoy pintxos in their natural habitat: a crowded Basque bar.

α Note

IN SPAIN, pintxos with names that consist of a description of their ingredients may be ordered in Spanish or in the Basque language, Euskara, depending on the linguistic preference of the person ordering. For pintxos with a proper name, the Spanish (not the Basque) is generally used when ordering. In this book, however, I've included both the Spanish and the Basque names for many of these dishes. I chose to do this when the pintxo's name has a significant meaning, such as El Velero (*belaontzia* in Basque, meaning "sailboat"), which helps to give the pintxo context. Proper names such as Gilda and Filomena have generally not been translated. In fact, though, very few pintxos were ever given proper names in the Basque language, and the only example of one in this book is Limoia Ber Bi (page 294); in this case, the Basque has been translated to Spanish.

The Basque language is ancient and mysterious, and on paper, it can be slightly intimidating. Take the word *pintxo*—the "tx" combination is the hardest to wrap your head around, but it's really nothing more than a simple "ch" sound, every time. Z, a common consonant, is pronounced as a soft, snakelike "ess." The combination of "tz" sounds like the double "zz" in the word *pizza*. The "tt" is quite difficult to pronounce; it has a strange sound like a wet, muffled version of "tx"—when in doubt, pronounce it as "ch."

On the Spanish side of Basque Country, Euskara is one of two official languages, along with Spanish, so one will find place-names given in both Spanish and Basque. Sometimes they are similar (as in the Spanish *Zarauz* and the Basque *Zarautz*), and sometimes they are totally unrelated (as in the Spanish *Vitoria* and the Basque *Gasteiz*). In this book, you will find a mix of Basque and Spanish place-names, just like in the larger cities where the pintxo was born and evolved.

THE PINTXO
COMMANDMENTS

The Institute of the Pintxo was formed in 2019 to help define and protect the pintxo as a cultural identity marker. The committee of local celebrities and chefs that established the institute combined their singular vision to create a Ten Commandments–style set of requisites for a true pintxo:

4

With a personality that reflects its establishment.

2

MADE IN-HOUSE

i.e., not commercially.

1

Small in size with a lot of flavor.

3

At the forefront of creativity and evolution.

5

A fresh bar counter and

HOT PINTXOS

made à la minute.

7

Friendly, professional service behind the bar.

9

Eaten at the bar counter.

6

Made with high-quality ingredients.

8

With a clearly marked price that reflects its quality.

10

ENJOYED

in company, with locals and in an authentic

BASQUE

ambience.

THE HISTORY OF THE PINTXO

Pintxos didn't just spontaneously appear in all their glory across the bartops of San Sebastián's Old Town. They've been evolving over the past century, catching on and changing with trends, tastes, and sociopolitical and economic influences. And they didn't get to be so good by accident. Here's how it happened, as told by those who have lived it.

1920s ↓ 1960s

The Birth

Pinpointing the birth of the pintxo is not just difficult, it's impossible. It is often said that the first pintxo was the Gilda (page 39), and that it was created in the bar Casa Vallés in 1946. However, posters advertising "hot and cold" banderillas (the original name for toothpick pintxos) at Bar Nido, where they were served by the great-grandmother of the present-generation owners of La Espiga (see page 64), date back to 1920. A pintxo more or less identical to the Gilda appears in a photo in Bar Martínez from the early 1940s. And, to get quite nitpicky about it, Rita Hayworth's movie *Gilda*, which inspired the name, didn't appear in Spain until its premiere in Madrid two days before Christmas Day in 1947. The urban legend of the Gilda likely originates from an article in the local paper, *Diario Vasco*, written in 2007. Who doesn't love a tidy origin story, after all?

"It's a black hole in history; nobody knows the how or the why."

—JESÚS CASTRO, LA ESPIGA, ON THE BIRTH OF THE PINTXO

But the real origin of the pintxo is a lot more, well, alcohol-fueled and ambiguous. In the early decades of the twentieth century, the streets of San Sebastián were filled with ultramarinos, sidrerías, and bodeguillas. These shops sold foodstuffs, hard cider, and bulk wine by the glass, jar, or bottle. Bodega Donostiarra, a now-classic pintxo bar, opened its first bulk wine shop in 1924 on Calle 31 de Agosto, where people would bring their own snacks to eat with their wine, and where the grandfather of Manu Marañón (see page 72) invented the Jardinera, serving anchovies to clients. Bar Nido, La Espiga, Ezkurra, and a few others also opened their doors around this time. The tradition of *poteo*, going from bar to bar to have a *pote* (glass) of wine, was born.

The Spanish Civil War (1936–1939) wreaked havoc and caused extreme poverty throughout the country. In the 1940s, the Old Town of San Sebastián was still a mess of muddy streets, donkeys, and their attendant flies. It also, however, saw the opening of some now-legendary bars: Martínez, Casa Tiburcio, Paco Bueno, Casa Alcalde, and La Cueva, among others. The tradition of pintxo hopping started with the movements among these shops and bars called *txikiteo*, a custom in which *kuadrillas*, groups of Basque friends, would meet after work or on the weekend and go from place to place before lunch and dinner, taking turns paying for rounds of *txikitos*, small glasses of wine served in thick-bottomed tumblers. The typical ten to thirty rounds of txikitos were considered par for the course, but of course that would have been a bit too much without something to line the stomach—enter pintxos. At first these could be simply hard-boiled eggs (el huevo del txikitero is a Bilbao institution), olives, or grilled sardines, in the case of the cider houses, but they were eventually laced together with toothpicks and given the name *banderillas*.

Times were still tough after the war—you'll find accounts of Gildas made with only half an anchovy each and potatoes replacing bread as the base—but better days came after World War II. Basque Country began its march toward the industrial powerhouse it is today, and a newly salaried citizenry stepped out to spend their earnings. This is when pintxos began to slowly shift from a mere afterthought to a trend. The foundations of pintxos were set: part of a social act, enjoyed standing up and on the move, as a precursor to a "real" meal, taken at family-run bars or taverns.

1920s → 1960s

ABOVE Paco Bueno, San Sebastián

ABOVE Bar Martínez, San Sebastián

1960s ↓ 1980s

The Evolution

"Ahh, they don't have more than three or four Gildas!"

—JOSÉ IGNACIO,
GANBARA, AND
A PHRASE HE COINED
FOR BARS WITHOUT
A SATISFACTORY
PINTXO SELECTION

The toothpick, the bread, the hopping from bar to bar—all this formed the reality of the pintxo entering into the 1960s. It was a time of contrast, of evolution, of past and present overlapping. A poster went up in Bar Martínez prohibiting bringing outside food in, signaling a transition from serving just alcohol to offering food as well. María Salud at La Cueva, one of the first pintxo bars in the Old Town of San Sebastián, went beyond chorizo on bread, serving Moorish kebabs (page 237) and gambas al ajillo, turning heads and spawning dozens of copycats. At that time, La Cueva was nestled not below a dining society and a jai alai court, as it is now, but under a chicken and rabbit abattoir, and it wasn't uncommon for customers to have to pick up the occasional escaped chicken head as it rolled onto the terrace.

More bars dedicating themselves to pintxos began to open in San Sebastián's Old Town, like Astelena, with its mouthwatering selection of freshly made toasts, squid, battered asparagus, and stuffed peppers. This is when *pincho*, from the Spanish word for "to skewer," came to replace the term *banderilla* in popular usage, a change some say was spurred by visitors from the rest of Spain. By the 1970s, each bar had become known for its signature pintxo—more competition meant the need to stand out, in part by seeking out fancier products like txaka (king crab; see page 111) and setting their pintxos on the bar to tempt clients. Nevertheless, making pintxos was still considered just another job—not glamorous, not for recognition, sometimes even relegated to the cleaning lady.

Throughout the 1970s, the price of pintxos began to rise in San Sebastián's Old Town. Its other neighborhoods, though, as well as the surrounding Basque capitals, were just waking up. In Gros, a newer neighborhood whose far corners were still a bit of a wasteland, Aloña and Hidalgo opened, precursors to Aloña Berri (see page 182) and Hidalgo 56 (see page 261). Bar Eme (see page 171) planted its roots in what was then middle-of-nowhere Bilbao, Pamplona served up its first pintxos, and Vitoria pioneered fried foods on a stick at Trafalgar (see page 83), an early outpost of that city's pintxo movement.

And in the early 1980s, the son of the owners of Hidalgo, Juan Mari, presented the first menu of hot pintxos in San Sebastián, consisting of individual-sized versions of their cazuelitas and raciones. Change, and an appetite for novelty, was in the air.

1980s
↓
2010s

The Golden Age

As Spain emerged from the decades-long Franco dictatorship, a hungry public created new demand for pintxos. Murmurs about the increasingly elaborate bites grew among professionals in the hospitality sector, further amplified in 1989 by a restaurant seminar organized by the Cofradía Vasca de Gastronomía, where thirteen local bars displayed their banderillas and pintxos, as well as by the I Concurso de Banderillas de Gipuzkoa, the first Competition of Banderillas in Gipuzkoa.

The pintxo, propelled by growing consumer demand and buying power, did what it does best—captivated the hearts, minds, and stomachs of anyone in its path. It also proved to be an economic boon, and it didn't take long for bars from Gros to Bilbao to start copying the trend. Bar owners like José Ramón Elizondo (see page 182) and Patxi Bergara and his wife, Blanca (see page 216), gave the pintxo the Nueva Cocina Vasca treatment, combining Basque tradition with haute cuisine techniques, and real innovation began to take place beyond Old Town. In 1992, *Pintxos Donostiarras* by Pedro Martín Villa was published, and it served as a blueprint for all of Basque Country.

All this coincided with a decline in political violence and a boom in tourism, especially toward the turn of the century. With the outsiders came further changes. In 1989, Txakoli was given its own Denominación de Origen, Getariako Txakolina, raising the quality of what had once been a rough table wine, and the wines served at pintxo bars began to improve dramatically. A full bar attracted clientele, and so the bars in the more touristy parts of the Basque capitals began to stack plates of pintxos practically on top of one another, random combinations of bread, preserves, and cheese, with paper signs describing the dozens of pintxos available.

On December 21, 1999, the Day of Santo Tomás, a tiny bar quietly opened in a corner of San Sebastián's Old Town with nothing set out on the counter and just a chalkboard menu. But the pintxos that came out of the kitchen at La Cuchara de San Telmo (see page 251) were revolutionary, and they marked yet another turning point in the evolution of the pintxo. Chefs from the world of haute cuisine began to shift their gaze to the pintxo's

"The pintxo has moved gradually, almost without us realizing, from the slice of bread to the plate. It has freed itself from that oval corset upon which it undeniably had to be placed, in order to be developed in different formats. The pintxo is no longer something you take with your hand, it no longer stains our lapels. You order it, you wait, and you eat it with a fork and knife."

—JOSEMA AZPEITIA,
PINTXOS DE VANGUARDIA A LA DONOSTIARRA

possibilities, experimenting with new techniques and ingredients. A pintxo no longer had to be something that was just a companion for a drink, eaten with one's hands; it could be a bit of braised meat with a lovely, shiny demi-glace—a miniature portion of what would normally be a main event. That opened the door to the idea of eating pintxos as a meal, a true sea change for this style of eating. It also led, inevitably, to the creation of sweet pintxos, something that would have been unimaginable mere decades before.

As menus of hot pintxos spread, the world of molecular gastronomy began to make its appearance as well. No longer having to display pintxos on the bartops opened up the possibilities significantly. Bars across Basque Country began to experiment with gels, foams, and spherifications in pintxo format, spurred on by the trophies now on offer at annual pintxo competitions across the region. The innovative A Fuego Negro (see page 157) pulled the pintxo to uncharted frontiers, from salads to soups in shot glasses, along with black napkins and extra-long toothpicks. Those years truly seemed like the golden age of the pintxo—the sky was the limit, many chefs and owners were in it for the love of the game, and the locals of San Sebastián and beyond embraced the ever-changing pintxo with curiosity and a good appetite.

1980s → 2010s

ABOVE Bar Charly, Pamplona

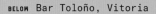

ABOVE La Cuchara de San Telmo,
San Sebastián

ABOVE PerretxiCo, Vitoria

2010s

↓

THE PRESENT

The Current State

"There's demand. In any neighborhood, you can find a blackboard with a list of hot pintxos. Quality can vary, but the pintxo has spread far and wide."

—PAUL ARRILLAGA, ZAZPI, ON THE FUTURE OF THE PINTXO

By the 2010s, innovation in the creation of pintxos seemed to have come to a head. Tourism levels in Basque Country reached new heights, encouraged by government-led promotions and, at least nationally, by a ceasefire that gradually resulted in a disarmament of ETA, the Basque separatist group. This period coincided with a changing of the guard of sorts—many of the cooks, couples, and families that had been behind their bars for thirty or forty years were ready to retire, and often they had no one to take their place. Also disappearing were the last groups of txikiteros; and the fallout from the 2008 recession, along with healthier eating habits, left the streets and the bars less crowded with locals than ever before.

The internet has also revolutionized the pintxo map. Tourists are a larger part of the clientele, and they come with their route already planned out or hop onto one of the many pintxo tours. Atari (see page 297) became a magnet for both foreigners and locals and could sell up to a thousand bar pintxos in a single summer service. What was formerly a foreign entity, the restaurant group, has begun to sprout up in San Sebastián and Bilbao, buying up various pintxo bars and preparing most of their pintxos in a central location—great for economics, not so much for character. In 2004, the phenomenon of "pintxo pote" was born in Vitoria when ten bars came together to offer a pintxo and a drink for a euro during a specified period each afternoon. The concept spread like wildfire, reaching its pinnacle in the neighborhood of Gros in San Sebastián, where it remains a Thursday-night event that features a drink and a pintxo (typically of low quality) for €2, and while it has drawn large crowds, it is missing the culinary spirit that defines the pintxo.

Today locals are looking toward preserving the pintxo, rather than innovating it. The Institute of the Pintxo was founded in 2019 to set ground rules for what defines a good-quality pintxo. And its creation came just in time—the COVID-19 pandemic, which effectively shut down Spain, put the pintxo in serious danger. Eating small bites left out in the open air elbow to elbow with strangers may be the least pandemic-friendly way of dining in the world. Pintxo bars were shuttered, and then cautiously reopened with table seating only, a crushing blow for the tiny bars of Basque Country. Several bars closed permanently or changed owners due to a well-timed retirement. Today the story of the pintxo is still evolving, but the ritual has more fans and fierce defenders than ever.

HOW TO EAT PINTXOS LIKE A LOCAL

Should you find yourself at a pintxo bar in Basque Country, there are a few rules you should observe:

1 DON'T BE SHY. Depending on the neighborhood, the establishment, and the time of day, you may need to weave your way through a crowd to get to the bar. Be polite, but don't be timid! Make eye contact with the bartenders if they're busy, so they know you are waiting.

2 EAT STANDING UP. Pintxos are meant to be eaten standing up at the bar.

3 ONE BAR, ONE PINTXO, ONE DRINK. The idea behind the pintxo is to keep moving. Locals have a drink and a pintxo to match, and then move on to the next bar. OK, maybe they have two pintxos— but do *not* order five at the first bar you walk into!

4 TRY THE SPECIALTY. If you don't know what pintxo a bar is famous for, ask the waiter, or simply look around. The best bars have one special item that everyone stops in for.

5 NAPKINS ON THE GROUND. Discreetly tossing your used napkins under the bar is the norm. It is considered more hygienic than leaving dirty napkins on the counter with the pintxos.

6 DON'T PAY UNTIL YOU HAVE FINISHED EATING. You shouldn't be asked to settle up before you are finished. But be sure to keep track of what you've ordered, as you will likely be asked even if the waiter knows.

7 CHAT AND RUB ELBOWS. The whole point of pintxos is to socialize. If you don't have a companion, strike up a conversation with someone next to you.

31

COMPETITIONS

There are innumerable pintxo competitions, from the Traditional Pintxo Championship to the Idiazabal Cheese Pintxo Contest—it seems like every village has its own version. Critics claim the contest world is now a mess of sponsors and chefs who present pintxos that have never seen the light of a pintxo bar. However, love them or hate them, pintxo contests have had the undeniable effect of spurring innovation and effort behind the bar.

The contests were started in order to institutionalize criteria for high-quality pintxos, and having world-famous, Michelin-starred chefs passing judgment on pintxos was major for the pintxo's reputation. Many bar owners acknowledge that pintxo competitions were the impetus for them to become more creative, especially at the beginning.

ABOVE Awards on display at Bar Bergara, San Sebastián

They had the added effect of spreading knowledge before cell phones and the internet existed, enabling chefs to be aware of and keep abreast of trends.

At these often days-long competitions, chefs and bar owners prepare their pintxos for a sitting jury of chefs and journalists, who score the entries and deliberate to decide the winner. The earliest recorded mention of a pintxo contest is in the Centro de Atracción y Turismo Report from 1971, which references the Primer Concurso de Banderillas de San Sebastián, won by La Espiga. However, there is no evidence of further competitions until the Concurso de Banderillas de Gipuzkoa in 1989. Pamplona hosted its first contest, I Concurso de Pinchos y Banderillas, in 1992, which in 1996 was succeeded by the Feria del Pintxo, whose winner was determined by popular vote instead of by a jury of professionals.

Here are the major pintxo contests by region.

BASQUE COUNTRY

◆

Campeonato de Pintxos
de Euskal Herria

Est. 2006

ARABA

◆

Semana del Pintxo de Álava

Est. 2014

Preceded by Concurso Alavés
de Pinchos y Banderillas

Est. 1993

GIPUZKOA

◆

Campeonato de Pintxos,
Banderillas y Cocina en
Miniatura de Gipuzkoa

Est. 2021

Campeonato de Pintxos
de Gipuzkoa

Est. 1999

NAVARRA

◆

La Semana del Pincho

Est. 1999

BIZKAIA

◆

Campeonato de Pintxos
de Bizkaia

Est. 2017

Preceded by Concurso de
Pintxos de Bilbao Bizkaia

Est. 1997

SPAIN
(Valladolid)

◆

Concurso Nacional
de Pinchos y Tapas

Est. 2005

TOOTHPICK

CHAPTER ONE

PINTXOS

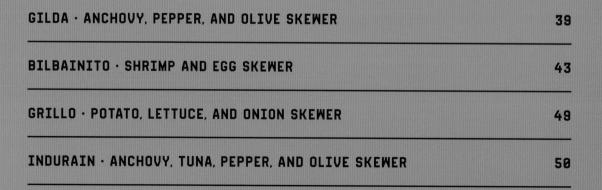

If this book is a bible of pintxos, then this chapter is most certainly the book of Genesis. While the characteristics that define a pintxo can be slippery at times, and controversial at others, no one will ever argue against two or three ingredients laced onto a toothpick being a pintxo. Why? Because that is how this entire way of eating began.

The word *pintxo* comes from the Spanish verb *pinchar*, meaning "to prick, poke, inject, needle, or stab." And indeed, the first incarnation of this type of miniature cuisine is the visual manifestation of the verb: nothing more than a pantry staple or two skewered on a wooden toothpick. Beautiful in its simplicity, this ground zero of the pintxo is anonymous in its origin, despite the many urban legends that nail it down to one moment or another. The most popular tale conveniently sets the invention of the first pintxo in Casa Vallés, in San Sebastián, in the 1940s, by a clever man named Txepetxa. Photographic proof from years earlier, however, disproves this theory. The truth is that no one knows who was the first to string together pickled vegetables, olives, cured fish, and anything else lying around on a sharp stick.

Nowadays toothpick pintxos aren't nearly as common, having been pushed aside to make room for flashier versions. But that doesn't take away from their perfection as an appetite awakener, as well as their ease factor. Any number of combinations is possible, using myriad ingredients—such as salted anchovies, cured tuna, pickled peppers, cocktail onions, and sun-dried tomatoes, to name some of the most popular.

This style of pintxo was originally called *banderilla*, a reference to the barbed sticks used in bullfighting. The literal translation is "small flag," which is fitting—nothing feels quite as patriotic as skewering together some of Basque Country's best foodstuffs into a beautiful, vinegary band of color . . . and then biting into it.

Gilda

ANCHOVY, PEPPER, AND OLIVE SKEWER

If a bar has only one pintxo on offer, it's likely to be the Gilda. The Gilda is nothing more than guindilla pepper, cured anchovy, and green olive served on a stick, yet this specific combination has eclipsed all other toothpick pintxos, thanks in no small part to its savvy link to Rita Hayworth's character in the eponymous 1946 film. Urban legends calling the Gilda the first pintxo, or attributing its invention to Casa Vallés (see page 40), are just that: legends. However, it is true that this was one of the first bites to grace the bartops of San Sebastián, with evidence dating it as far back as the 1920s. The key to making the best Gilda is the selection of ingredients: the guindilla should be delicate, thin, and smooth; the anchovy should have no visible bones; and the olive oil should be extra-virgin and fresh.

MAKES 4

8 pickled guindilla peppers
    (see below)
8 green manzanilla olives, pitted
4 anchovy fillets packed in olive oil,
    preferably Cantabrian
Good-quality extra-virgin olive oil
    for drizzling

Cut the stems off the peppers. Cut each pepper crosswise in half.

With a long toothpick, pierce one olive through its center, followed by 2 pieces of pepper. Add an anchovy, threading it onto the toothpick in an S shape. Add 2 more pieces of pepper and finish with another olive. Repeat with the remaining ingredients to make 3 more Gildas.

Serve at room temperature on a platter, drizzled generously with olive oil.

NOTE

Choose your toothpick wisely. While flat toothpicks were originally used to make pintxos, both the size and the aesthetic complexity of the pintxo have evolved since then. The best pintxo toothpick is around 4 inches (10 cm) long and has only one pointed end, which is used to pierce the ingredients.

PIPARRAK / GUINDILLA PEPPERS / GUINDILLAS

The most celebrated guindillas, a type of pepper in the *Capsicum frutescens* species, are grown in and around the village of Ibarra and begin to appear in Basque markets at the beginning of summer. They are a bright, verdant green, with smooth, tender skin, and can be anywhere from 2 to 6 inches (5 to 15 cm) long. In season, fresh guindillas are typically flash-fried or pickled for use year-round, and they are a vital addition to many traditional pintxos, such as the Gilda. The closest substitution would be pickled banana peppers, although their texture and flavor are somewhat different.

CASA VALLÉS, SAN SEBASTIÁN

✦

Casa Vallés holds a hallowed place in the slim written history of the pintxo, thanks to a local newspaper article that attributed the invention of the Gilda to the bar. Regardless of the veracity of this urban legend, Casa Vallés is one of San Sebastián's oldest still-functioning pintxo bars. Blas Vallés, a winemaker from Olite in Navarra, founded the bar in 1942 as a place to sell the wine he produced (records show that wine had been sold in the same location as early as 1936). The bar has long been an object of affection and even debate among donostiarras (the Basque term for residents of San Sebastián). In 1973, the bar caught fire and the owners had to throw out more than a hundred hams that were damaged in the blaze. The city was abuzz that March with a debate about whether these hams couldn't just have been sold as a peculiar "smoked" variety.

The bar has been in the same family for four generations, and it still retains a feeling of authenticity. The interior, with terrazzo flooring and a slatted wooden bar and walls, is hung with cured hams and medieval-looking chandeliers, giving it the impression of being frozen in time. And in a way, it is—the most classic of pintxos still top its bar, along with plates of sandwiches, with jars of preserves and hunks of cheese in the corner.

Banderillas and Bullfighting

❖

Toothpick pintxos, with their piles of
colorful ingredients, are said to resemble
banderillas, the barbed sticks used in
bullfighting that are wrapped with colorful
paper easily visible to the crowd in the
bullring. A traditional Spanish bullfight
has three separate parts, and the middle
one is the tercio de banderillas, in which
the matador or the banderilleros go after
the bull, intent on driving the sharp end
of the stick into its back and shoulders
and reenergizing it for the final face-off.

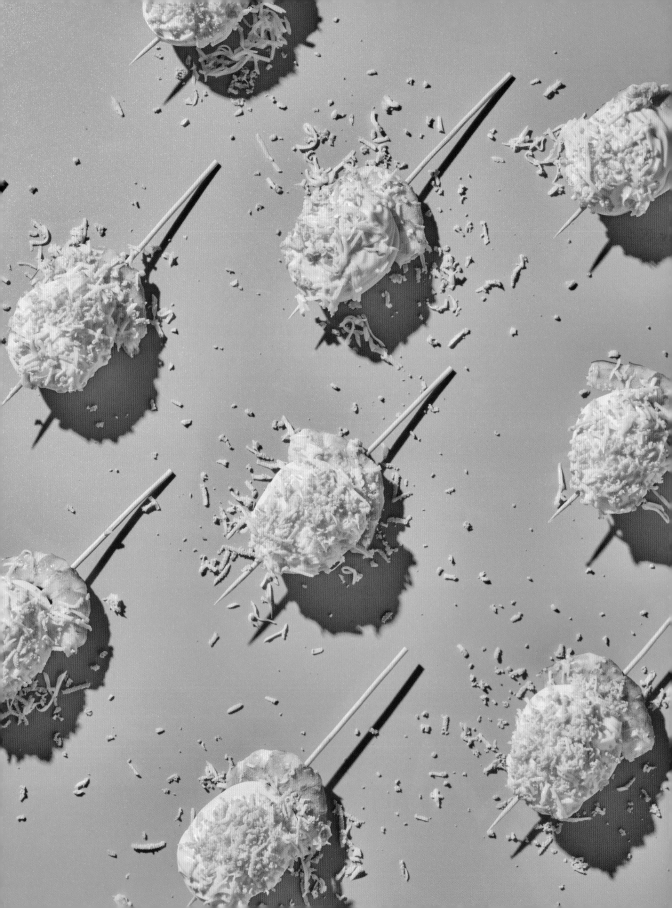

Bilbainito

SHRIMP AND EGG SKEWER

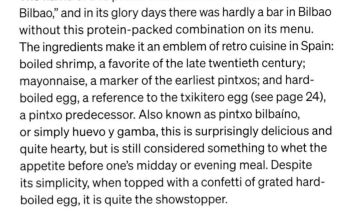

The name of this pintxo translates to "the little one from Bilbao," and in its glory days there was hardly a bar in Bilbao without this protein-packed combination on its menu. The ingredients make it an emblem of retro cuisine in Spain: boiled shrimp, a favorite of the late twentieth century; mayonnaise, a marker of the earliest pintxos; and hard-boiled egg, a reference to the txikitero egg (see page 24), a pintxo predecessor. Also known as pintxo bilbaíno, or simply huevo y gamba, this is surprisingly delicious and quite hearty, but is still considered something to whet the appetite before one's midday or evening meal. Despite its simplicity, when topped with a confetti of grated hard-boiled egg, it is quite the showstopper.

MAKES 6

4 large eggs
Kosher salt
6 large shrimp
¾ cup (165 g) mayonnaise, preferably homemade (recipe follows)

SPECIAL EQUIPMENT

A pastry bag fitted with a decorative piping tip (optional)

Bring a large saucepan of water to a boil. Carefully lower the eggs into the water and cook for 12 minutes, maintaining a gentle boil. Drain the eggs, run under cold water to stop the cooking, and let cool.

Gently crack and peel the eggs. Cut 3 of the eggs lengthwise in half; leave the remaining egg whole.

Bring a large pot of heavily salted water (it should taste like the ocean) to a boil over high heat. Meanwhile, fill a large bowl with equal parts ice and salted water. When the water is boiling, add the shrimp and cook for 2 minutes. Remove the shrimp with a slotted spoon and transfer to the ice bath. Allow the shrimp to cool completely, then drain and peel, removing and discarding the shells and heads (if any). Devein the shrimp if desired.

With a long toothpick, pierce one shrimp through its center, followed by one egg half (skewer it lengthwise so that the toothpick pierces the white twice). Repeat with the remaining shrimp and egg halves.

Arrange the pintxos on a serving platter. Place a generous dollop of mayonnaise on top of each one (use a pastry bag fitted with a decorative piping tip for a refined retro effect). Using the medium-small holes of a box grater, grate the remaining egg over the pintxos to finish. Serve at room temperature.

CONTINUED →

Mayonesa Casera

HOMEMADE MAYONNAISE

MAKES ABOUT 1 CUP (220 G)

1 large egg, at room temperature
¾ cup (180 ml) sunflower or other neutral oil
Juice of ½ lemon, at room temperature, or more to taste
Pinch of salt, or more to taste

Crack the egg into a tall cylindrical container and add the oil, lemon juice, and salt. Insert an immersion blender into the container so it touches the bottom and, without moving it at all, blend on the lowest setting to emulsify the ingredients. When the mayonnaise is almost totally emulsified, move the blender slowly up and down to fully incorporate the remaining oil. (Alternatively, combine the egg, lemon juice, and salt in a conventional blender and, with the blender running, slowly stream in the oil through the hole in the lid.)

Taste for seasoning, adding more salt and/or lemon juice if necessary. If the mayonnaise is too thick, stir in a bit of water.

Use immediately or transfer to an airtight container and store in the refrigerator for up to 3 days.

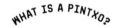

WHAT IS A PINTXO?

"Until recently, you didn't make pintxos to be the best or for a contest—it was your job. Just like cabinetmakers, there were pintxo makers."

—ANDER GONZÁLEZ, ASTELENA

SAN SEBASTIÁN

ABOVE Bar Txepetxa, San Sebastián

San Sebastián, the Basque capital, is where pintxos began. A city of just under 180,000 people, Donostia (as it is known in Euskara) somehow manages to have it all. The city's mixture of belle epoque and modern architecture butts up against the crescent-shaped shoreline of La Concha Bay, which is framed by beautifully green mountains that rise rather dramatically from the ocean.

Since it became a favored vacation spot for the Spanish monarchy at the turn of the nineteenth century, the city has relied on commerce and tourism as its main industries. The wealthy traveling class also exposed the city to a high level of cuisine very early on, when royals and noblemen would bring their French or French-trained chefs along with them. Their knowledge rubbed off, and some of these chefs even stayed behind, beginning what would be San Sebastián's march to global culinary fame.

The tradition of the city's pintxos has its nexus in the Parte Vieja (Alde Zaharra in Euskara), the Old Town. Other neighborhoods, such as the glitzy Centro and the seaside Gros, have also played an important part in the history of the pintxo and are still home to some of the city's best pintxo bars. These bars stay afloat not because of tourism but because of local clients—this is a city where people are obsessed with food. From the fresh markets to the festival days, everything centers around eating, appropriately enough in a city that claims to have held, off and on, the world title for both number of bars and number of Michelin stars per capita.

ABOVE San Sebastián

ABOVE Bar Martínez, San Sebastián

BELOW Calle 31 de Agosto, San Sebastián

Grillo

POTATO, LETTUCE, AND ONION SKEWER

Cri, cri, cri . . . that's the sound crickets make in Spanish, and some say it's the sound you make biting into this crisp, fresh pintxo, whose name means "cricket" in Spanish. Others claim it was christened the *grillo* because the ingredients (lettuce, onion, and potato) are "cricket food," a statement accurate only in the sense that the omnivorous insects are skilled scavengers and this pintxo was born in a time of hunger and scarcity. It is the result of ingenuity at the beginning of the pintxo age: putting together pantry staples, dressing them with oil and vinegar, and piling them up in eye-catching displays. The grillo fell out of favor as pintxos evolved, but it has returned to some bartops in Bilbao, where it is jokingly referred to as the first vegan pintxo.

MAKES 6

3 fingerling or other small potatoes, peeled
Kosher salt
¼ cup (60 ml) extra-virgin olive oil
2 tablespoons white wine vinegar
1 spring onion (see Note)
6 green-leaf lettuce leaves

Place the potatoes in a large saucepan and add cold water to cover them completely. Salt the water generously and bring to a boil over high heat. Reduce the heat to low and cook the potatoes at a simmer until tender, about 20 minutes; a fork should slide effortlessly into a potato. Drain and allow to cool.

Meanwhile, in a small bowl, whisk together the olive oil and vinegar with a pinch of salt.

Cut the potatoes crosswise in half. Transfer to a small bowl, sprinkle with salt, and toss with half the vinaigrette.

Trim off the green parts of the onion, cut off the root, and slice the onion in half. Separate the layers of the onion. Trim off the loose, ruffled edges of the lettuce leaves, leaving the crisper middle section.

With a long toothpick, skewer 2 pieces of onion. Tear one of the trimmed lettuce leaves into 2 or 3 bite-size pieces and add to the skewer. Pierce a piece of potato lengthwise through its center, so the flat side will face down when the pintxo is served. Repeat with the remaining ingredients to make 5 more pintxos.

Arrange the pintxos on a serving platter, drizzle the remaining vinaigrette over them, and serve.

NOTE

If spring onions aren't available, use the mildest onion you can find, such as Vidalia, and use just half the amount called for in the recipe—here, that would be ½ mild onion.

Indurain

ANCHOVY, TUNA, PEPPER, AND OLIVE SKEWER

A cyclist may not be the first thing that comes to mind when you see the beauty of a platter stacked with this glistening pintxo. But the Indurain gets its name from Miguel Induráin, one of cycling's greats. The athlete from Navarra holds the record for most consecutive wins of the Tour de France, and his titles from 1991 to 1995 are reflected in the five guindilla peppers stacked on top of the chunk of cured tuna that forms the base of this pintxo—which was renamed in his honor. This beautifully simple pintxo showcases the best of local *conservas*, or preserves. The pantry ingredients come together in a flash and can be assembled ahead of time, making it great for entertaining.

MAKES 6

1 spring onion (see Note, page 49)
6 green manzanilla olives, pitted
30 pickled guindilla peppers
    (see page 39), stemmed
1 jar or can (about 7.7 ounces/220 g)
    tuna in olive oil, drained
6 anchovy fillets in olive oil, preferably
    Cantabrian
Extra-virgin olive oil for drizzling

Remove the roots and green parts of the spring onion and cut the bulb into a 2-inch (5 cm) length. Cut it lengthwise in half and separate the layers. If the bulb is large, you may need to quarter it, so that each piece is about 1 inch (2.5 cm) wide. Reserve 6 pieces of onion and set the rest aside for another use.

With a long toothpick, pierce one olive through its center, followed by a piece of onion and 5 guindillas.

Separate the tuna into blocks about 1 inch (2.5 cm) wide and 3 inches (7.5 cm) long; you want 6 pieces of tuna. Drape an anchovy over a piece of tuna and skewer the anchovy and tuna with the toothpick. Repeat with the remaining ingredients to make 5 more pintxos.

Arrange the pintxos on a platter, drizzle generously with olive oil, and serve.

HEGALUZEA / TUNA / BONITO

•

The prized fish of Basque waters is the tuna. Not just any tuna, however—white albacore tuna, *Thunnus alalunga*, known as *bonito del norte* in Spanish. It has dark blue, almost black skin, which fades to white along its underside, and its meat is juicy and flavorful. Summer marks the season for fresh tuna, although most of the catch is preserved in olive oil, a prized ingredient in pintxo making.

BODEGA DONOSTIARRA, SAN SEBASTIÁN

✦

In 1924, Valentín Suso Susunaga and Javier Ibarrolaburu Arrese started
a business selling wine on Calle 31 de Agosto that would turn into an empire.
Their *bodegas donostiarras*, or San Sebastián wine cellars, spread quickly
across the city to ten different locations. Their clientele got into the habit
of bringing charcuterie and other snacks with them to accompany the wines
they were tasting, beginning the tradition of small bites and drinks. These
storefronts gradually turned into informal snack bars, with the location on Calle
Peña y Goñi growing in fame from 1976 at the hand of Miguel Mendieta and Pili
Mintegi (as well as Eladio Marañón, who would later go on to head the famed Bar
Txepetxa). Known for excellent canned seafood and traditional cuisine, Bodega
Donostiarra remains a stalwart today, now in the hands of Miguel Montorio.
The Indurain always graces the marble bartop, and you will want to order either
it or the completo, its sandwich counterpart featuring the same ingredients
served in a mini baguette.

Myths of the Toothpick

❖

There are many myths and a lot of false notions surrounding the purposes of the toothpick in pintxos eating. The toothpicks are not to be saved while you are eating and then proudly displayed to the waiter so he will know what to charge you. And they are not color-coded according to the ingredients. If you find yourself in a bar that happens to be promoting one of these practices, your best bet is to wave "Agur" and head to another establishment.

The Industrialization
of an Institution

❖

As simple as toothpick pintxos are to make, some companies have made a business out of packaging "pre-pierced" pickled items and cured seafood. Since the late twentieth century, bar owners have been able to purchase premade Gildas and other banderillas. While in San Sebastián this shortcut is considered practically sacrilegious, other parts of Spain have embraced it, with stalls in markets piled high with different pre-assembled combinations. Bombas, Lagartos y Cohetes, a company based in Madrid that sells to all of Spain, is the hippest example of packaged toothpick pintxos, with its colorful and snappy choices.

SHARP AND ACIDIC

(choose one from each category)

FATTY AND OILY

Black Kalamata olive

Green manzanilla olive

Gordal olive stuffed with red pepper

Sun-dried tomato

RICH AND MAYONNAISE-Y

(choose one from each category)

MEAT/FISH

Boiled shrimp

Fried calamari

Canned tuna

Jamón ibérico

EGG

Hard-boiled egg half

Hard-boiled quail egg

CANNED SEAFOOD

Albacore tuna

Salt-cured anchovies

Vinegar-cured anchovies

Sardines

PICKLED

Guindilla peppers

Red peppers

Pickles

Cocktail onions

Quail eggs

OLIVE OIL

A good drizzle of high-quality extra-virgin olive oil is a must to finish this type of pintxo.

MIX–AND–MATCH
TOOTHPICK PINTXOS

Toothpick pintxos can be divided fairly cleanly into two camps: those with sharp and acidic flavors, like the Gilda (page 39), and those that are rich and mayonnaise-y, like the shrimp and egg skewer (page 43). Depending on which type you prefer, you can riff off the most common ingredients and mix and match them to make your own creations. Follow the basic formulas shown here to make perfect toothpick pintxos.

VEG

Olives

Roasted peppers

Sun-dried tomatoes

Jarred artichoke hearts

MAYO

A dollop of mayonnaise, applied with a spoon or piped with a pastry tip, is an excellent finish.

BREAD

PINTXOS

Bread has been a building block in the Iberian diet for centuries, so it's no surprise that the pintxo jumped from a toothpick to a slice of crusty baguette. In restaurants, cafés, bars, and bodeguillas, the Spanish version of a baguette, called *barra*, is always available, a natural companion to the usual snacks of cured seafood, cheeses, and vegetables.

Today an edible base of bread still defines one of the most popular pintxo formats. Purists love it because it represents the classic definition of a pintxo: no plate, no cutlery, just a couple of bites. And bar owners love it because it opens up a world of opportunities to create and differentiate their offerings without a big investment or, really, much effort at all. When anchovies in olive oil, piquillo peppers, and white asparagus are arranged together on a slice of bread, the pintxos fly off the proverbial shelf.

The tradition of putting ingredients on a slice of bread to create a pintxo began simply: bread, a piece of cheese or an anchovy, and that was it. Both in times of scarcity and during long drinking sessions, that base of bread helped fill stomachs. Slices of a barra from a neighboring bakery were the first base for bread pintxos, but white sandwich bread soon began to make its appearance as well. A symbol of finery, the soft, snowy slices are popular foils for luxury ingredients, such as salmon (see page 90) or crab in mayonnaise. It eventually became popular to fry pintxo-sized pieces of bread in olive oil until golden and crispy, making the bread base sturdier and giving it a delicious, oily crunch. Specialty breads, from the mollete to pan de cristal (see page 60), also find a place on more innovative bartops. Today many modern bars use artisan loaves or make their own bread.

This chapter includes many of the most well-loved bread-based pintxos, some of which feature quirky names like La Delicia (page 62) and Antxopi (page 81). Many of them are based on combinations of popular local ingredients that you will find at nearly every pintxo bar in some shape, form, or fashion, like the Brie pintxo (page 89) and the baby eel pintxo. All of them are visually stunning, which is one of the pintxo's most important attributes.

THE BREADS

It all started with the barra, the Spanish version
of the baguette. While it remains the primary pintxo vessel,
a few other breads are also used as the base of various pintxos.

BARRA

This crusty baguette-style
white loaf is the most
popular bread in Spain,
accounting for about
60 percent of all bread
sold across the country.
Anywhere from 1½ to
2½ feet (45 to 75 cm) long,
it is a classic bread, made
with flour, water, yeast,
and salt. Its neutral flavor
and soft crumb make it a
good base for pintxos.

SPANISH BAGUETTE

The main difference between a barra and
a Spanish baguette is size. The baguette is longer
and thinner than the barra. While it is made with
the same ingredients, the baguette's proportions
make the dough more flexible, allowing
it to be shaped into a longer loaf.

PAN DE MOLDE

This white sandwich bread is most often used
either untoasted or deep-fried in olive oil
until golden. Some bars use an artisan pan
de molde, while others use a more industrial
version, almost identical to American white
bread. And some bars, such as Bar Eme
in Bilbao (see page 171), bake their own.

PAN DE CRISTAL

Pan de cristal is a specialty bread
that is popular in more modern
pintxo bars; its name translates
to "glass bread." It has an ultra-
fine, ultra-crispy crust and a soft,
barely there crumb. Invented
in 2004 by Catalán baker Jordi
Nomen, it is widely served as an
accompaniment to Spanish jamón,
thanks to its delicate form
and flavor.

BRIOCHE

Pan brioche is similar to pan de molde but enriched with eggs, milk, butter, and sugar. Sweet, light, and spongy, it comes in both rectangular and round loaves. It's most often seen in modern pintxo bars.

PAN DE PASAS Y NUECES

Pan de pasas y nueces is studded with raisins and walnuts and often made with whole wheat or rye flour. Although this bread is synonymous with holiday time, it appears year-round as a base for pintxos made with foie gras, cheeses, and other luxe, fatty ingredients.

MOLLETE

This soft, flat Andalucían white bread remains somewhat of a novelty in the northern part of Spain. Made with flour, yeast, salt, water, and olive oil, it is often eaten at breakfast in the south, but in pintxo bars, it serves as an unexpected base for more contemporary pintxos.

BAO

The bao is quite trendy in Spain now, popping up in the most unexpected places, including pintxos. This steamed Vietnamese bun is favored by young chefs as an innovative way to present pintxos made with stewed meats and loose, mayonnaise-y components.

PAN DE LEÑA

Pan de leña (wood-fired bread) has a similar size (about 1½ feet/ 45 cm long and weighing around 8 ounces/226 g) and crumb as the barra. However, pan de leña is baked in a stone oven, giving the crust a chewier, more rustic feel.

The Spanish Baking Tradition

❖

It is widely believed that bread was first introduced into the Iberian Peninsula in the third century BCE by Celtiberians. During the Mozarabic period, wheat was grown in Spain and bread was a basic part of the diet. *Panaderías*, or bakeries, date to the twelfth century. During the nineteenth and twentieth centuries, bread making went through a major industrialization process, and many artisan village bakeries closed, taking with them an incredible variety of *panes de pueblo*. But the twenty-first century has seen a return to traditional baking methods.

La Delicia

THE DELICACY

When a classic pintxo has been around for nearly a hundred years and still flies off the bar counter, you can bet it is special. La Delicia, from Bar La Espiga in San Sebastián (see page 64), is a perfect pintxo. The salt-cured anchovy is rich in umami, while the sharp bite of the delicate onion-parsley vinaigrette balances out the richness of the mayonnaise and hard-boiled egg. The splash of Worcestershire, a more recent touch dating back to the 1980s, is optional, but almost everyone asks for it.

MAKES 6

3 large eggs
½ onion
½ cup (30 g) fresh parsley leaves
¼ cup (60 ml) white wine vinegar
Kosher salt
Sunflower or other neutral oil
    for drizzling
12 anchovy fillets in olive oil,
    preferably Cantabrian
½ baguette, sliced on an angle
    into 6 pieces
¾ cup (165 g) mayonnaise,
    preferably homemade
    (page 44)
Worcestershire sauce

Bring a large saucepan of water to a boil. Carefully lower the eggs into the water and cook for 12 minutes, maintaining a gentle boil. Drain the eggs, run under cold water to stop the cooking, and let cool.

Gently crack and peel the eggs. Remove the yolk from one egg and discard (or enjoy it as a snack). Finely chop the white in a food processor and transfer the white to a small bowl (no need to clean the food processor bowl here).

Slice the 2 remaining eggs lengthwise into 4 slices. Cut the 2 middle slices of each egg (with the most yolk) crosswise in half; discard the other slices or reserve for another use.

Pulse the onion in the food processor until finely chopped. Transfer to the bowl with the egg white. Pulse the parsley in the food processor until finely chopped. Add to the bowl with the onion and egg white. Pour the vinegar over the top and sprinkle with salt. Drizzle generously with sunflower oil, stir, and set aside to macerate for at least 15 minutes. (You can make this vinaigrette up to 1 day ahead; cover and refrigerate.)

To assemble, arrange 2 anchovies on each piece of bread. Dab a bit of mayonnaise in the center of each anchovy and place a slice of egg on top. Place a generous dollop of mayonnaise on top of the egg slice. Working in batches, scoop up a bit of the onion vinaigrette with your hands and squeeze out the excess liquid, then arrange a spoonful of the mixture over the anchovies on either side of the egg.

Right before serving, splash each pintxo with Worcestershire sauce. Cut them in half, if desired, and serve.

NOTE

This vinaigrette is super versatile—it's amazing on white asparagus or grilled shrimp, or almost anything, really. Feel free to up the quantities and save some in your fridge, as it will keep for a week or two.

GRAN BAR LA ESPIGA, SAN SEBASTIÁN

✦

La Espiga and the family behind it are, without a doubt, pioneers in the world of the pintxo. On November 17, 1928, two young newlyweds, Jesús Castro and María Luisa San Martín, took over a bar located in a former wheat warehouse for the equivalent of €70 (about $80). Luisa took her cues for the menu from her best friend, a cook at the famous Casa Nicolasa, and her own mother, Simona, a renowned restaurateur who had been at the helm of El Nido. At this emblematic bar, which Simona had run since 1917, she was known for her banderillas. Luisa's own creations, a selection of fritos (fried snacks) like the chorrera (ham and hard-boiled egg, battered and fried), La Delicia (page 62), and more, remained on the menu when her son, José Mari, and daughter-in-law, Garbiñe, took over. Garbiñe had met her husband-to-be while working as a waitress in Bar Aralar, a classic of the Parte Vieja.

However, La Espiga is far from caught in a time warp. Renovated in 2008, it feels fresh and modern but nods to its past with a dark wood bartop (cut in a very contemporary shape) and a floor made of the city's emblematic hexagonal sidewalk tiles. You can find the third generation hard at work here every day of the week, with Jesús, Txema, and Luma tending the bar and the dining room and Koro in the kitchen. But tradition is king at La Espiga, so much so that not even a fryer has been allowed into the small kitchen. The tons of fritos served by the bar are fried one by one in the same type of pan that Luisa used back in 1928.

ABOVE Bar Toloño, Vitoria-Gasteiz

ABOVE Bar Txepetxa, San Sebastián

ABOVE Bar Txepetxa, San Sebastián

Anchoa en Salazón

SALT-CURED ANCHOVY

This pintxo has had a place of honor at Antonio Bar since it opened in 1969. The savory combination of salty cured anchovies, sweet green peppers, and spicy green chiles will hold well if you want to assemble these before your guests arrive.

Antonio Bar uses jarred green guindillas riojanas preserved in sunflower oil with garlic, and if you have access to these (see Notes), use them! If not, the recipe below includes instructions for confiting fresh hot green chiles. The anchovies are the other secret ingredient: they are preserved in salt every spring by a fisherman in the village of Getaria, who has been supplying the bar since it opened in 1969, despite the fact that he is now retired. But any good-quality anchovies will work in this pintxo.

SERVES 6

2 sweet Italian green peppers, such as Cubanelle
½ cup (120 ml) extra-virgin olive oil
Kosher salt
¼ cup (60 ml) white wine
2 fresh long green hot chiles, such as serranos (or guindillas riojanas preserved in oil and garlic; see Notes)
1 garlic clove, sliced
½ baguette, sliced on an angle into 6 pieces
12 anchovy fillets in olive oil, preferably Cantabrian

NOTES

If you can get the jarred guindillas they use at Antonio Bar, skip the confit step and simply chop the peppers.

You can prepare the peppers well ahead of time—store them in the refrigerator in their cooking oil once cooled.

Remove the stems and seeds from the Italian peppers. Halve them lengthwise and then crosswise so that you have 8 pieces of pepper.

Heat ¼ cup (60 ml) of the olive oil in a sauté pan over medium-low heat. Add the Italian peppers and a pinch of salt. When the peppers begin to simmer, flip them and press them flat. Reduce the heat to the lowest setting, cover, and cook, flipping the peppers occasionally, until they are tender, about 20 minutes. Remove from the heat.

Drain the oil from the peppers into a small container; set aside. Return the sauté pan with the peppers to medium-high heat, splash the peppers with the white wine, and simmer until the wine is nearly gone, about 5 minutes. Transfer the peppers to the container with the olive oil and allow to cool completely.

Meanwhile, heat the remaining ¼ cup (60 ml) olive oil in a saucepan over medium-low heat (if you have jarred guindillas riojanas, skip this step). Add the fresh hot chiles and a pinch of salt and stir. When the chiles begin to simmer, flip them and reduce the heat to the lowest setting. Add the sliced garlic, cover, and cook, flipping the chiles occasionally, until they are tender, about 20 minutes. Remove from the heat and allow to cool completely.

CONTINUED →

While the peppers and chiles cool, preheat the broiler. Arrange the slices of bread on a baking sheet and broil until just toasted on the edges; the centers should remain soft and chewy. Remove from the broiler.

Cut the chiles (or jarred guindilla peppers) into ½-inch (1.5 cm) pieces.

To assemble the pintxos, lay 2 anchovies across each slice of toasted bread, flush against the edges on one side of the slice with the rest of the anchovies hanging over the opposite edge. Place a piece of green pepper on top of the anchovies on each toast, arrange 2 to 4 pieces of chile (or guindilla) on top, and fold the green peppers over them. Then fold the overhanging ends of the anchovies over the top. Slice each pintxo crosswise in half down the middle, if desired, and serve.

Antonio Bar, San Sebastián

✦

Seen from the street, Antonio Bar doesn't exactly draw you in. The signage is modern and discreet, and the bar itself is so small, you could easily miss it. Opened on July 7, 1969, by Antonio Royo, the bar changed hands in 1995 when Antonio retired and passed the keys to Ramón Elizalde and Humberto Segura. These two friends had met while working at Hotel Europa, drawn together by a similar work ethic and belief in the value of good customer service.

The story of Antonio Bar is one of optimization—Antonio and then Ramón and Humberto spent year after year making many tiny improvements, resulting in one of San Sebastián's best pintxo bars. Some of the traditional pintxos have stayed, such as the cured anchovy toast, which, despite its simplicity, is a real show. New classics have been born too, such as langoustine ravioli and a fried brick pasta stuffed with oxtail, the bar's most popular hot pintxos. In the world of pintxos, Antonio's is on the slow food end of the spectrum— pintxos assembled to order, twenty-eight-egg Spanish omelets that take an hour to cook, Ibérico ham toasts prepared à la minute. And it won't take many visits for the staff to remember not just your name but how many spicy peppers you like on your anchovy toast.

Anchoa con Pate de Oliva

ANCHOVY WITH OLIVE PÂTÉ

If it weren't for a scare on the highway, the recipe for San Sebastián's most famous anchovy (and most closely guarded pintxo secret) may have been lost forever. One night, after Manu Marañón and his mother experienced a close encounter with a semitrailer, they looked at each other and thought the exact same thing: the anchovies. Manu and his mother were (and still are) the only two humans on the planet who know how to make what many call the world's best marinated anchovies. The day after that fateful near miss, they went to a notary, signed and sealed the recipe, and locked it away in a safe for the next generation.

Suffice it to say, this is *not* the recipe from Bar Txepetxa (see page 72). However, it is the closest you are likely to get at home, and it makes quite a delicious pintxo. The olive-topped anchovy was one of four original pintxos created by Manu's parents. Allowing the anchovies to rest overnight after marinating lets the flavor mellow and settle, but for those eager to eat their freshly marinated anchovies, you can skip that step.

SERVES 6

½ cup (120 ml) apple cider vinegar
¼ cup (60 ml) water
1 teaspoon kosher salt
6 fresh anchovies
Extra-virgin olive oil for storing
    the anchovies
¼ onion, minced
2 tablespoons white wine vinegar
1 cup (3½ ounces/100 g) black olives,
    pitted
2 tablespoons olive oil
½ baguette, sliced on a sharp angle
    into 6 pieces

In a shallow bowl, mix together the apple cider vinegar, water, and salt. Set aside in the refrigerator.

Fill a bowl with equal parts water and ice. To clean the anchovies, twist the head of each one about 90 degrees, then delicately pull on it to remove it from the body. The spine and tail should follow, leaving you with 2 fillets. (If the head breaks off without the spine and tail, simply discard it, then delicately pinch the tip of the spine and lift to remove it.) Run the anchovy fillets under cold water to remove any traces of blood. Inspect the fillets for bones and remove any you find, then put the fillets in the bowl of ice water.

Allow the anchovies to sit for about 5 minutes, then drain off the water and refill the bowl with more water and ice as needed. Repeat this process twice, soaking the anchovies for about 5 minutes after each water change, then drain once more. This will help remove all traces of blood from the fish.

CONTINUED →

Add the anchovies to the chilled vinegar marinade and refrigerate for 2 to 3 hours. Check the anchovies after 2 hours, as their size will determine the length of time they need to marinate; the ideal marinated anchovy should be almost (but not quite) totally white all the way to the center. When the anchovies have reached this point, drain off the marinade and pat them dry with a paper towel.

Transfer the anchovies to an airtight container, cover with a layer of extra-virgin olive oil, and refrigerate overnight (or for up to 1 week).

In a small bowl, combine the onion with the white wine vinegar. Set aside to macerate for at least 30 minutes or up to overnight.

Add the olives and olive oil to a food processor and pulse until the olives are very finely minced and the mixture resembles a smooth pâté.

When ready to serve, preheat the broiler. Arrange the slices of bread on a baking sheet and broil until just toasted on the edges; the centers should still be chewy. Remove from the broiler.

Arrange 2 anchovy fillets atop each slice of bread. Smear a generous amount of olive pâté, about a tablespoon per slice, over the middle. Place a spoonful of the macerated onions in the center of the olive pâté. Serve immediately.

WHAT IS A PINTXO?

"For me, the perfect pintxo would be like a perfect piece of sushi. None of this garbage with a thousand creams—no, something more simple, the perfect mouthful in a bar."

—ALEX MONTIEL,
LA CUCHARA DE SAN TELMO

ANTXOA / ANCHOVY / ANCHOA

•

Anchovies are highly prized by the Basques. They are eaten in three forms: fresh (only in season, of course), grilled, fried, or anything in between; salt-cured, the fillets tiny and brown and packed with umami; and vinegar-cured, white and deliciously tart (these are also known as *boquerones*). The local anchovies are incredible any way you eat them, and it's easy to see why Basques worship the antxoa.

The curing process is an age-old tradition first practiced by the Italians who came to Spain in search of seafood to preserve and found anchovies and tuna. European anchovies (*Engraulis encrasicolus*) reproduce between May and June, and that is the best time to eat them. The choicest cured anchovies are the hand-cleaned Cantabrian ones, smaller than anchovies from other waters and without a bone in sight. They have a pleasant oceany taste and melt like butter in your mouth.

BAR TXEPETXA, SAN SEBASTIÁN

✦

At traditional pintxo bars like Txepetxa, in San Sebastián's Parte Vieja, it may seem like time stands still. That, however, is a mirage. It takes a lot of blood, sweat, and missed holidays to keep the quality of the food on the countertop the same, day in and day out. That is exactly what each successive generation has managed to do at Txepetxa. Josetxo Marañón and his wife, Mari Carmen Ramos, who founded the bar in 1972, came from San Sebastián hospitality industry royalty—Josetxo's father, Valentín Marañón, worked at the old Bodega Donostiarra (see page 52), and his mother opened Bar Bergara in Gros with a friend. Now Txepetxa is in the capable hands of Josetxo and Mari Carmen's son, Manu Marañón, who has been behind the bar since the age of eight—when he used to make the Gildas.

Despite the bar's ongoing success, Manu maintains the same schedule he always has: He starts each day at 6:00 a.m. with a call to his anchovy man. They meet outside the bar with the catch, and then Manu prepares the star of Txepetxa's menu—the vinegar-cured anchovies—in complete solitude. He finishes before any of the staff arrive, then painstakingly locks up the ingredients to preserve their secrecy. The effort (and the hype) is worth it—these anchovies are delicate epiphanies that win over even ardently professed anchovy haters.

The Jardinera (literally "gardener") was the first anchovy pintxo on offer at Txepetxa: a slice of toast with vinegar-cured anchovies and a pepper-onion vinaigrette. After ten years of serving the Jardinera, Josetxo and Mari Carmen began experimenting, expanding their offerings to four different anchovy toasts by the late 1990s, and now there are more than a dozen different versions. The bartop is decorated with ceramic replicas of the anchovy pintxos rather than the real thing, because they are all toasted and assembled to order—one reason they are so good.

DRINKING WITH FRIENDS

What to drink with pintxos? The classic answer is wine. For most of the twentieth century, it was de rigueur to have either white or clarete, a dark rosé from Navarra, by day, and then move to red wine in the evening. As Txakoli, the local Basque wine made from Hondarrabi Zuri grapes, gained in respectability and quality, however, it became a very common accompaniment to the *poteo*, the tradition of going from bar to bar and drinking a glass of wine at each spot. Nowadays both red and white wine are drunk throughout the day, but beer is also a common option—you can even order a pintxo-friendly mini beer called a zurito. Mosto, or grape juice, is a popular nonalcoholic choice, served with an olive garnish. Basque hard cider and vermouth are other options, with vermouth served mostly at

midday. The most popular red is Rioja, of which you can choose from reserva, crianza, and del año. The white wines are often Verdejo, typically from Rueda, or Chardonnay from Navarra.

ABOVE Haizea, San Sebastián

Queso, Membrillo y Nueces

CHEESE, QUINCE PASTE, AND WALNUTS

Back when pintxo bars were just for drinking, wedges of cured local cheese often sat in the corner, waiting to be sliced up and offered to those imbibing. Eventually, the slices were tossed atop some slices of bread to form the original version of this pintxo, which also happens to be a bite-size version of a traditional dessert still served in Basque cider houses. Walnuts, Idiazabal cheese, and quince (or sometimes apple) paste is a classic combination, and with good reason—the bright fruit paste cuts the fatty, grassy flavor of the cheese, and the walnuts lend an appealing crunch. It's easy to put together, which makes this a crowd-pleaser for pintxo parties at home.

MAKES 6

½ baguette, sliced on an angle into 6 pieces

3 ounces (85 g) quince paste (membrillo; see Resources, page 302)

2 ounces (55 g) Idiazabal cheese (see Note)

Walnut halves (about 12)

Preheat the broiler. Arrange the slices of bread on a baking sheet and broil until just toasted on the edges; the centers should still be chewy. Remove from the broiler and let cool.

Cut the quince paste into thin slices and then into evenly sized rectangles, about 1 by 2 inches (2.5 by 5 cm).

Remove any rind from the cheese and cut the cheese into evenly sized triangles.

Reserve 6 walnut halves. Finely chop the remaining walnuts.

Divide the quince paste among the slices of toast, top with the cheese, and place a walnut half in the center of each pintxo. Sprinkle with the chopped walnuts. Pierce each pintxo with a toothpick, if desired, and serve.

NOTE

You can use either smoked or cured Idiazabal. If you can't find Idiazabal, substitute another cured sheep's-milk cheese, such as Manchego.

To Toast or Not to Toast

❖

While the bread for many pintxos is lightly toasted, which keeps it from getting soggy and collapsing, there are exceptions. Some pintxos, because of the consistency of their ingredients, are served on untoasted baguette slices.

What to drink with
PİNTXOS

WINE!

WHITE	CLARETE	RED
(Verdejo, Albariño, Chardonnay)		(Rioja reserva, crianza or del año, Ribera del Duero)

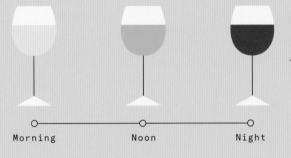

Morning   Noon   Night

BEER!

TXAKOLI!

CAÑA   ZURITO
(big!)   (small!)

CIDER!   VERMOUTH!

OR

OR TRY A NONALCOHOLIC DRINK

Mosto!

Pimiento Relleno de Bonito

TUNA-STUFFED PEPPER

This pintxo is more than the sum of its parts—a sweet, jewel-like piquillo pepper, roasted and stuffed with bonito del norte (tuna preserves) mixed with tartar sauce. The Martínezes of Bar Martínez (see page 78) disclosed the recipe, "more or less," emphasizing that the tartar sauce for this legendary pintxo is a secret. The recipe below comes extremely close to the original, however, as the real secret to success when crafting this pintxo lies in using the highest-quality ingredients. Use a light hand with the mayonnaise, or the mixture will ooze out of the pepper rather than stuff it.

MAKES 12

1 baguette, sliced into 12 pieces
¼ cup (60 ml) extra-virgin olive oil
1 tablespoon sherry vinegar
Kosher salt
1 jar or can (about 7.7 ounces/220 g) tuna in olive oil
¼ cup (about 50 g) minced onion
2 tablespoons minced cornichons
1 tablespoon minced capers
¼ cup plus 2 tablespoons (80 g) mayonnaise, preferably homemade (page 44), plus a little more if needed
½ teaspoon dried tarragon
Freshly ground black pepper
12 piquillo peppers (from one 190 g jar; see Note)

Preheat the broiler. Arrange the slices of bread on a baking sheet and broil until just toasted on the edges; the centers should still be chewy. Remove from the broiler and let cool.

Whisk together the olive oil and sherry vinegar in a small bowl. Season with salt. Set aside.

Drain the tuna and, using your hands, break it into tiny pieces into a medium bowl. Add the onion, cornichons, and capers, then add the mayonnaise, tarragon, and a generous pinch of black pepper and stir until the mixture comes together. If it looks dry, you can add a bit more mayo, but you want the mixture to hold together, not leak out of the peppers. Season with salt.

Distribute the mixture among the piquillo peppers, filling them gently with a spoon.

Arrange the toasted bread on a serving plate and place a stuffed pepper atop each piece. Sprinkle with salt. Drizzle generously with the sherry vinaigrette, allowing it to pool on the plate so the bread can soak it up from the bottom too. Serve immediately.

NOTE

While this recipe will work with any small red pepper, the true pimiento del piquillo is from Lodosa in Nafarroa (Navarra) and has its own protected designation. The smoky flavor of these peppers comes from the fires used for roasting them before removing the skin. Smaller and more delicate than red bell peppers, they make for perfect bite-size stuffed peppers.

BAR MARTÍNEZ, SAN SEBASTIÁN

✦

Bar Martínez is the oldest pintxo bar in San Sebastián's Old Town, now run by the third generation of the same family that opened it on May 13, 1942, on Calle 31 de Agosto. Manuel Martínez and Juliana Gil, who moved to San Sebastián from the Rioja, were able to open it then despite quite a bit of bureaucratic red tape, due to the fact that the former bar in the same location, Amiguet, had been owned by a madame and was a center of "suspicious" activity. Once it overcame the suspicions of the local wives, however, Bar Martínez prospered. Manuel, a painter, sculptor, and woodworker, had a fondness for giving nicknames to the bar's innovative bites, such as the so-called Basque caviar (hake roe). You can spot him in a 1943 photo that hangs proudly over the bar to this day, standing beside a bartop full of pintxos that include the Gilda (page 39), proof that this famous pintxo actually existed before its purported birth date of 1946.

Bar Martínez is ground zero for many of the city's other well-known bars—various family members kept arriving from the Rioja, working at Martínez and sleeping in a back room. One of them, Manuel's brother, eventually went on to open Tamboril (see page 234). Bar Martínez was a bright spot in Old Town, especially during times of scarcity in the mid-twentieth century, a place where fishermen, neighbors, and famous musicians alike rubbed elbows.

In the late 1960s and early 1970s, Manuel and Juliana's three sons, Urbano, Manuel Jr., and José Ignacio, took over and gave the bar a radical facelift, transforming it into a modern, luxurious spot with waiters in bow ties and a bar heavy with shrimp, crayfish, goose barnacles, frog's legs, and calamari. It was the golden age, with the brothers inventing avant-garde pintxos and introducing luxury items such as smoked salmon and Russian king crab (the latter after seeing it on the bar of Borda Berri; see page 248). On any given Sunday, they could go through eighteen bottles of vermouth and twenty-six pounds of mushrooms for one of their most famous pintxos (page 232). Eventually José Ignacio founded Ganbara (see page 178) and Urbano established a few of his own restaurants, while Manuel Jr. and his wife, Nieves Saa, remained at Bar Martínez.

Currently Mikel, Manuel Jr.'s son, heads the family business, after a twenty-year career in software. His focus is on finding the absolute best raw materials and crafting a wine menu with rare and special selections, bottles that he and his cousin Amaiur (from Ganbara) want to drink themselves.

THE 5 W'S (AND 1 H) OF SLICING BREAD

Like Basque cuisine itself, the things that seem the simplest often hold the most secrets. The plain piece of bread that serves as a base for so many pintxos is not just *any* piece of bread, and knowing exactly how to slice it is key to achieving pintxo perfection.

1

WHY. The way you slice the bread, its thickness and shape, will have an important effect on the size and look of your pintxo.

2

WHO. Many pintxo bars have a team dedicated solely to the pintxos served on the bar. Often one team member is charged with slicing and toasting all the bread first thing in the morning. It's not uncommon for a popular bar to go through fifty to a hundred baguettes in a single service, so this is quite a job.

3

WHAT. Although a few bars have an electric bread slicer at their disposal, most cut the bread by hand with a serrated knife.

4

WHERE. In the land of daily bread, a nifty cutting board with slats, which allows the crumbs to fall into a box below as the bread is sliced, shouldn't come as a surprise. If you don't have one of these boards, a regular cutting board will, of course, suffice.

5

WHEN. One of the things that separates an average bread pintxo from a great one is cutting the bread as close to the moment of assembly and serving it as soon as possible. Bread is alive, and it dries out and hardens with exposure to air.

6

HOW. The cut of the bread slice is supremely important. Usually the baguettes for pintxos are sliced on an angle, typically about ¾ inch (2 cm) thick. Some pintxo makers use a barely angled cut, about 60 degrees, while those who want more surface area and a larger slice of bread may sharpen the angle to about 30 degrees. Experiment with different pintxos and find the right angle for each one.

Antxopi

ANTXOPI

Sometimes the creation of a new pintxo gets crowdsourced. At El Rincón de Luis Mari (see page 83), owner Luis Mari Puelles offered a carefully selected menu of preserved seafood, charcuterie, and cheese; anchovies to die for; and some of the best piquillo peppers out of Navarra. However, he also had a problem: people didn't order the ingredients he had taken such care to source.

One day, one of his clients suggested he stack together some of the items on a piece of bread, so Luis Mari began to experiment, laying a salted anchovy over a ruby-red piquillo, sprinkling it all with a little bit of this, a little bit of that. Finally he came up with a combination he loved and christened it the Antxopi, and the rest is history. It remains one of the bar's most famous pintxos, and they sell about a hundred and fifty of them during an average weekend lunch service. The recipe for the mayonnaise used to decorate the pintxo is a house secret, but this version comes close enough to give the pintxo its signature taste.

MAKES 6

½ baguette, sliced on an angle into 6 pieces
1 large egg
¼ cup (60 ml) olive oil
1 garlic clove, sliced
6 jarred or canned piquillo peppers
½ cup (110 g) mayonnaise, preferably homemade (page 44)
Worcestershire sauce
½ lemon (optional)
Kosher salt (optional)
6 anchovy fillets in olive oil, preferably Cantabrian
Parsley Oil (recipe follows)

SPECIAL EQUIPMENT

A squirt bottle or a pastry bag fitted with a fine tip

Preheat the broiler. Arrange the slices of bread on a baking sheet and broil until just toasted on the edges; the centers should still be chewy. Remove from the broiler and let cool.

Bring a large saucepan of water to a boil. Carefully lower the egg into the water and cook for 12 minutes, maintaining a gentle boil. Drain the egg, run it under cold water to stop the cooking, and let cool.

Gently crack and peel the egg. Remove the yolk and crumble it into a small bowl. Finely chop the white. Set aside.

In a large skillet, combine the olive oil and garlic and heat over medium heat until the garlic turns a light golden color. Remove it with a slotted spoon and set aside.

Add the peppers to the pan and cook slowly over medium-low heat for about 10 minutes to confit them slightly. Reduce the heat so that the oil is just barely bubbling, flip the peppers, and cook for about 5 minutes more. Remove from the heat.

CONTINUED →

In a small bowl, mix the mayonnaise with 5 or 6 dashes of Worcestershire sauce. If using store-bought mayonnaise, you may want to add a squeeze of lemon juice and a pinch of salt as well. Transfer the mayonnaise to a squirt bottle or a pastry bag fitted with a fine tip. (If you don't have either of these, you can use a ziplock bag; snip off the tip of one of the bottom corners.)

To assemble, place a pepper on each slice of bread. Lay an anchovy across the center. Pipe the mayonnaise into a loop-de-loop pattern all the way around the edges of each pintxo. Sprinkle the egg yolks and whites over the pintxos. Drizzle parsley oil in a circle around the edges of the pintxos.

Arrange the pintxos on a platter and serve.

Aceite de Perejil

PARSLEY OIL | PERREXIL OLIOA

MAKES ABOUT ½ CUP (120 ML)

Leaves from 1 bunch parsley
1 garlic clove, sliced
½ cup (120 ml) olive oil

Combine the parsley, garlic, and olive oil in a food processor and process until the parsley is in tiny pieces, or process the ingredients using an immersion blender.

Transfer to a squirt bottle (for easy dispensing) or a jar with a lid. The parsley oil will keep in the refrigerator for up to a week.

WHAT IS A PINTXO?

"For me, a pintxo
is an exquisite snack,
one that shouldn't
ruin your appetite."

—SANTI RIVERA, LA VIÑA

EL RINCÓN DE LUIS MARI, VITORIA

✦

It all began with a lucky soccer bet. Playing La Quiniela, a Spanish soccer betting game, Luis Mari Puelles won enough money to open a bar in the old town of Vitoria-Gasteiz in 1957. He and his wife, Adita Asarta, opened and ran Trafalgar and were some of the great innovators of the city's somewhat provincial dining scene. Luis Mari was always testing new ideas on his clients, both at Trafalgar and at Autobuses, his second (very busy) bar in the Vitoria bus station. One of these innovations has endured for more than half a century: banderillas calientes. A play on toothpick pintxos, these banderillas were skewers threaded with fried bites.

The four versions served at Trafalgar are all still available today at El Rincón de Luis Mari, which opened in 1990 and was the first bar in Vitoria to be dedicated to *picoteo*, or snacking. Their banderillas calientes thread together croquetas, artichokes, stuffed peppers, eggs, and ham in different combinations, four to a skewer, then batter and fry them. Today Luis Mari's son Iñigo heads the bar, also famous for its Ibérico ham—which explains the acorns decorating the wall tiles and the gated corner where up to a hundred Jabugo hams hang, waiting their turn to be sliced. Thanks to the high-quality and tradition-steeped offerings of Luis Mari and his son, generations of clients return year after year, bringing their children and then their grandchildren to El Rincón.

VITORIA

Bar Deportivo Alavés, Vitoria

Vitoria is the capital of Álava and the seat of the Spanish Basque government. Landlocked between Rioja wine country and the greener hills of the north, the city of 250,000 does not share the tourism of other Basque capitals, but it is lively with locals. The nucleus is the almond-shaped medieval quarter with its embarrassment of riches, from the Gothic-style cathedral to the Arquillos colonnade.

Vitoria has always been an important place for trade—nearly a quarter of its inhabitants work in industrial jobs. The city expanded wildly in the 1960s, with a surge of immigration from the rest of Spain to fill the growing demand for factory workers.

The sweeping Plaza de la Virgen Blanca, which is the site of Vitoria's patron saint fiestas on August 4, serves as the heart not just of the city itself but of the dining scene as well. The streets that stretch out from it wind like snakes to the city's best pintxo bars. Innovative pintxos came late to Vitoria, with Spanish omelets and banderilla-style pintxos being just about the only thing on offer at the bars until the mid-1990s. In contrast to those found in the other, more cosmopolitan capitals, pintxos in Vitoria are generally both less refined and more filling. A signature of the city is the tortilla manchada (literally "stained Spanish omelet"), served with a nub of chorizo and a bit of the reddish-orange cooking juices drizzled on top. Many of the pintxos feature the trinity of ingredients local to Álava—eggs, potatoes, and wild mushrooms or truffles—in surprising forms.

ABOVE Plaza España, Vitoria-Gasteiz

Seta, Jamón y Guindilla

OYSTER MUSHROOM, HAM, AND PEPPER

The secret to this pintxo lies in the ajilimójili, a sauce originating in Andalucía. Its most basic iteration is a garlicky dressing made with oil and vinegar; it is not emulsified, mayonnaise-style, but left loose and liquid. Be sure to let the mushrooms caramelize during cooking, and you'll find this simple pintxo is quite a revelation.

This pintxo was once served at the classic Bar Narrika, in the Old Town of San Sebastián. Known both for its mushrooms and the endearing grouchiness of its owners, Josemi and Mari Carmen, the bar specialized in this pintxo and in baguette sandwiches, or bocadillos.

MAKES 6

½ cup plus 1 tablespoon (140 ml) olive oil

2 tablespoons apple cider vinegar

2 garlic cloves, halved and green germ removed

2 parsley sprigs

6 fresh guindilla peppers (see Note)

Kosher salt

6 oyster mushrooms, stems trimmed

3 slices jamón ibérico, cut crosswise in half

½ baguette, sliced on an angle into 6 pieces

SPECIAL EQUIPMENT

A squirt bottle

Combine ⅓ cup (80 ml) of the olive oil with the vinegar, garlic, and parsley in a food processor or blender and blend well. Transfer the ajilimójili to a squirt bottle.

Pour the remaining olive oil into a sauté pan and heat to about 350°F (175°C). To test the oil temperature without a digital thermometer, add a single pepper to the oil; if it sizzles on contact, the oil is ready. Add all the peppers to the pan and cook without moving them for 30 to 60 seconds, then flip them over and continue to cook, turning them as needed, for about 1 minute more, or until they are well blistered with a few touches of gold. Remove the peppers with a slotted spoon and transfer to paper towels to drain. Sprinkle generously with salt.

Wipe the pan clean and heat over high heat until hot. Add the mushrooms and drizzle generously with some of the ajilimójili. Sear the mushrooms on one side, without moving them, until golden brown, about 2 minutes. Reduce the heat to medium, flip the mushrooms, and drizzle with more ajilimójili. Cook until the mushrooms are golden, about 1 minute more. Remove from the pan and set aside.

Add the ham to the pan and cook, turning once, for about 30 seconds on each side, until the fat has rendered a bit. Transfer to a plate.

Add the slices of bread to the pan and toast them on one side, allowing them to soak up the juices. Remove from the heat.

To assemble, place one mushroom on the toasted side of each piece of bread. Squirt them with a drizzle of the ajilimójili and place the ham on top of the mushrooms. Top each one with a fried pepper. Serve immediately.

NOTE

If you can't find fresh guindilla peppers, you can substitute other small, mild green peppers, such as pimientos de Padrón or shishito peppers.

Brie, Jamón y Mermelada

BRIE, HAM, AND JAM

Perhaps more than any other food, pintxos are about eating with your eyes. This pintxo is a beauty, with a zigzag of balsamic glaze contrasting with the white of the Brie and sesame seeds. Decorating bartop pintxos with a colorful jam is a popular technique, and this recipe incorporates eye-catching dollops of red and yellow atop the slices of Brie. These pintxos are easy to put together, universally appealing, and lovely when arranged on a platter.

MAKES 6

½ baguette, sliced on an angle into 6 pieces
4 ounces (113 g) Brie cheese
6 slices jamón ibérico
1 tablespoon apricot jam
1 tablespoon strawberry or raspberry jam
Balsamic Glaze (page 224) for drizzling (optional)
White sesame seeds for sprinkling (optional)

Preheat the broiler. Arrange the slices of bread on a baking sheet and broil until just toasted on the edges; the centers should remain chewy. Remove from the broiler and let cool.

Cut the Brie into 6 equal rectangular slices.

Drape one piece of ham over each slice of toasted bread, folding it as necessary so that the edges barely hang over the bread, and place a piece of Brie on top. Using a small spoon, dollop a bit of apricot jam (about ½ teaspoon) on one side of the Brie on each pintxo, and repeat on the other side with about ½ teaspoon of the strawberry or raspberry jam.

Arrange the pintxos on a platter. Drizzle them with balsamic glaze in a zigzag pattern and sprinkle with sesame seeds, if desired. Pierce each pintxo with a toothpick, if desired, and serve.

URDAIAZPIKOA / HAM / JAMÓN

Jamón ibérico is one of the world's most celebrated and most expensive ingredients. Made in southern regions of Spain such as Andalucía and Extremadura, this dry-cured ham has hundreds of years of artisanal tradition behind it. The highest-quality Spanish ham is jamón ibérico de bellota de pata negra, a name that refers to the specific type of pig (Iberian, with black legs) and its diet—acorns. The hams are dried for a couple of weeks under a layer of salt and then air-dried for 4 to 6 weeks. Then the long aging process begins, which requires at least a year and can take up to 4 years. Served from morning to night, jamón is ubiquitous in Spain.

Salmon Marinado

MARINATED SALMON

With this pintxo of marinated salmon rolled up around a potato salad with tartar sauce, El Globo won the first pintxo competition in Bilbao, in 1998, receiving a perfect score of 10 from renowned San Sebastián pintxo chef José Ramón Elizondo (see page 182). The secret to its exquisite simplicity lies in the marinade, which mellows the flavor of the fish and lends it touches of dill and black pepper.

Use a very sharp knife to cut thin slices from the chilled marinated salmon. If you are unable to cut slices that are thin enough, you can cut thicker rectangles and pound them lightly between sheets of plastic wrap to get thin pieces of the right size.

MAKES 6

Kosher salt

1 small potato, such as Yukon Gold

1 large egg

½ spring onion (see Note, page 49), finely diced

2 tablespoons finely chopped capers

2 tablespoons finely chopped cornichons

½ cup (110 g) mayonnaise, preferably homemade (page 44)

1 teaspoon Dijon mustard

½ lemon

Kosher salt and freshly ground black pepper

3 slices white sandwich bread, crusts removed

6 slices Cured Salmon (recipe follows)

¼ cup (10 g) chopped fresh dill

SPECIAL EQUIPMENT

A squirt bottle or a pastry bag fitted with a small plain tip

Bring a large saucepan of salted water to a boil. Add the potato and then carefully lower the egg into the water. After exactly 12 minutes, remove the egg and run it under cold water to stop the cooking; let cool. Continue cooking the potato at a gentle boil until tender, a total of 20 to 25 minutes. Drain the potato and let cool until you can handle it.

Gently crack and peel the egg. Finely chop it.

Remove and discard the potato skin and finely chop the potato.

In a small bowl, combine the egg, potato, spring onion, capers, and cornichons. Add ¼ cup (55 g) of the mayonnaise, the mustard, a squeeze of lemon juice, and a pinch each of salt and pepper. Stir until well combined.

Cut the bread slices lengthwise in half.

To assemble the pintxos, divide the potato salad among the slices of salmon, placing it near a longer edge of each one. Roll the salmon up around the potato and place seam side down atop the bread.

Transfer the remaining ¼ cup (55 g) mayonnaise to a squirt bottle or pastry bag fitted with a small plain tip. Squeeze a zigzag of mayo atop the salmon on each pintxo and sprinkle generously with the chopped dill. Serve.

CONTINUED →

NOTE

The salmon can be cured up to a week ahead. After slicing it, coat it generously with a neutral oil, such as sunflower, and store in an airtight container in the refrigerator until ready to serve.

Cured Salmon

½ cup (100 g) sugar
½ cup (135 g) kosher salt
2 teaspoons freshly ground black pepper
¼ cup (10 g) chopped fresh dill
One 10-ounce (285 g) piece skin-on salmon fillet,
    any bones removed (see Note)

In a medium bowl, combine the sugar, salt, pepper, and dill and whisk to mix.

Put half the sugar-salt mixture in the bottom of a glass baking dish, spreading it into a rectangle about the size of the piece of salmon. Place the salmon on top of it and spread the remaining sugar-salt mixture over the fish, making sure it is completely covered, to the point where you can't see any pink. Cover with plastic wrap, pressing it directly against the salmon, and set a can of tomatoes or something similar on top to weight it down slightly.

Transfer the salmon to the refrigerator and let marinate for 36 hours.

Remove the fish from the baking dish and rinse it well under cold water. Pat dry with paper towels. Using a very sharp knife held almost horizontal to the cutting board, slice the salmon on an angle into very thin sheets; aim for pieces approximately 3 by 4 inches (7.5 by 10 cm). Cover and return to the fridge until ready to use.

"What is a pintxo?
The perfect companion for
a glass of wine or beer."

—JESÚS CASTRO, LA ESPIGA

BAR EL GLOBO, BILBAO

✦

Bar El Globo began on a blind date. Mónica Padró's sister set her up with Luis Aranduri in part because he and Mónica shared a dream of opening a restaurant. In 1997, not long after they met, they opened El Globo together on what would prove to be a choice corner in Bilbao's central district—although they didn't actually admit their romantic feelings to each other until a few months later. For years, Luis had had his eye on Bar Eboga, an institution in Bilbao where *tertulias*, or social gatherings, devoted to conversing about bulls and opera, among other topics, led to the founding of ABAO, La Asociación Bilbaína de Amigos de la Ópera, in 1953. The couple gave the downtrodden bar a makeover and named it El Globo ("the globe") to represent the type of establishment they hoped to create: a meeting place for people from around the world.

In mid-'90s Bilbao, that was a faraway dream, but when the Guggenheim Museum opened a branch there, it meant Luis and Mónica were in the right place at the right time. Mónica created exquisite pintxos with international touches that have become modern classics, and Luis worked the bar, chatting up visitors in several languages. El Globo's pintxos won contest after contest, but Mónica always insisted on presenting only pintxos that she could replicate on the bartop day after day. El Globo's counter remains the envy of all Bilbao, even though the couple retired in 2022, passing their little corner of the Ensanche (neighborhood)—and the thousands of visitors they receive every year—on to new owners.

Bacalao al Pil-Pil

SALT COD IN PIL-PIL SAUCE

Sometimes the inspiration for a pintxo comes from a classic dish. Salt cod with pil-pil sauce is universally adored by Basques, so it's no surprise to find a miniature version in pintxo bars everywhere there. The word *pil* is an onomatopoeia for the sound of the olive oil bubbling around the salt cod as it cooks. The gelatin that the fish releases emulsifies with the olive oil to create a thick, luxurious yellow sauce.

Although purists insist that the pil-pil sauce thicken on its own, with just the perfect flick of the wrist to emulsify the fish's gelatin and the oil's fat, this recipe employs a secret weapon: a fine-mesh strainer, which ensures a creamy, emulsified sauce every time. Dollop the sauce atop the tender salt cod and garnish it with golden garlic nuggets. This pintxo is the best of Basque Country in one bite.

MAKES 6

½ baguette, sliced on an angle into 6 pieces
3 garlic cloves, peeled
1 cup (240 ml) extra-virgin olive oil
3 jarred or canned piquillo peppers
8 ounces (225 g) salt cod fillet, desalted (see Notes)
½ dried guindilla pepper, sliced into rings
Coarse salt if necessary
Chopped fresh parsley for garnish

NOTES

Desalting the cod will take 12 to 48 hours, so plan ahead. For the process, see page 96.

If whisking the sauce fails, an immersion blender can bring the sauce together. Be careful not to blend it too much, though, or the pil-pil will thicken to a mayonnaise-like consistency.

Preheat the broiler. Arrange the slices of bread on a baking sheet and broil until just toasted on the edges; the centers should still be chewy. Remove from the broiler and let cool.

Slice one of the garlic cloves. In a large skillet, heat 2 tablespoons of the olive oil and the sliced garlic over medium heat until the garlic turns a light golden color; remove it with a slotted spoon and set aside. Add the piquillo peppers to the pan and cook for about 10 minutes to confit them slightly. Reduce the heat so that the oil is just barely bubbling, flip the peppers, and cook for about 5 minutes more. Remove from the heat.

Mince the remaining 2 garlic cloves. In a large sauté pan or a medium pot with straight sides, heat the remaining ¾ cup plus 2 tablespoons (210 ml) olive oil and the minced garlic over medium heat. When the garlic starts to "dance," bubbling in the oil, and color lightly, reduce the heat to low and cook until the garlic is a uniform golden color. Remove the garlic with the slotted spoon and drain on a paper towel.

Add the salt cod fillet to the pan, skin side up (it should not sizzle; if it does, turn the heat down), followed by the guindilla. Cook the fish for 3 to 4 minutes on the first side, then turn it over and cook for another 3 minutes. Transfer the fish to a plate.

CONTINUED →

You will see two different liquids in the pan: the golden olive oil and the watery, milky gelatin the fish has released. Pour most of the oil into a heatproof container and then begin to move the pan gently but continuously in a back-and-forth motion over low heat. After a minute or two, the fillet will have released a bit of liquid onto the plate. Pour this liquid into the pan and use the bottom of a fine-mesh sieve to whisk it briskly, keeping the sieve in contact with the surface of the pan. Gradually add the reserved oil back to the pan, little by little, whisking continuously until the sauce is emulsified and thick (see Notes). Taste for seasoning and add a bit of salt if necessary. Remove from the heat.

Halve the piquillo peppers lengthwise so you have 6 triangular pieces.

Remove the cod from the pan and cut into 6 equal pieces.

Place a piece of piquillo pepper on each slice of bread and place a piece of cod on top. Dollop a generous amount of the sauce over each piece of fish, allowing it to drip down over the edges. Sprinkle with the minced garlic, garnish with the chopped parsley, and serve.

Preparing Salt Cod

It's not obvious how to use salt cod, which is sold salt-crusted and dry. The key is to desalt it before using it, a process that is extremely simple, requiring nothing more than cool water and time. When you plan to serve salt cod, be sure to incorporate into your prep timeline the 12 to 48 hours it will take to draw out the excess salt.

Twenty-four to 48 hours before you are going to use the salt cod, run it under cold water to remove the excess salt on its surface. If necessary, cut the cod into evenly sized pieces (always work with pieces of similar size, or they will end up unevenly salty). Place the cod in a large bowl, add cold water to cover, and set aside to soak in a cool place—generally desalting will take longer in the refrigerator than at cool room temperature.

Depending on the size of the pieces of cod and its saltiness, desalting will take anywhere from 12 to 48 hours; change the water every 8 to 12 hours. After the first 12 hours, taste a piece of the cod for saltiness and then, if necessary, keep soaking it and tasting it every 6 hours. When it tastes well seasoned, neither overly salty nor bland, drain the cod, pat dry with paper towels, and proceed as directed in your recipe. If you must store the cod after desalting, treat it like fresh fish and refrigerate it for no more than a couple of days.

WHAT IS A PINTXO?

"With a good pintxo, it is the pleasure of good eating in a tiny dose. Something that awakens your sense of taste and sight, something to accompany a good drink."

—MIKEL MARTÍNEZ, CAFÉ BAR BILBAO

CAFÉ BAR BILBAO, BILBAO

Severo Unzué Donamaría came to Bilbao from San Martín de Unx in Navarra to open a small bodeguilla, a wine shop for both wholesale and retail sales that often served as a makeshift bar. His first spot, in the Ledesma area of Bilbao, did well, and so his empire began. Severo's successful formula of elegant bars with Andalucían decor (starting with Café Iruña; see page 238) resulted in some of the city's most emblematic establishments, including Café Bar Bilbao. Since 1910 (or 1911, depending on who you ask), this bar in the city's porticoed Plaza Nueva has seen civil war, the rise and fall of nationalism, floods from the nearby estuary, and, later, floods of tourists come and go.

Café Bar Bilbao has always been a favorite gathering spot, and it maintains the classic tradition of being open and offering full service from morning to night. In 1991, Pedro Martínez took over the business, and it continues safely in the hands of his sons, Mikel and Joserra. But even the bar's ornate molded ceilings and patterned wall tiles can't compete with the visual attraction of the bartop stacked with pintxos—normally there are anywhere from twenty to thirty different types available. Bacalao is a specialty, coming in several forms: pil-pil, ajoarriero (stewed with peppers and tomatoes), and stuffed into piquillo peppers.

Tosta de Bogavante

LOBSTER TOAST

Essentially a Connecticut-style lobster roll with a Mediterranean mayo dollop, tosta de bogavante is luxurious down to the smallest detail. Seared lobster is piled on top of grilled bread and dressed with a parsley oil redolent of garlic.

MAKES 6

1 large egg, at room temperature
¾ cup (180 ml) sunflower or other neutral oil
Kosher salt
1 tablespoon cava, at room temperature
1 tablespoon fish or lobster stock (see Notes)
A lemon wedge (optional)
Extra-virgin olive oil
½ small round rustic loaf or ciabatta, sliced into 6 pieces
9 ounces (255 g) freshly cooked lobster meat (from arms and knuckles; see Notes), broken into bite-size pieces (about 2 cups)
¼ cup (60 ml) Parsley Oil (page 82)
Flaky sea salt

SPECIAL EQUIPMENT

A pastry bag fitted with a small plain tip or a ziplock bag

Crack the egg into a tall cylindrical container. Add the sunflower oil and a pinch of kosher salt. Insert an immersion blender into the container so it touches the bottom and, without moving it, blend on the lowest setting. Once the mayonnaise is almost totally emulsified, move the blender slowly up and down to incorporate the remaining oil. (Alternatively, use a regular blender: Combine the egg and salt in the blender and, with the blender running, slowly stream in the oil through the hole in the lid.) Add the cava and stock and blend well. Taste for seasoning, adding more salt and/or lemon juice if necessary.

Transfer the aioli to a pastry bag fitted with a small plain tip or a ziplock bag. If making ahead of time, refrigerate until ready to use; if using a ziplock bag, cut off the tip of one of the bottom corners before piping the aioli.

Heat a bit of olive oil in a large sauté pan over high heat. Add the slices of bread and toast, allowing them to color slightly before turning them to toast the other side. Transfer to a plate.

Add a bit more olive oil to the pan, then add the lobster, in batches if necessary to avoid crowding, and sprinkle lightly with kosher salt. Sear for about 45 seconds on each side. Remove from the heat and let cool slightly.

Pipe a zigzag bed of aioli onto each piece of bread. Divide the seared lobster among the pieces of bread, drizzle with the parsley oil, and sprinkle with flaky sea salt. Serve.

NOTES

You can buy already-cooked lobster or cook a 1½-pound (680 g) lobster yourself. Be careful not to overcook it. If cooking a whole lobster, instead of using fish stock for the aioli, after removing the meat from the shell, boil the lobster shells in a pot of water for about 5 minutes. Strain and use the resulting lobster "stock" in the aioli.

If using frozen precooked lobster, allow it to thaw completely before using it here.

BAR ZERUKO, SAN SEBASTIÁN

✦

The road paved by early pintxo innovators like Bar Bergara (see page 216) and Aloña Berri (see page 182) leads directly to the door of Bar Zeruko. Zeruko built a fantasy world atop the foundations laid by those greats—a bar trembling under the weight of stacks and stacks of avant-garde modernist pintxos, pieces of edible art whose ingredients were rarely immediately discernible to the naked eye.

Bar Zeruko opened its doors at number 10 Calle Pescadería in 1982. Félix Calvo, a fisherman, and his wife, Perfe, named their bar after the family boat and, from their newly established business, happily served traditional Basque cuisine for years. But Zeruko truly came into its own when their children took over—Joxean led a sea change from the kitchen, and Marili became a powerful presence in the bar, a sharp-tongued matriarch whose tough love inspired both awe and affection in everyone who stepped into Zeruko.

Some years later, a facelift gave the bar a modern look—a smooth white counter, nearly a dozen small tables crowded where only a few should really have fit, and a chalkboard wall featuring a rotating list of fabulous creations: the Lobster Rose, with "green leaf" bread and dehydrated strawberry petals, stuffed with lobster and foie cream, served on a shot-glass vase smoking with the aroma of rose essence; suckling pig with mustard; the Hoguera (page 253); foie gras mousse wrapped in a sherry gel and topped with a bronzed piece of crunchy Idiazabal; and on and on. Zeruko functioned slightly differently from many other pintxo bars—most of the bar pintxos you selected would be whisked away when you ordered, sent to the kitchen to be warmed and finished, and brought to you looking more like a plated restaurant dish. Joxean brought spherifications, foams, and other trappings of Ferran Adrià's modernist cuisine to the pintxo, winning several awards and competitions in the process. Zeruko's owners eventually expanded to Barcelona, opened a restaurant alongside its tiny bar, and even toyed with the idea of opening a location in New York City. Unfortunately, however, the bar closed its doors permanently in 2019.

MIX-AND-MATCH
BREAD PINTXOS

Pintxos served atop bread allow for endless creativity. The combinations are easy to create and customize, depending on what ingredients you have on hand.

If you want to riff on the idea and go a little pintxo crazy, lightly toast a slice of baguette, choose an ingredient from each of the rows below, and make your own! Start with the items from row 1 and continue stacking the ingredients in that order, finishing with a garnish from row 4.

4

Strip of piquillo pepper

Onion-pepper vinaigrette, such as the one on page 240

Green olive

Sesame seeds

Poppy seeds

Chopped fresh parsley

3

Fried calamari

Grated hard-boiled egg

Dollop of mayonnaise

Walnuts

Jam (raspberry, apricot, kiwi, etc.)

Cherry tomato

Sliced deli ham

2

Fried guindilla or Gernika pepper

Pickled guindilla pepper

Slice of hard-boiled egg

Boiled shrimp

Hard-boiled quail egg

Jamón ibérico

Quince paste

Sautéed mushrooms

1

Stuffed piquillo pepper

Cured tuna

Cured anchovies

Smoked sardines

Ensaladilla rusa (page 106)

A mayonnaise-based salad (shrimp, leek and ham, txaka, etc.)

Smoked salmon

Spanish or Basque cheese

Blood pudding

Spanish omelet

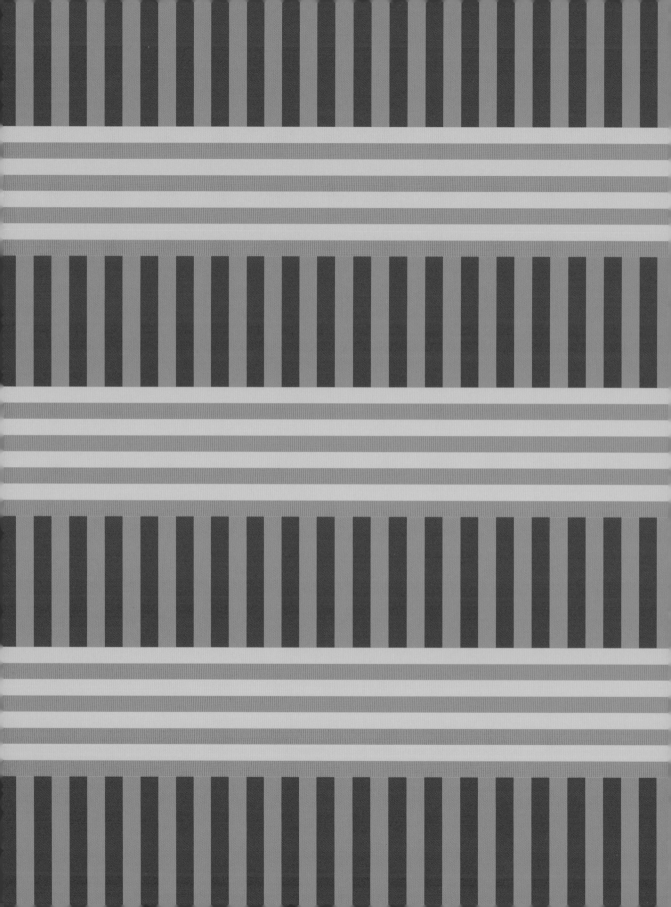

ENSALADILLA

CHAPTER THREE

PINTXOS

¡Ah, ensaladilla! The word itself is a diminutive of the Spanish word *ensalada*, or salad, used in both Spanish and English to refer to a combination of ingredients dressed with vinegar and oil. The word *ensaladilla*, however, refers to a much more mysterious, luxurious mixture of various chopped ingredients bound with a creamy mayonnaise. Ensaladillas can be made of nearly anything, although they tend to be potato- or seafood-centric. They can be served family style, to be scooped up with forks and pieces of bread, or as a pintxo, mounded atop a slice of bread. And they're found in nearly every bar in Spain.

The most popular version is the Ensaladilla Rusa (page 106), but there are many other good options. Imitation crab (see page 111), shrimp, tuna, ham, or chopped hard-boiled egg—they all blend beautifully with mayonnaise into creamy white mounds, typically perched on bread, but also found atop a base of puff pastry or pâte brisée.

Almost any ingredient can be turned into an ensaladilla, which may be why this style of pintxo has been a major vessel for chefs' creativity. Even before Nueva Cocina Vasca, Basque Country's haute cuisine movement that began in the 1970s, had trickled down to pintxo bars, chefs were arranging fiddly garnishes to create ensaladilla masterpieces. Some of these ensaladillas had grown almost baroque in nature, part of a more-is-better aesthetic that came to mark the era.

When it comes to ensaladillas of any type, the mayonnaise is key. The best mayonnaise for an ensaladilla is homemade, light, and subtly flavored. Sunflower oil is the oil most commonly used to make a mayonnaise destined to bind various vegetables and seafood. You can also add a drizzle of extra-virgin olive oil to give the mayo just a touch more flavor.

These mountains of mayonnaise-based salads may seem a fright to those accustomed to counting calories, but in the diet of northern Spain, they are viewed as the perfect way to quiet a rumbling stomach before lunch or dinner. And ensaladillas are refreshing, especially when served cool, making them the perfect summertime pintxos.

Ensaladilla Rusa

RUSSIAN POTATO SALAD

Ensaladilla rusa is, after the tortilla, the most ubiquitous and popular pintxo in Spain. With its creamy mishmash of potatoes, hard-boiled egg, mayonnaise, and various canned vegetables and seafood mounded on a piece of bread, it's a crowd-pleaser. The possible variations are endless: the type of mayonnaise, the cut of the vegetables, the proportions, and the inclusion of ingredients from canned peas to olives to carrots to red peppers. This recipe approximates the ensaladilla from Bar Ezkurra (see page 108), widely considered one of the best in San Sebastián. Make it as written a few times, and then experiment to find your own signature mixture.

MAKES 15

Kosher salt

3 large potatoes (about 550 g), preferably Yukon Gold, peeled

1 carrot

7 large eggs

¼ cup (40 g) drained canned tuna belly in escabeche

¼ cup (50 g) drained canned green peas

2 cups (500 g) mayonnaise, preferably homemade (page 44), plus about 1 cup (250 g) for garnish

1 baguette, sliced on an angle into 15 pieces

SPECIAL EQUIPMENT

A pastry bag fitted with a decorative piping tip or a ziplock bag

NOTE

If you use homemade mayo, the potato salad will keep for up to 2 days in the refrigerator, though it's always better to make it on the day you are going to eat it. With store-bought mayo, it will keep for up to 3 days.

Bring a large pot of salted water to a boil over high heat. Add the potatoes and carrot and cook for 8 minutes. Carefully add the eggs and boil for exactly 12 minutes more—20 minutes total. Use a slotted spoon or a spider to remove the eggs and run them under cold water to stop the cooking. Set aside.

Pierce one of the potatoes with a fork; if it slides in easily, the potatoes are ready. Drain the potatoes and carrot and let cool.

When the eggs are cool enough to handle, peel them.

Chop the potatoes into a medium dice. Cut 5 of the eggs and the carrot into a small dice. Place the potatoes, diced eggs, and carrot in a large bowl. Add the tuna, breaking it up, along with the peas and a generous pinch of salt.

Add 1½ cups (375 g) of the mayonnaise to the bowl and stir gently. Add the remaining ½ cup (125 g) mayonnaise a few tablespoons at a time, stirring until the mixture is creamy and smooth. Cover and refrigerate for at least 1 hour before serving (see Note).

Scoop generous spoonfuls of the salad onto the baguette slices, forming little mountains. Remove the yolks from the remaining 2 eggs (put the yolks aside for another use) and, using the small holes of a box grater, grate the whites over the pintxos, covering them with a layer of grated egg white.

Transfer the mayonnaise for garnish to a pastry bag fitted with a decorative piping tip, or transfer to a ziplock bag and cut off the tip of one of the bottom corners. Squeeze a dollop of mayonnaise onto each pintxo. Serve immediately.

BAR EZKURRA, SAN SEBASTIÁN

✦

The history of Bar Ezkurra, in San Sebastián's Gros neighborhood, dates back to 1933. It was opened by a man named Eguren, who later had to flee the city for political reasons when the Spanish Civil War broke out. He left the bar to a brother-in-law named Ezkurra ("acorn" in Basque), who put his own last name on it. When he put the bar up for sale in 1960, the Balda family, from the village of Betelu, bought it, on a tip from an uncle who lived in San Sebastián. The Baldas have run the bar ever since: first Joakin Balda, with his three sons, José María, Alejandro, and Enrique; and then Joseba, José María's son, who took over when the second generation retired in 2002.

Today the bar retains a traditional atmosphere, with a dark wooden bar, clay-colored terrazzo floor, and tables for four designed for card playing, although some relics of the past, like the mounted heads of wild game, have given way to photographs of San Sebastián and other decor. The peculiar spelling on the bar's sign, which reads EZKUŔA, is a reflection of grammatical usage that predated the standardization of Euskara in 1968. The bartop remains crowded with traditional pintxos, as it has been since the very beginning, and ensaladilla rusa is the specialty. Ezkurra sells up to 175 pounds of potato salad on busy days, such as New Year's Eve. Joseba swears by a high proportion of potato and hard-boiled egg in the mix, along with canned peas and a scattering of tuna. But he claims the secret to the popular pintxo is the mayo, from a recipe of his uncle Alejandro's, letting slip only that it contains pasteurized egg.

WHAT IS A PINTXO?

"There's a definition out there that it's
a food eaten in two or three bites, and that's it,
but I would say it's a food that doesn't reach the
amount of a *media ración*, or small plate.
It's about defining the quantity, because from
there, nowadays a pintxo can be anything."

—JOSEBA BALDA, EZKURRA

The Ensaladilla Rusa Debate

❖

There is an ongoing, spirited debate about what an ensaladilla rusa should and should not contain. In fact, the choice of ingredients is part of the statutes of the Observatorio de la Ensaladilla Rusa (ODER), a not-for-profit (and tongue-in-cheek) institution devoted to this humble dish. ODER asserts that ensaladilla rusa is defined as boiled potatoes in a light mayonnaise. Carrots and peas are approved but optional ingredients. ODER also approves the sparing use of preserved seafood, including tuna and mackerel. It does not, however, endorse the addition of red peppers, olives, shrimp, onion, parsley, chives, corn, or other commonly used ingredients.

The History of Russian Salad

❖

Russian salad has a controversial origin. Recipes for it can be found in English sources as far back as the 1840s, showing that a widespread claim that Russian chef Lucien Olivier was its inventor is bogus. (He was still a young boy at that time.) In fact, in 1815, French chef Antonin Carême published a book with a recipe for a salad of vegetables mixed with mayonnaise. And a mayonnaise salad appeared on written menus in Spain as early as the 1850s. However, it is true that the salad rose to fame from the kitchens of Olivier's restaurant, Hermitage, in Moscow, although his version contained caviar, capers, and partridge. According to ensaladilla legend, Olivier would create elaborate salads drizzled with mayonnaise only to see his diners mix everything together before eating them, which gave him the idea to serve this salad already mixed together. One of its earliest mentions in Spanish cookbooks was in the 1893 *Manual de Cocina Práctica* by M. L. Lassus. And the word *ensaladilla* was accepted into the official Spanish lexicon by the Real Academia Española in 1936, defined as "a cold food similar to ensalada rusa."

Ensaladilla de Txaka

CRAB SALAD

Txaka's story begins in the cold waters of the Bering Sea, off the peninsula of Kamchatka. Red king crab was abundant in these waters, and the company Chatka was born in 1930 to take it to market. As word of the high-quality crabmeat spread, Chatka began preserving it in cans and shipping it worldwide. Quite expensive and difficult to find, it was highly prized. During the mid-twentieth-century times of scarcity in San Sebastián, cans of Chatka crabmeat were among the products smuggled across the border to the city from France.

It wasn't until surimi was first fashioned into "crabmeat" in the 1970s, making the ingredient more accessible and affordable, that this pintxo began to gain greater popularity. The small sticks of processed fish were intended to resemble crab legs—white cylinders tinted at the edges with smoked paprika. Chopped txaka (as the word is often written now) mixed with mayonnaise and topped with hard-boiled egg is something akin to Basque comfort food. It's refreshing and cool, making it perfect to serve when it's hot outside.

MAKES 9

3 large eggs
½ baguette, sliced on an angle into 9 pieces
7 ounces (200 g) imitation crab sticks
½ cup (110 g) mayonnaise, preferably homemade (page 44)
Kosher salt

Bring a large saucepan of water to a boil. Carefully lower the eggs into the water and cook for 12 minutes, maintaining a gentle boil. Drain the eggs, run under cold water to stop the cooking, and let cool.

Meanwhile, preheat the broiler. Arrange the slices of bread on a baking sheet and broil until just toasted on the edges; the centers should still be chewy. Remove from the broiler and let cool completely.

Chop the crab sticks into tiny pieces, or pulse in a food processor until finely chopped. Transfer to a medium bowl.

Gently crack and peel the eggs. Separate the yolks from 2 of the eggs and reserve. Finely chop the 2 egg whites and add the whites to the chopped crab sticks. Add the mayonnaise and stir well. Season with salt to taste.

Arrange a heaping spoonful of the mixture atop each piece of bread. Grate the remaining egg and the reserved yolks on the medium-small holes of a box grater over the pintxos. Serve at room temperature.

VARIATION

To add a bit of retro glam, garnish each toast with a small boiled shrimp and a sprig of parsley, or a thin strip of cured salmon and a sliver of piquillo pepper.

Mayonesa sin Huevo

EGGLESS MAYONNAISE | ARRAUTZARIK GABEKO MAIONESA

If you are worried about leaving pintxos out at room temperature for hours, or you will be feeding people with special dietary requirements, you may want to sub this recipe for traditional mayonnaise. Made with milk and oil and no eggs, it is a safe bet and, when used in any of the recipes in the book, a very convincing substitute.

MAKES ABOUT 2 CUPS (440 G)

⅔ cup (160 ml) cold whole milk
1 small garlic clove, peeled
1½ cups (360 ml) sunflower or other neutral oil
2 teaspoons white wine vinegar
Kosher salt

Put the milk and garlic in a tall cylindrical container and add the sunflower oil. Insert an immersion blender into the container so it touches the bottom and, without moving it at all, blend on the lowest setting to emulsify the mixture. When the mayonnaise is almost completely emulsified, move the blender slowly up and down to incorporate the remaining oil. Add the vinegar and a pinch of salt and blend until combined. Taste for seasoning. (Alternatively, combine the milk, garlic, vinegar, and salt in a regular blender and, with the blender running, slowly stream in the oil through the hole in the lid.)

The mayonnaise will keep for several days when stored in an airtight container in the refrigerator.

El Velero

THE SAILBOAT

Sometimes the creative process of a pintxo seems to work backward. That is the case with El Velero, a pintxo from La Cepa, in San Sebastián, which consists of a slice of deli ham rolled around potato salad and garnished with shrimp and jamón ibérico. During a television interview for the channel La Sexta, one of the bar's career waiters, Gonzalo, was asked to make a pintxo. He improvised, finishing by garnishing it with a slice of ham in the shape of a sail. He called it "The Sailboat," and when pressed by the interviewer to say why, he invented a story about a boat of his that had sunk in a storm. After the interview was televised, clients wanted to try the pintxo, so La Cepa began to make it for the masses. The pintxo itself is a simple combination, with the added bonus of being quite substantial, perfect to eat after a few drinks when you need something in your stomach.

MAKES 6

½ baguette, sliced on an angle into 6 pieces
1 large egg
Kosher salt
12 medium shell-on shrimp
1 cup (275 g) Ensaladilla Rusa (page 106)
6 slices deli ham
¼ cup (55 g) mayonnaise, preferably homemade (page 44)
6 slices jamón ibérico

SPECIAL EQUIPMENT

A pastry bag fitted with a decorative piping tip

Preheat the broiler. Arrange the slices of bread on a baking sheet and broil until just toasted on the edges; the centers should still be chewy. Remove from the broiler and let cool.

Bring a large saucepan of water to a boil. Carefully lower the egg into the water and cook for 12 minutes, maintaining a gentle boil. Drain, run the egg under cold water to stop the cooking, and let cool.

Gently crack and peel the egg. Set aside.

Bring a large pot of heavily salted water to a boil (you want to use at least ¼ cup/75 g salt). Prepare an ice bath with equal parts ice and salted cold water.

When the water is boiling, add the shrimp and cook for 2 minutes. Remove the shrimp with a slotted spoon and transfer to the ice bath. Allow the shrimp to cool completely, then drain and peel, discarding the heads (if any) and shells. Devein the shrimp, if desired.

Place a heaping spoonful of ensaladilla rusa on one of the shorter edges of a piece of deli ham and roll the ham up around the salad into a cylinder. Place it seam side down on one of the slices of toasted bread. Repeat with the remaining deli ham and potato salad.

CONTINUED →

Transfer the mayonnaise to a pastry bag fitted with a decorative piping tip and squeeze a dollop onto both sides of each ham roll. Nestle a shrimp next to each dollop.

Using the small holes of a box grater, grate the egg over the top of the pintxos. Thread each piece of Ibérico ham onto a long toothpick, forming an S shape, with the ham at the top of the toothpick so it looks like a sail. Pierce the middle of each ham roll with one of the toothpicks to fasten the "sails" to the pintxos, and serve.

LA CEPA, SAN SEBASTIÁN

✦

La Cepa sits, virtually unchanged over the past seventy years, on San Sebastián's historic Calle 31 de Agosto. The bar opened in 1948, and Joaquin Pollos and his wife, Loren Astiazaran, took it over in 1999. They had experience running cafés and nightclubs in the city, but with La Cepa, they'd had a clear mission: to maintain tradition. They removed some of the mounted bull heads and bullfighting posters, relics from the former *torero* owner Santi Mayor, but the bar retains its terra-cotta tiles, whitewashed walls, and stained wood accents.

La Cepa has always been known for its ham, and cured legs of jamón ibérico still hang in a row above the wooden bar. Ham on a baguette, plates of sliced ham, pintxos with ham— many of the older generation of La Cepa clients have been coming here for jamón for half a century. The menu itself has hardly changed, with a mix of traditional cazuelitas, earthenware dishes of stews, salt cod, potatoes, and fried eggs, simple but delicious offerings made with good local products. In 2021, the family sold the bar to Bernardo Beltrán, a seasoned restaurateur of the Old Town and the founder of Beti Jai and Bernardo Etxea.

Ensaladilla de Puerro y Jamón

LEEK AND HAM SALAD

This ensaladilla is typical of Basque Country, likely due to the predominance of leeks in Basque gardens, where most of Spain's leeks are grown. They form the base of many traditional dishes, as well as this common pintxo, which combines leeks with a bit of ham and a generous scoop of mayonnaise to make a light, refreshing bite.

MAKES 6

Kosher salt

2 leeks, white and light green parts only, rinsed well

1½ ounces (42 g) sliced deli ham (about 3 slices)

½ spring onion (see Note, page 49), white and light green parts only

⅓ cup (75 g) mayonnaise, preferably homemade (page 44)

½ teaspoon Dijon mustard

½ baguette, sliced on an angle into 6 pieces

2 sun-dried tomatoes, thinly sliced (for a total of 12 slices)

Bring a large pot of salted water to a boil.

Slice the leeks lengthwise in half and cut into thin slices. Add the leeks to the boiling water and blanch them for 3 minutes. Drain in a colander, rinse under cold water to stop the cooking, drain again, and then pat dry.

Cut the ham into pieces similar to the slices of leek.

Cut the spring onion into the thinnest slices possible.

In a medium bowl, stir together the mayonnaise and mustard. Add the leeks, ham, and onion and stir well. Season to taste with salt.

Preheat the broiler. Arrange the slices of bread on a baking sheet and broil until just toasted on the edges; the centers should still be chewy. Remove from the broiler and let cool completely.

To serve, arrange a heaping scoop of the ensaladilla on top of each baguette slice. Smooth the ensaladilla with a spatula or spoon so it has a nice round appearance. Garnish each pintxo with 2 strips of sun-dried tomato and serve.

THE "SECRET" INGREDIENT

Once upon a time, up into the 1950s, the mayonnaise in pintxo bars and restaurants was mixed by hand. But the advent first of food processors and, later, of immersion blenders, mechanized the process. Then, after the first salmonella cases caused by raw eggs hit northern Spain in 1985, laws were passed that ended restaurants' use of raw eggs in mayo, decreeing: "Eggs will be substituted with pasteurized egg products . . . house-made mayonnaise, in addition to being made with pasteurized egg products, must have an acidity below 4.2 pH in the final product." Now Huevina and other brands of pasteurized eggs are the norm when it comes to making mayonnaise.

MIX–AND–MATCH
ENSALADILLA RUSA
PINTXOS

Ensaladilla rusa can reach the level of art with the addition of a few garnishes. Although some purists may say any topper beyond the traditional grated hard-boiled egg is anathema, there are others who take ensaladilla art quite seriously. If you'd like to decorate your ensaladillas with a final flourish, here are some options. You can mix and match these ingredients to garnish a single pintxo, or you can serve the entire ensaladilla in a serving dish and get even more elaborate with the garnish.

Fresh chives, whole or chopped

Fresh parsley, sprigs or chopped

Preserved fish— tuna, mackerel, or anchovies

Mini breadsticks

Olives, pitted or stuffed with pimientos, whole, halved, or sliced

Cornichons, whole or chopped

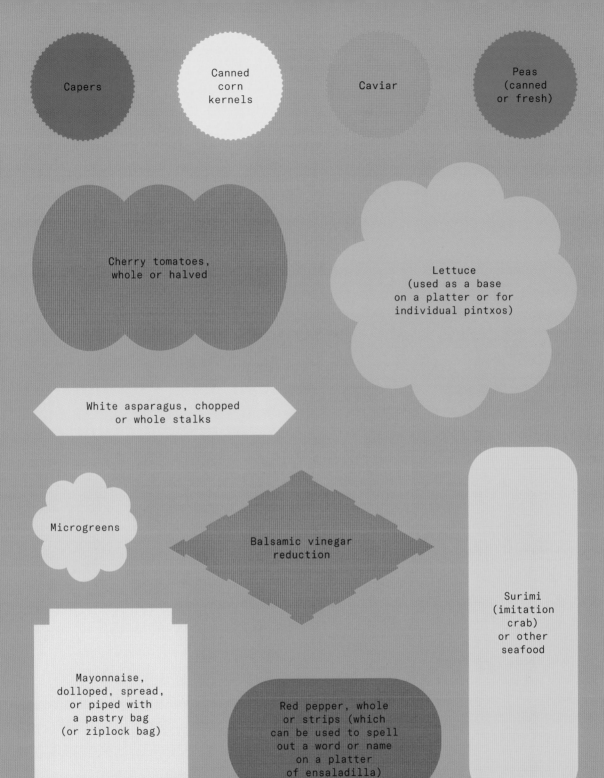

Capers

Canned corn kernels

Caviar

Peas (canned or fresh)

Cherry tomatoes, whole or halved

Lettuce
(used as a base
on a platter or for
individual pintxos)

White asparagus, chopped
or whole stalks

Microgreens

Balsamic vinegar
reduction

Surimi
(imitation
crab)
or other
seafood

Mayonnaise,
dolloped, spread,
or piped with
a pastry bag
(or ziplock bag)

Red pepper, whole
or strips (which
can be used to spell
out a word or name
on a platter
of ensaladilla)

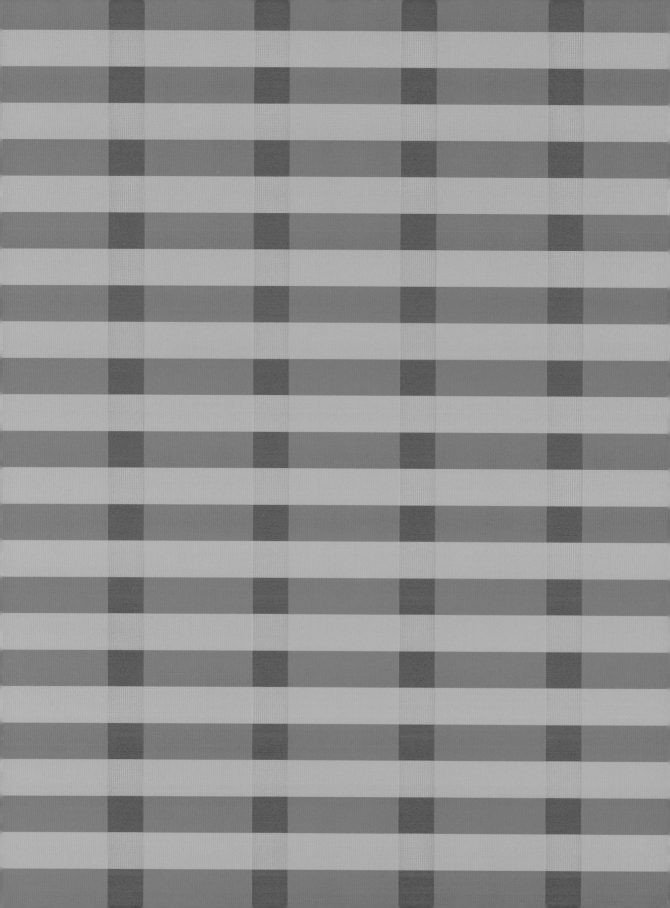

FRIED

CHAPTER FOUR

PINTXOS

In the land of olives, oil is abundant and free-flowing. That is one of the reasons frying is such an integral part of Spanish cuisine. From the pescadito frito of southern Spain to the fried pintxos of the north, the art of cooking ingredients submersed in hot oil is on full display morning, noon, and night.

Nearly every bar serves fried pintxos. They are the workhorses of the bar, the bites that are guaranteed to soak up the glasses of wine. But pintxos are often enjoyed by the whole family, and croquetas, bolas, and other traditional fried pintxos are a crowd-pleaser for all ages. The children act like mini adults, oohing and ahhing over croquetas as they sip their grape juice (mosto) or gather in the corners to amuse themselves.

Many of the fried pintxos you can order today actually predate the concept of pintxos. Before banderillas (see page 41) were set out on plates at the bar counter, fried seafood, croquetas, and fried breaded meats were sold at drinking holes as far back as the late 1800s. They came into their own in the mid-twentieth century, when creativity collided with scarcity in the form of simple foods, combined and fried in endless variations, including the Moscovita (page 135) and Gavilla (page 149). In Vitoria, the Puelles family at Bar Trafalgar gained fame for their spin on the banderilla, in which croquetas, bolas, fried shrimp, and more stood in for the traditional pickled vegetables. Today the level of artistry evident in fried pintxos runs a huge gamut, from frozen industrial battered shrimp to homemade béchamel croquetas, breaded to order as at Bar Fitero in Pamplona (see page 221).

Recipes for fried pintxos in all their variations could fill an entire book. This chapter offers the most famous fried bites from cities across Basque Country.

FRYING 101

It may be what's on the inside that counts, but a golden, crispy exterior is a must for a perfect fried pintxo. A good masa (batter) or rebozado (breading) is held in veneration, spoken of with awe, in almost religious reverence. But the truth is that the trick is almost never in the recipe—it is in the raw materials and in the hands of the experienced fryer, who knows instinctively when the oil temperature is right and coddles each nugget to a golden brown.

The Batters

Here are the common types of batters and coatings used for fried pintxos.

BREADCRUMBS

The Spanish love their fine breadcrumb coatings, as evinced by the ample offering of different styles, sizes, and flavors of preground breadcrumbs in the grocery store. A simple fine breadcrumb coating, after a dip in flour and an egg wash, is considered the breading par excellence. Homemade breadcrumbs are a rarity, even at the finest establishments. Panko does make an appearance, but only in more modern places.

EGG WASH

A dip in nothing but an egg wash is a favorite treatment for seafood, resulting in a pillowy exterior that complements the briny sea flavor. Unlike pintxos with other coatings, some argue, these pintxos are even more delicious served at room temperature.

MASA ORLY

This fermented batter can be made with yeast or beer. It is extremely popular for frying seafood, vegetables, and balls of béchamel. The yeast version often also includes an egg white beaten to stiff peaks.

TEMPURA Made with cold water and flour, this batter is seen only in more modern pintxo bars; it is never used for traditional fried pintxos.

Double Dipping

❖

It's perfectly fine to reuse your frying oil. In fact, using it
at least twice is common practice, especially where olive oil is
concerned. Allow the oil to cool and then strain it into a jar
or bottle and seal it with the lid. If you don't have a strainer,
allow the sediment to settle to the bottom of the pot and then
leave that behind when you transfer the oil.

Fry Right

❖

The temperature of the oil is of utmost importance when making
fried pintxos, and the ideal temperature is 350°F (175°C). If
the oil is too hot, whatever you are frying will get too brown
on the outside while remaining undercooked on the inside. If the
oil is too cold, the exterior won't set up quickly enough and
the pintxo will absorb the oil, resulting in a grease overload.
If the oil is at the perfect temperature, a crispy exterior will
form quickly, preventing the pintxo from absorbing the oil, and
the time required to brown the exterior will be perfectly matched
to the time needed to heat the interior or cook it through.
To test the oil temperature, you can either use an instant-
read thermometer or try the traditional trick of tossing a few
breadcrumbs into the hot oil to see if they sizzle vigorously.

Frying Oils

❖

Which oil is best for frying battered fish and croquetas is
hotly contested among the frito cognoscenti. Some swear by
olive oil, but the truth is, many restaurants and bars prefer
to use sunflower oil, the Spanish answer to vegetable oil. From
a nutritional standpoint, though, olive oil is almost always
preferable. Extra-virgin olive oil maintains its healthful
qualities even when heated to higher temperatures. When it
comes to the finished product's taste, however, the real bottom
line is maintaining the correct temperature, using good frying
techniques, and, of course, starting with good-quality raw
ingredients.

Bola de Carne

MEAT FRITTER

This pintxo looks unassuming; it's a simple browned meatball. However, in the case of the bola de carne, it's what's on the inside that counts. The interior is like a croqueta on steroids: béchamel holds together ground beef, spices, and peppers. The Alegria Riojana peppers in the filling add a tiny bit of heat to keep things interesting. In Pamplona, these are often called fritos de pimiento.

MAKES 18 TO 20

1 tablespoon extra-virgin olive oil

½ onion, finely diced

½ sweet Italian green pepper, such as Cubanelle, minced

1 garlic clove, minced

Kosher salt

1 pound (454 g) ground beef

½ beef bouillon cube, crushed

2 hot red Alegria Riojana peppers, minced

⅓ cup (80 ml) white wine

½ teaspoon pimentón, dulce or picante (sweet or hot)

2¾ cups (345 g) all-purpose flour, plus more for dredging

2 cups (480 ml) whole milk

1¼ cups (300 ml) beer, preferably lager

2 tablespoons sunflower or other neutral oil

Olive oil for deep-frying

In a large skillet, heat the extra-virgin olive oil over medium-high heat. Add the onion, green pepper, garlic, and a pinch of salt and cook, stirring occasionally, until the vegetables begin to turn translucent, about 5 minutes. Add the beef, another pinch of salt, and the crushed bouillon cube and cook, breaking up the meat with a wooden spoon and stirring occasionally, until it is thoroughly cooked through, 7 to 8 minutes.

Add the hot red peppers, white wine, and pimentón and simmer until the liquid has reduced by about half.

Add ¾ cup (95 g) of the flour and cook, stirring well, for about 1 minute. Add the milk little by little, stirring constantly. When all the milk has been added, cook for a few minutes longer to thicken the mixture. Season to taste with salt. Remove from the heat, press a piece of plastic wrap directly against the surface of the mixture, and let cool completely.

ALEGRIA RIOJANA PEPPERS

•

Alegria Riojana peppers can range from 50,000 to 100,000 on the Scoville scale. They are generally sold in small (2.8-ounce/80 g) cans or jars. These peppers are similar to the guindillas of Basque fame, allowed to ripen and turn red before being wood-fired and jarred. They are native to the Rioja region, as the name indicates, where heat is generally tolerated much better than in Basque Country. If you can't find canned Alegria Riojana peppers (see Resources, page 302), substitute fresh cayenne or red Thai chile peppers.

Meanwhile, sift the remaining 2 cups (250 g) flour into a medium bowl. Add a generous pinch of salt. Whisk in the beer little by little until you have a smooth batter. Whisk in the sunflower oil, mixing well. Cover the bowl with plastic wrap and chill for at least 1 hour or up to overnight.

Form the meat mixture into spheres the size of a golf ball (about 1½ ounces/45 g each) and set aside on a plate.

In a large heavy saucepan, heat 2 inches (5 cm) of olive oil over high heat until it reaches about 350°F (175°C). Use a thermometer to test the oil, or throw in a bit of the batter; if it sizzles on contact, the oil is ready. Spread some flour on a plate.

Working in batches to avoid crowding the pan, one by one, dredge the meatballs in the flour, shaking off the excess, then pierce with a toothpick, if desired, dip in the chilled batter, and add to the hot oil. Fry the meatballs, turning them occasionally for even cooking, until golden brown, about 3 minutes. Remove with a slotted spoon and drain on paper towels. Sprinkle immediately with salt.

Transfer the meatballs to a platter and serve warm.

How to Eat a Fried Pintxo

❖

The nature of fried pintxos means that they are served, for the most part, directly from the kitchen. There are some establishments that reheat fried pintxos that have been sitting out on the bar, but this practice is frowned upon by in-the-know locals. This means the pintxos typically come hot, on a plate handed to you by the bartender. They may or may not have a toothpick protruding—if so, grab one by the toothpick and take a bite! If not, hands and fingers are fair game for picking up and eating the pintxo. Some fried pintxos come with a fork, which, of course, is acceptable to use but not mandatory.

Merluza Rebozada

BATTERED HAKE

Battered hake falls squarely into the classic pintxo camp. Also known as *merluza frita* (fried hake) or *merluza a la romana* (Roman-style hake), the fish undergoes a dusting of flour and a dip in egg before being fried to golden perfection in bubbling olive oil. Tender sautéed green peppers and a dollop of mayonnaise are a common garnish.

If you can't find hake, cod or flounder makes a fantastic substitute. The freshness of the fish is the foundation of this dish.

MAKES 6

3 tablespoons olive oil
2 sweet Italian green peppers, such as Cubanelle, julienned
Kosher salt
¼ cup (60 ml) white wine
1 pound (454 g) hake fillet(s)
1 large egg
Flour for dusting
½ baguette, sliced on an angle into 6 pieces
½ cup (110 g) mayonnaise, preferably homemade (page 44)

In a medium sauté pan, heat 1 tablespoon of the olive oil over medium-high heat. Add the peppers with a pinch of salt and sauté, stirring occasionally, until tender, 10 to 15 minutes. Add the white wine and simmer until the liquid has evaporated. Remove from the heat and set aside.

Cut the hake into 6 equal rectangular portions. Beat the egg in a shallow bowl. Spread the flour on a plate.

In another medium sauté pan, heat the remaining 2 tablespoons olive oil over medium-high heat. Working in batches to avoid crowding the pan, sprinkle the pieces of hake lightly with salt, pass each piece through the flour, turning to coat and shaking off the excess, dip into the egg, coating it completely and letting the excess drip off, and add to the hot oil. Cook, turning once, for 2 to 3 minutes on each side (depending on size), until golden brown. Drain on paper towels.

Place a piece of fish atop each of the bread slices. Arrange a pile of sautéed green peppers on one end of each piece and spoon a dollop (or decoratively pipe a large dot) of mayonnaise on the other end. Serve immediately.

Gamba a la Gabardina

FRIED SHRIMP

Gabardina means, literally, "trench coat." And these shrimp, dipped in a batter known as masa orly, appear to be sporting a fashionable outer layer when they emerge from the hot cooking oil. The most famous gambas a la gabardina in Basque Country come from the kitchen of Paco Bueno (see page 132), where the closely guarded secret behind this perfect bit of fried shellfish has been in the family for more than seventy years, passed down from generation to generation.

This recipe is only an approximation, but the Bueno family shared a few tips for its execution. Most important, of course, is to use the best shrimp you can find, preferably fresh. A not-insignificant hint is that at Paco Bueno, they make the tempura batter twice a day, a few hours before each service; this resting time is key to the quality of the finished product, so make your batter at least an hour ahead of time if you can. And finally, mix the batter with a light touch—in the Paco Bueno kitchen, they've been known to use their hands to mix it with care.

MAKES 6

⅓ ounce (10 g) compressed fresh yeast
1¼ cups (300 ml) lukewarm water
2 cups (250 g) all-purpose flour
1½ teaspoons sugar
1½ teaspoons table salt
Olive oil for deep-frying
12 extra-large shrimp, peeled, tails left on
Kosher salt

To prepare the tempura batter, mix the yeast with a bit of the lukewarm water in a large bowl and let sit for a few minutes, until foamy.

Add the rest of the water to the bowl, then sift the flour, sugar, and table salt little by little into the liquid. Set the batter aside to rest at room temperature for at least 20 minutes or, ideally, an hour or more.

When ready to fry the shrimp, pour about 2 inches (5 cm) of oil into a deep heavy saucepan and heat over high heat until it reaches 350°F (175°C). Use a thermometer to test the oil, or toss in a bit of the batter; if it sizzles on contact, the oil is ready.

Season the shrimp with kosher salt. Working in batches, dip the shrimp in the batter, a few at a time, add to the hot oil, and fry, turning once, until lightly golden, 2 to 3 minutes. Drain on paper towels.

When they are cool enough to handle, thread 2 shrimp onto each of six long toothpicks. Serve immediately.

PACO BUENO, SAN SEBASTIÁN

✦

Paco Bueno had a promising boxing career ahead of him—he was poised to compete in the 1936 Olympics in Berlin—until the Spanish Civil War began and he was taken prisoner. Once released, he watched helplessly with gloves off as the Second World War broke out on the European continent. When that war finally ended, his boxing career had been stalled for too long, and at age thirty-four, the need to find a living beyond boxing led Paco to open his namesake bar on San Sebastián's Calle Mayor in 1950. Hospitality ran in the family—Paco's mother ran the successful Café La Paz in nearby Errenteria, and his mother-in-law joined him in the kitchen of his new bar.

Athletics run in the family too—Paco Jr., who helped out behind the bar starting at the age of fourteen, played on Spain's national rugby team. He

took over when Paco retired, alongside his wife, Mariaje. Today, their son Gorka runs the day-to-day operations of Bar Paco Bueno and works in the kitchen. For four generations, and more than seventy years, this family has put in fifteen-hour days, making thousands upon thousands of the famous gamba a la gabardina pintxo, with the same recipe used since the beginning. All the pintxos are classics—including tortillas made with potatoes still peeled by Paco Jr. himself, banderillas, chorizo, ensaladilla rusa, and more.

The History of the Croqueta

❖

The oldest reference to this beloved fried item dates
from France in the 1600s, when a mixture of leftovers was
formed into the first croquette. (*Croquette* because, yes,
this most Spanish of snacks is French in origin.) The
name, loosely translated, means "little crunchy thing."
The first written recipe came from a chef who cooked
for members of Louis XIV's court, and the croquette was
indeed fit for a king: a mixture of truffles, shortbread,
and cheese, bound with egg. The first reference to
béchamel sauce, the croqueta's traditional binding agent,
is believed to have appeared in 1733. Croquetas arrived
in Spain in the early 1800s, and the rest is history.

Gracias por su visita

Moscovita

MUSCOVITE

Made with nothing but hard-boiled eggs, cured jamón, and Swiss cheese, this pintxo is simple to prepare, requiring just a dip into a leavened batter and a bubbling deep-fry. The combination is as filling as it is delicious, so you only need to allot one pintxo per person.

This has been served up at Hostería del Temple (see page 136) in Pamplona's Casco Viejo since the bar first opened its doors. Owner Luis christened the pintxo after a friend of his from Moscow whom everyone called El Ruso. Its appearance may also play a role in its name, as some say this big fried chunk looks like a piece of Muscovite mica.

MAKES 6

2 cups (250 g) all-purpose flour, plus more for dredging
Kosher salt
1¼ cups (300 ml) beer
2 tablespoons sunflower or other neutral oil
3 large eggs
2½ ounces (75 g) Emmental cheese (see Notes)
6 slices (about 1½ ounces/45 g) jamón serrano (see Notes)
Olive oil for deep-frying

Sift the flour into a large bowl and add a generous pinch of salt. Whisk in the beer little by little, until you have a smooth batter. Whisk in the sunflower oil, mixing well. Cover the bowl with plastic wrap and chill for at least an hour or up to overnight.

Bring a large saucepan of water to a boil. Carefully lower the eggs into the water and cook for 12 minutes, maintaining a gentle boil. Drain the eggs, run under cold water to stop the cooking, and let cool.

Cut the cheese into twelve 1-inch (2.5 cm) cubes.

Gently crack and peel the eggs. Cut lengthwise in half.

Pierce a piece of cheese with a long toothpick or round skewer, then fold a piece of ham into an S shape and skewer it next to the cheese. Add an egg half, piercing it through the middle of the yolk, and follow it with another piece of cheese. Repeat with the remaining ingredients to make a total of 6 skewers.

Pour about 2 inches (5 cm) of olive oil into a deep heavy saucepan and heat over high heat until it reaches about 350°F (175°C). Use a thermometer to test the oil, or toss in a bit of the batter; if it sizzles on contact, the oil is ready.

Spread some flour on a plate. Working in batches to avoid crowding the pan, pass each skewer through the flour, turning to coat and shaking off any excess, then dip the skewers in the batter, turning to coat completely, and add to the hot oil. Fry the pintxos until golden brown, a minute or two on each side. Remove with a slotted spoon and drain on paper towels.

Transfer the skewers to a platter and serve warm.

NOTES

Emmental is the classic Swiss cheese, but you can use any Swiss-style cheese you like here.

Although Hostería del Temple uses serrano ham, you can sub prosciutto, jambon de Bayonne, or even jamón ibérico—they're all delicious in this!

HOSTERÍA DEL TEMPLE, PAMPLONA

✦

Luis Fernandez and Mercedes Santa Cruz decided to open a dining establishment in Pamplona's old town in 1965. They took over Bar Goñi, a restaurant that had served simple, traditional lunches, and gave it a makeover. They chose the name Hostería del Temple (Temple Inn) as an homage to the Knights Templar, whose presence in Navarra dates back to 1133, and to the Camino de Santiago, which passes right by the restaurant's front door. They renovated the bar in a medieval style with local decorator Alejandro Gomez, restoring dark wooden beams for the ceiling, installing a copper hood behind the bar, and hanging paintings of castles and scenes from the Middle Ages.

The walls are lined with ceramic tiles from Teruel in Aragon, which are more somber than the bright Andalucían tiles, and look right at home in Hostería del Temple's small, dark bar. When they opened their doors, Luis and Mercedes offered the fritos that Pamplona is known for and, before long, kept their bar lined with tortillas, pintxos, and earthenware dishes of offal. Today this venerable spot is an institution in Pamplona, now run by the second generation: Clara, Carlos, and Maite.

PAMPLONA

ABOVE Bar Gaucho, Pamplona

Pamplona is the capital of Navarra, the purported birthplace of the Basque people. Iruña, as Pamplona is known in Euskara, is a town of just more than 200,000 people and is perhaps most famous for the "running of the bulls" during its San Fermín celebration. Casco Viejo, the celebrated old quarter, has more than its fair share of buildings dating back to the Middle Ages, giving it an ancient, unflappable air.

The city is the nucleus of the province, the beating heart of its financial, commercial, and industrial sectors. It's also home to several universities, ensuring a year-round atmosphere of revelry and a thriving street life. The Catholic influence is still felt strongly, in no small part thanks to the religious pilgrims who pass through the city on the Camino de Santiago.

Pamplona's pintxo scene centers around its fritos, or fried things. This category includes anything deep-fried in oil, from croquetas, with their béchamel-based fillings encased in breadcrumbs, to gambas gabardina, shrimp dipped in a tempura batter and puffed to golden perfection. The city boasts a collective claim to expertise in the crunchy golden exterior and a gift for frying that matches that of Andalucían housewives, who can, according to urban legend, fry the wind. In modern times, Pamploneses enjoy a wider variety of options, like black fritos made with squid ink, or even a "fried ceviche"—proving that even the oldest pintxo traditions can evolve with the times.

ABOVE Pamplona's Casco Viejo

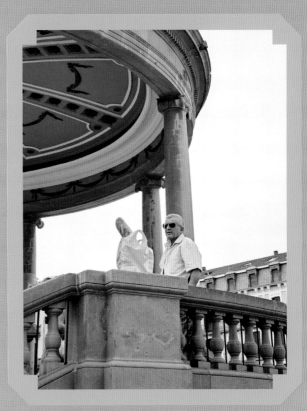

ABOVE Plaza de Castillo, Pamplona

ABOVE Plaza de Castillo, Pamplona

ABOVE Bar Fitero, Pamplona

Mejillón Relleno

STUFFED MUSSELS

In Bilbao and other parts of Basque Country, mussels are popularly known as *mojojones*. The mussels for this pintxo are chopped and simmered in a mixture of paprika-spiced caramelized onions, then spooned back into their shells, capped with a thick béchamel, breaded, and fried. When they have a spicy bite, they are known as *tigres*, or tigers, but this version from Baste is somewhat milder. Fried seafood is a staple of the Sunday *poteo* on the streets of Bilbao's Zazpikaleak, or Old Town, and on a busy Sunday, Baste might see hundreds of these flying out of the fryer by the plateful, steaming and satisfying.

MAKES 12

8 medium to large mussels (see Notes)
4 tablespoons (60 ml) extra-virgin olive oil
½ cup (120 ml) white wine
½ onion, diced
¼ cup plus 2 tablespoons (47 g) all-purpose flour, plus more for dredging
1 teaspoon pimentón dulce (sweet)
1 teaspoon pimentón picante (hot)
Kosher salt
1 tablespoon tomato sauce (see Notes)
¼ cup (60 ml) Cognac or other brandy
1½ teaspoons cornstarch
1 tablespoon unsalted butter
1½ cups (360 ml) whole milk, warmed
Freshly ground white pepper
Freshly ground black pepper
1 large egg
About 3 cups (300 g) dry breadcrumbs
Sunflower or other neutral oil for deep-frying

Rinse the mussels and scrub off any barnacles. Soak the mussels in a bowl of cold water for about 20 minutes.

Drain the mussels and remove any "beards" by pulling down sharply on each; discard. Rinse the mussels and drain well.

In a small pot, heat 2 tablespoons of the olive oil over high heat. Add the mussels, place a lid on the pot, and cook for about 1 minute. Pour in the white wine, shake the pot, and cook the mussels for another 1 to 2 minutes, until they open. Discard any mussels that remain closed. Remove the mussels from the pot and reserve the cooking liquid.

Open the mussels and remove the meat; reserve the shells, separating the two halves. Finely chop the meat and set aside.

In a sauté pan, heat the remaining 2 tablespoons olive oil over medium heat. Add the onion and sauté until tender and beginning to take on a golden hue, about 10 minutes. Add 2 tablespoons of the flour, both pimentóns, and a pinch of salt and cook, stirring, for a few minutes. Add the tomato sauce and cook, stirring, for a minute or two.

Add the mussels, the reserved cooking liquid, and the Cognac and bring to a simmer. Mix the cornstarch with a tablespoon or so of cold water to make a slurry and add to the pan. Cook, stirring, until the mixture is homogeneous and begins to pull away from the sides of the pan, 3 to 5 minutes. Remove from the heat and allow to cool.

In a large sauté pan, melt the butter over medium-high heat. Add the remaining ¼ cup (30 g) flour and cook, stirring with a whisk, for about 1 minute, being careful not to let the flour color. Whisking vigorously, add the milk little by little, until it has all been incorporated. Add a generous pinch each of salt, white pepper,

and black pepper. Taste the béchamel and add a bit more salt, if desired. Remove from the heat.

Arrange the 12 mussel shells on a tray. Divide the mussel mixture among them, filling them to just above the top edge. While the béchamel is still warm, scoop a spoonful of it over the top of each filled shell. Allow to cool completely at room temperature, or refrigerate for quicker cooling.

Set up your breading station: Cover the bottom of a shallow bowl with flour. Beat the egg with a bit of water in another shallow bowl. Place the breadcrumbs in a third shallow bowl.

Remove any béchamel hanging over the edges of the mussel shells. Dredge the mussels in the flour, shaking off the excess, then dip in the egg, allowing the excess to drip off, and finally roll in the breadcrumbs to coat. Place the coated mussels on a clean dry plate or baking sheet and set aside until ready to fry.

Pour about 2 inches (5 cm) of sunflower oil into a large heavy saucepan and heat over high heat until it reaches about 350°F (175°C). Use a thermometer to test the oil, or throw in a few breadcrumbs; if they sizzle on contact, the oil is ready. Working in batches to avoid crowding the pot, add the mussels to the hot oil and fry, turning them occasionally for even cooking, until light golden brown, 3 to 4 minutes. Remove with a slotted spoon and drain on paper towels.

Transfer the mussels to a platter and serve warm.

The Day of the Croqueta

❖

Every January 16, the Día Internacional de la Croqueta is celebrated in bars throughout Spain and across social media. The International Day of the Croqueta originated, as many such celebratory days do, as part of a publicity campaign. Created for a Madrid restaurant, La Croqueta, by its marketing team, the campaign quickly went viral, as people argued over the best recipe and the ins and outs of making this favorite dish.

BASTE, BILBAO

✦

In 1969, the brothers Basterretxea opened this small bar off Plaza Miguel de Unamuno after putting in time at Guria, Bilbao's temple of classic cuisine, and Juanito Kojua, one of San Sebastián's top restaurants at the time. They created a menu of classics, from their famous stuffed mussels to salt cod and squid, that endures today. Their niece, Mari Carmen Samblas, and her husband, José

María Martín, have worked in the bar since nearly the beginning, and they took over the reins in 2003 with their friend and now-partner, Óscar Zarzosa. While the decor was changed, leaving only the original stone walls, the cuisine has remained faithful to Basque tradition. Mari Carmen and José María are still behind the stoves, cooking up bacalao al pil-pil, lamb sweetbreads, porcini scrambles, and croquetas based on their famous béchamel. Baste has long been an obligatory stop for many Bilbao families.

Croqueta de Pollo

CHICKEN CROQUETTE

Croquetas are the Proustian madeleine of Spain—crunchy golden nuggets filled with a silky béchamel that remind everyone of their childhood and their mother's cooking. Every bar has a croqueta, and the blank-palette nature of béchamel makes croquetas endlessly customizable—whether flavored with jamón, porcini, blood sausage, and salt cod, along with more interesting combinations like blue cheese and walnut. Chicken croquetas are a common version, with slightly retro overtones; the béchamel, studded with tender pieces of chicken and hard-boiled egg, is made in the same pan used for cooking the chicken, making it extra flavorful.

Making croquetas can be a bit involved, requiring constant stirring of the béchamel, cooling of said béchamel, and then the three-step breading of the individual croquetas. The good news is, these bites are more than worth the trouble, and they also freeze well. This recipe yields nearly three dozen for that very reason—if you plan ahead, a single afternoon of croqueta making can yield many future moments of pure fried enjoyment.

MAKES 30

5 large eggs
1 tablespoon extra-virgin olive oil
Two 6-ounce (170 g each) boneless chicken breasts
Kosher salt
3 tablespoons unsalted butter
½ onion, finely diced
1 cup (125 g) all-purpose flour, plus more for dredging
4 cups (960 ml) whole milk, warmed
2 cups (220 g) fine dry breadcrumbs (see Notes)
Sunflower or other neutral oil for deep-frying

SPECIAL EQUIPMENT

A large pastry bag (optional)

Bring a large saucepan of water to a boil. Carefully lower 2 of the eggs into the water and cook for 12 minutes, maintaining a gentle boil. Drain the eggs, run under cold water to stop the cooking, and let cool.

Meanwhile, heat a large sauté pan over medium-high heat and add the olive oil. Season both sides of the chicken breasts with salt and place them in the pan. Cook, turning once, until firm to the touch, about 5 minutes per side. Transfer the chicken breasts to a plate to cool (set the pan aside), then chop the chicken into small pieces.

Gently crack and peel the hard-boiled eggs. Finely chop them and set aside.

Add 2 tablespoons of the butter to the sauté pan and melt over medium heat, scraping up any bits of chicken from the bottom. Add the onion and cook until translucent and very tender, about 15 minutes.

CONTINUED →

Increase the heat to high and add the chopped chicken, stirring to combine. Add the flour and stir constantly with a whisk for about 1 minute. Whisking vigorously, add the milk, little by little at first, and then working up to ½-cup (120 ml) increments, until it has all been incorporated. Add ½ teaspoon salt and the remaining tablespoon of butter, stirring to melt it. Taste the béchamel and add a bit more salt, if desired. Stir in the chopped hard-boiled eggs.

Transfer the mixture to a baking pan, cover with plastic wrap, pressing it directly against the surface, and refrigerate for at least 1 hour or up to overnight. (Chilling will make it easier to form perfectly shaped croquetas.) Or transfer the mixture to a large pastry bag and chill, if you'd like to pipe out the filling, a faster option.

When ready to shape and fry the croquetas, beat the remaining 3 eggs in a bowl with a bit of water. Spread the breadcrumbs on a rimmed baking sheet or large plate. Spread flour on a large plate for dredging.

If your croqueta base is in a baking pan, scoop up about 2 tablespoons of the mixture and form it into a small ball. Roll it back and forth between your palms to form a cylinder. Dredge the croqueta in the flour, shaking off the excess, then dip it in the egg, allowing the excess to drip off, and finally roll it in the breadcrumbs to coat. Set the croqueta on a clean large plate or baking sheet. Repeat with the remaining mixture, and set aside until ready to fry.

If your croqueta base is in a pastry bag, if necessary, snip the tip from the bag to leave an opening about 1 inch (2.5 cm) in diameter. Pipe roughly 3-inch-long (7.5 cm) logs of the mixture onto the plate with the flour, cutting them apart as you go with a butter knife or other straight edge. Sprinkle with more flour to coat and then, working with one piece at a time, dip them in the egg, allowing the excess to drip off, roll them in the breadcrumbs to coat, and set on a clean large plate or baking sheet.

The breaded croquetas can be refrigerated, tightly covered, for up to 3 days. They can also be frozen for up to 3 months, and then can go straight from freezer to fryer when desired. To freeze, put the croquetas on a baking sheet and freeze until solid, then transfer to a freezer bag.

Pour about 2 inches (5 cm) of sunflower oil into a large heavy saucepan and heat over high heat until it reaches about 350°F (175°C). Use a thermometer to test the oil, or throw in a few breadcrumbs; if they sizzle on contact, the oil is ready. Working in batches to avoid crowding the pan, fry the croquetas, turning them occasionally for even cooking, until golden brown. Remove with a slotted spoon and drain on paper towels; sprinkle immediately with salt.

Transfer the croquetas to a platter and serve warm.

URKABE, SAN SEBASTIÁN

✦

From its post at the back of Gros, far from the beach and the city's Old Town, Urkabe still serves up the same menu as when it opened in 1982. It is the definition of a neighborhood bar—family-run, simple, dependable, and filled with a loyal clientele. Now headed up by Javi Dominguez, the bar was opened by his wife's parents, Máximo Muñiz and Vicenta Saralegui. The specialty is the chicken croqueta, although the salt cod version, the Spanish omelet, and the Urkabito (a large piece of fried salt cod with red pepper and béchamel) are also popular. Decorated with a few plants and pictures of San Sebastián, it's a small bar with a retro vibe. Javi's motto is "If something works, don't change it," and the constant flow of regulars, whom he greets with a shout and a smile, proves he's right. Urkabe holds the distinction of being one of the only bars in the city's central neighborhoods that is closed on the weekends.

Gavilla

SHEAF

For this pintxo, a combination of pork tenderloin, cured ham, and melty Swiss cheese is covered in béchamel and deep-fried. There is no way it could be anything but delicious, but its hold on the residents of San Sebastián goes beyond simple taste. At the time of its creation, it was a revelation that took the ubiquitous croqueta to new levels. The easiest way to coat the skewers of pork and cheese with the béchamel is to dip them into the sauce while it is still hot, then lay the skewers on a plate to cool.

MAKES 8

1 tablespoon extra-virgin olive oil
Two ¼-inch-thick (6 mm) slices pork tenderloin (about 4 ounces/113 g total)
Kosher salt
4 slices jamón serrano (see Note)
4 slices Swiss cheese
4 tablespoons (60 g) unsalted butter
½ onion, finely diced
2 cups (250 g) all-purpose flour
4 cups (960 ml) whole milk, warmed
2 large eggs
1½ cups (165 g) fine dry breadcrumbs
Sunflower or other neutral oil for deep-frying

NOTE

Jamón serrano is made in a way very similar to ibérico, but it comes from commercially raised pigs, not a heritage Spanish breed. The meat of those pigs is of a lower quality, and therefore jamón serrano (while delicious) is seen as a more workaday cured ham, often used in cooking or fed to children. You can use other types of cured ham for this pintxo, from the finer ibérico to ham from Bayonne, or even prosciutto.

Heat the olive oil in a sauté pan over medium-high heat. Sprinkle the pork tenderloin slices with salt and sauté, turning once, for 2 minutes on each side, or until cooked through. Remove from the heat and let cool.

Cut each tenderloin slice into quarters, trimming away any excess fat. Cut the slices of jamón in half. Cut the Swiss cheese slices in half.

Pierce a piece of ham with a long toothpick, folding it in half twice to make it bite-size. Fold a piece of cheese in half and skewer it with the toothpick, sliding it next to the ham. Finally, add one of the pieces of tenderloin. Repeat with the remaining ingredients to make a total of 8 pintxos. Set aside.

Melt the butter in a sauté pan over medium heat. Add the onion and cook until translucent and very tender, about 15 minutes.

Increase the heat to high, add 1 cup (125 g) of the flour, and stir with a whisk for about 1 minute. Whisking vigorously, add the milk, little by little at first, then working up to ½-cup (120 ml) increments, until it has all been incorporated, then continue whisking until the béchamel is smooth and thick. Stir in ½ teaspoon salt, taste, and add a bit more salt, if desired. Remove from the heat and let cool slightly.

Dip each pintxo in the warm béchamel, rotating it to coat it on all sides, and transfer to a plate. Refrigerate until completely cooled (refrigerating the pintxos will cool them quickly and make them easier to work with).

Beat the eggs in a bowl with a bit of water. Spread the breadcrumbs on a rimmed baking sheet or large plate. Spread the remaining 1 cup (125 g) flour on another plate.

CONTINUED →

Dredge each pintxo in the flour, shaking off the excess, then dip it in the egg, allowing the excess to drip off, roll it in the breadcrumbs to coat, and set on a plate or baking sheet. Repeat with the remaining pintxos and set aside until ready to fry.

If you aren't frying them immediately, the pintxos can be covered and refrigerated overnight. They can also be frozen for up to 3 months and then can go straight from freezer to fryer when desired. To freeze, put the pintxos on a baking sheet and freeze until solid, then transfer to a freezer bag.

When ready to fry, pour about 2 inches (5 cm) of sunflower oil into a large heavy saucepan and heat over high heat until it reaches about 350°F (175°C). Use a thermometer to test the oil, or toss in a few breadcrumbs; if they sizzle on contact, the oil is ready. Working in batches to avoid crowding the pan, fry the pintxos, turning them occasionally for even cooking, until golden brown, 3 to 4 minutes. Remove with a slotted spoon and drain on paper towels. Immediately sprinkle with salt.

Transfer to a platter and serve warm.

Huevo Frito con Patata

FRIED EGG WITH POTATO

A fried egg with potatoes is perhaps the simplest, most homey dish in Spanish cuisine. This pintxo takes the concept and flips it—the potato is transformed into a paper-thin sheet that is wrapped around a raw egg yolk and pancetta, sprinkled with salt, and fried. To eat it, you pop the entire pintxo into your mouth, and with a single bite, it explodes, thrillingly.

This pintxo is the star of the menu at Sagartoki, sometimes dressed up with a slice of the local Álava truffle. On a busy Saturday, the bar has been known to sell more than a thousand of them.

MAKES 6

Kosher salt
1 large potato, peeled and chopped
1 tablespoon unsalted butter
¼ cup (60 ml) milk, warmed
6 thin slices bacon or pancetta
6 large eggs
Flaky sea salt
Extra-virgin olive oil for deep-frying

Preheat the oven (preferably in convection mode) to 195°F (90°C). Line a 13 by 18-inch (33 by 45 cm) baking sheet with a silicone baking mat or parchment paper.

Bring a medium saucepan of salted water to a boil. Add the potato and boil until nearly falling apart, about 20 minutes. Drain the potato (don't worry about getting the pieces super dry; a bit of water is OK) and transfer to a food processor or blender.

Add the butter and 2 tablespoons of the milk to the potatoes and process until smooth, adding up to 2 tablespoons more milk if necessary, until you get a runny puree. Season with kosher salt to taste.

Using an offset spatula, spread the potato puree over the prepared baking sheet in the thinnest-possible layer. Transfer to the oven to dehydrate for about 4 hours, until the edges are just beginning to brown; be sure to remove the sheet of potato puree from the oven before it is fully dehydrated so that it is still flexible. Allow the sheet to cool enough so that you can handle it.

Cut the potato sheet into 4 by 5-inch (10 by 12.5 cm) pieces. Transfer to a plate or tray and reserve.

Cut each piece of bacon in half and then make a cross out of the 2 halves. Separate the eggs and very gently place a yolk atop the center of each cross (discard the egg whites or reserve for another use). Sprinkle the yolks with flaky salt. One by one, lift up the corners of the crosses and lay them gently over each egg yolk.

Check on your potato squares. If they aren't flexible enough, spray them lightly with water to lend them a bit more flexibility. With a small metal spatula, place one egg yolk packet atop each of the potato rectangles. Lift a long side of one of the rectangles and fold it over the bacon-egg packet. Grasp the edges and fold them over again, in the same direction, so the packet is totally enveloped. Lightly moisten the edges of the other two sides to help them stick and fold them over in an envelope-like fold. Turn the packet seam side down and repeat with the remaining pintxos.

Pour about 2 inches (5 cm) of olive oil into a large heavy saucepan and heat over high heat until it reaches 350°F (175°C) on an instant-read thermometer. Place one pintxo in a slotted metal spoon or on a slotted spatula, seam side down, and gently dip it halfway into the oil. Hold it there for about 10 seconds to seal the seams, then fully submerge the pintxo in the oil and fry, flipping it once, for about 90 seconds, until it is an even golden color. Remove and place on paper towels to drain. (It is best to fry just one at a time until you get the hang of these delicate pintxos.) Repeat with the remaining pintxos.

Allow the pintxos to rest for about 1 minute, then serve.

SAGARTOKI, VITORIA

Senén González was raised behind a stove. His parents ran a small restaurant-bar in the village of Beasain (Gipuzkoa). Sagartoki was a cider house when Senén first took a job there in 2001, at the age of twenty, but by the time he was twenty-two, he had bought part of the restaurant and begun to update the pintxo roster—in his words, "copying what they were doing in San Sebastián." Soon Sagartoki started to enter pintxo contests and win. It was given the award for Best Pintxos Bar (La Mejor Barra de Pinchos) in 2005 at the Lo Mejor de la Gastronomía awards. The huevo frito con patata, born from a spark of inspiration Senén had while dining at the restaurant Rodero in Pamplona, won Best Tapa of España back-to-back in 2006 and 2007. In 2010, Sagartoki won a national award for the best Spanish omelet.

Senén is one of the only pintxo bar owners who has gone as far as to patent his creations. At his R & D space and factory (opened in 2020), he has created an entire line of heat-and-eat foods, as well as machines to automate the creation of tortillas de patata. Both the premade sheets of potato wrappers and the deep-fried egg pintxo are exported to countries from Belgium to Italy (see Resources, page 302).

Black Rabas

BLACK CALAMARI

On Sundays in the Old Towns of Basque Country (especially in Bilbao), you can smell the calamari frying. Passing around a plate of rabas is a weekend ritual in even the humblest *taberna*, or traditional bar.

These black *rabas* (the common term for fried calamari in the north of Spain) turn the traditional dish on its head, presenting a plate of pillowy rings that, at first glance, could pass for tempura-fried calamari. In fact, they hold a filling prepared in the style of the classic Basque dish called squid in ink. The squid is pureed, placed in circular silicone molds (a technique inspired by Xabi Gutierrez, head of R & D at Restaurante Arzak), and fried in a yeast batter. With its flavorful filling and steaming-hot crunchy exterior, this pintxo is an *alta cocina* nod to traditional cooking.

MAKES 60

1¾ pounds (800 g) cleaned squid

⅔ cup (160 ml) extra-virgin olive oil, plus more for deep-frying

⅔ cup (160 ml) sherry

2 large onions, chopped

1 sweet Italian green pepper, such as Cubanelle, cored, seeded, and chopped

3 garlic cloves, minced

Kosher salt

1 ounce (28 g) jamón ibérico, minced (about ¼ cup)

2 tablespoons tomato sauce, preferably homemade (page 209)

1¼ cups (300 ml) Fish Broth (recipe follows)

2 teaspoons squid ink (see Notes)

⅓ ounce (10 g) compressed fresh yeast

1¼ cups (300 ml) lukewarm water

2 cups (250 g) all-purpose flour, plus more for dredging

1½ teaspoons sugar

SPECIAL EQUIPMENT

60 silicone mini donut molds (with a diameter of 1½ inches/4 cm)

A pastry bag fitted with a large plain tip

Cut the squid into 1-inch (2.5 cm) pieces. Pat thoroughly dry with paper towels.

In a large sauté pan, heat 2 tablespoons of the olive oil over high heat. Once it is hot, add about a third of the squid (avoid crowding the pan) and cook, stirring occasionally, for a few minutes, until the squid has released most of its liquid and is beginning to sear. Add one-third of the sherry, stirring to deglaze the pan, and simmer to reduce the liquid for 30 seconds to 1 minute. Transfer the squid and any liquid to a bowl and return the pan to the heat. Repeat with the remaining squid and sherry in two more batches. Reserve the squid.

In a large pot, heat the remaining olive oil over medium heat. Add the onions, green pepper, garlic, and a pinch of salt and cook, stirring, until the vegetables are tender, about 20 minutes.

Add the ham and the tomato sauce and simmer for a minute or two. Add the squid and its liquid and stir. Add the fish broth and squid ink and bring to a simmer. Simmer for 15 minutes, or until the squid is tender. Taste, adding salt if necessary. Remove from the heat and allow the mixture to cool.

Transfer the squid mixture to a food processor and process until smooth. Let the mixture cool completely.

Arrange 60 silicone mini donut molds on two baking sheets. Transfer the filling to a pastry bag fitted with a large plain tip and pipe it into the molds. Transfer to the freezer and freeze completely.

CONTINUED →

Pop the squid rings out of the molds, transfer to ziplock bags or an airtight container, and freeze until ready to fry.

To prepare the batter, mix the yeast with a bit of the lukewarm water in a large bowl and let it sit for a few minutes, until foamy.

Add the rest of the water to the bowl, then sift in the flour, sugar, and ½ teaspoon salt little by little. Set the batter aside to rest at room temperature for at least 20 minutes or, ideally, an hour or more.

Pour about 2 inches (5 cm) of olive oil into a large heavy saucepan and heat over high heat until it reaches about 350°F (175°C). Test the oil with a thermometer, or drop a bit of batter into it; if it sizzles on contact, the oil is ready. Spread some flour on a plate.

Working in batches to avoid crowding the pan, add the squid rings (directly from the freezer) to the flour, shaking off the excess, then dip in the batter, allowing the excess to drip off, and add to the hot oil. Fry, turning once, until golden, 1 to 2 minutes. Remove from the hot oil with a slotted spoon and drain briefly on paper towels.

Arrange the fried squid on a platter and serve immediately.

Fumet

FISH BROTH | ARRAI SALDA

MAKES ABOUT 2 QUARTS (1.9 L)

Bones, head, and tail from 1 fish, preferably hake
1 carrot, chopped
1 leek, chopped and rinsed well
½ spring onion (see Note, page 49), chopped
3 parsley sprigs
Kosher salt

Thoroughly rinse the fish bones, head, and tail to remove any residue. Transfer to a stockpot.

Add the carrot, leek, spring onion, and parsley to the pot, then add enough water to cover completely and a generous pinch of salt. Bring the water to a boil, reduce the heat to maintain a gentle simmer, and cook for 20 minutes, skimming off any foam that forms on the top.

Remove the broth from the heat and allow it to steep a bit; about 10 minutes is sufficient.

Strain the broth through a fine-mesh sieve, discarding the solids. Use immediately, or let cool completely and transfer to airtight containers. It will keep in the refrigerator for up to 5 days or in the freezer for at least 6 months.

A FUEGO NEGRO, SAN SEBASTIÁN

Chef Edorta Lamo's avant-garde pintxo bar, opened in 2006, was an unlikely combination of a passion for soul music, underground culture, and the local food traditions of his grandparents. From the beginning, the bar Lamo opened with Amaia Garcia on Calle 31 de Agosto stood out from the pack. It wasn't just the innovative pintxos, from olives filled with vermouth gel to tiny hamburgers with bright red ketchup buns to salt cod marshmallows filled with piperrada reduction. It was the dark ambient lighting of the place, the hip-hop beats in the background, and the innovative plating inspired by both pop culture and Basque culture. Even some of the tiny details were groundbreaking and quickly copied, like the bar's black cocktail napkins and longer, more visually striking pintxo sticks.

The bar, which was a pioneer in every sense of the word, became a bastion of the San Sebastián pintxo scene, one that emphasized both modern cooking techniques and the special culinary traditions of the area. A Fuego Negro closed its doors in 2020, but Lamo continues his legacy at Arrea!, a farm-to-table restaurant in the rural province of Álava.

MIX-AND-MATCH
CROQUETAS

Croquetas are a pillar of Spanish snack cuisine. And it's
no wonder—their crunchy breadcrumb exterior gives way
to a gorgeously creamy interior, an addictive combination that
also has an element of nostalgia for many people. Another reason
for their popularity is their versatility. You can make a croqueta
with almost anything, thanks to the adaptable béchamel base.
Following the recipe below, make a béchamel and then mix in
5 ounces (140 g) of your desired ingredient, chopped. Spread the
mixture in a baking pan and chill for at least 1 hour; or transfer
it to a pastry bag, which will make it easier to form perfectly
shaped croquetas. Then bread and fry following the instructions
on page 146.

Here are some tips on how to get creative with the croqueta,
as well as some ideas to serve as inspiration.

BECHAMELA | BÉCHAMEL | BECHAMEL

This creamy béchamel makes the perfect versatile
base for any croquetas.

MAKES 4½ CUPS (1215 G), ENOUGH FOR ABOUT 30 CROQUETAS

5 tablespoons (70 g) unsalted butter
½ onion, finely diced
1 cup (125 g) all-purpose flour
3¼ cups (780 ml) whole milk
1 cup (240 ml) heavy cream
Kosher salt

In a large sauté pan, melt the butter over medium heat. Add the onion and cook
until translucent and very tender, about 15 minutes.

Increase the heat to high, add the flour, and stir with a whisk for about 1 minute.
Combine the milk and cream and whisk into the pan, little by little at first, working
up to ½-cup (120 ml) increments, until incorporated. Add a generous pinch of salt.
Taste the béchamel and add a bit more salt, if desired. Add any flavoring of your
choice before transferring the béchamel to a tray or storage container. Press plastic
wrap directly against the surface to prevent a skin from forming and refrigerate
until ready to form the croquetas.

Creation Techniques for Croquetas

INFUSION: Infusing the milk and/or cream for the béchamel is a great way to make your croquetas extra flavorful, and is especially recommended when it comes to more delicately flavored foods. You can use the ingredient of your choice, scraps, or even bones. Add to a saucepan with the milk or cream and bring to a simmer, then remove from the heat and set aside to infuse for at least 15 minutes or up to an hour. Strain the liquid to remove the solids before adding the infused milk or cream to the roux.

USE COOKING JUICES: When the principal ingredient must be sautéed or otherwise cooked before being incorporated into the béchamel, a great technique for amping up the flavor is to make your béchamel in the same pan (without cleaning it). The juices and the browned bits on the bottom of the pan will deepen the flavor of the béchamel.

CHOP AND ADD YOUR INGREDIENT: The next step in making many croquetas is adding the ingredient in question, in small pieces, to the béchamel. The rule of thumb here is that the ingredient must be ready to eat, so if it's something that needs to be cooked before eating, cook it before you add it to the béchamel. And don't add too much—the croqueta should just be studded with the ingredient, so that the béchamel still makes up most of the filling.

BREADING: The final step is the breading. Most croquetas are coated with dry breadcrumbs or, for a more modern style, panko. If you are using nuts in your croqueta filling, including them in the coating is also fair game. Popular variations include morcilla croquetas coated in ground pistachios and cheese croquetas with hazelnuts or walnuts. Grind up the nuts and use them instead of or mixed with breadcrumbs to coat the croquetas after the egg wash.

Ideas for Croqueta Fillings

Tuna

Salt cod

Blue cheese (such as Cabrales, a strong blue cheese from Asturias)

Cured beef

Chocolate

Spinach and shrimp

Walnuts

Idiazabal (cured sheep's-milk cheese from Basque Country)

Apple

Blood sausage

Pistachios

Chicken

Salmon

Mushrooms, especially porcini or oyster

Squid, tinted black with its ink

Pork sausage (such as sobrasada, a lightly cured sausage from the Balearic Islands)

Chorizo (or txistorra)

159

BAR

PINTXOS

In this chapter, you'll find pintxos that are neither pierced by a toothpick nor perched atop a slice of bread yet still retain a hallowed spot on a decked-out pintxo bartop. These are the items that you spot first when you walk into a pintxo bar. They sit in clusters, half a dozen deep (or more, depending on size), covering the bar completely. You can often just grab them yourself, but sometimes a waiter will insist on heating the pintxo (often by microwave, either in the kitchen or directly behind the bar) before serving it to you.

The creation of many of these dishes marked a turning point in the history of the pintxo. These dishes represented the first step out of the canon of traditional pintxo-dom and into a world of miniature culinary creativity. The small plate or individual earthenware casserole becomes a blank slate that offers a world of possibilities beyond toothpicks and sliced bread. These are pintxos that may necessitate silverware, a once unthinkable development.

The recipes in this chapter showcase enough creativity to make your head spin. From the Spanish omelet (page 166), that workhorse of the pintxo bar, to the gorgeous and luxurious foie gras nougat (page 199), they range from traditional to exquisitely modern. Some of these pintxos are deceptively simple, like the ham croissant (page 177), while others come off as undeniably gourmet (despite being quite easy to make), like the Idiazabal cheese soup with porcini (page 190). The one thing they all have in common is that they are both legendary *and* delicious.

THE
DISPLAY CASE

Glass display cases have appeared, disappeared, and reappeared throughout the history of pintxo bars. The national law Real Decreto 3484/2000, enacted on December 29, 2000, obligated bars to keep food under the correct conditions in terms of temperature, hygiene, and cleanliness, preventing "contamination by nearby waste or residue, smoke, toxic substances, and other strange substances." This was widely seen as a law implementing the use of glass cases. The legislation was enforced by occasional patrols, with fines that typically hovered around 500 to 1,000 euros. Most pintxos remained uncovered on bartops, however, and glass cases began to have a retro feel as bars complying with the law became fewer and farther between. The latest, most lasting change came about thanks to COVID-19. Following the lockdowns of 2020, almost every bar that has reopened has returned to keeping pintxos covered, employing everything from glass display cases to plastic tops.

ᴀʙᴏᴠᴇ Bar Gaucho, Pamplona

Tortilla de Patatas

SPANISH OMELET

The Spanish omelet, or potato tortilla, has a place of honor on virtually every bartop in Spain. The tortilla española is much more than the sum of its parts. Made of nothing more than potato, egg, olive oil, and, often, onion, it comes together in a soft, savory snack perfect for any time of day.

The trick to this simple pintxo lies not in quantifiable elements but in the cook's hand and their attention to the smallest sensory details when cooking it (as well as the nonstick qualities of the pan used). It's a dish that can take a few attempts to get the hang of, but it is worth every minute. Tortilla is perfect at any meal, served in wedges with a bit of bread on the side, or cut into bite-size squares for parties. The tortilla should be cooked on the outside but juicy and the tiniest bit runny when you cut into it.

SERVES 8

3 large potatoes, preferably Yukon Gold, Kennebec, or Monalisa, peeled
3 tablespoons extra-virgin olive oil, plus more if needed
2 onions, thinly sliced
2 teaspoons kosher salt
1 cup (240 ml) sunflower or other neutral oil
10 large eggs

Halve the potatoes lengthwise and then cut each half lengthwise into quarters. Chop into pieces about ½ inch (1.5 cm) wide; you should have about 4 cups (see Notes). Put the potatoes in a bowl, add water to cover, and set aside.

In a small sauté pan, heat 2 tablespoons of the olive oil over high heat. Add the onions, sprinkle with ½ teaspoon of the salt, reduce the heat to medium, and cook, stirring occasionally, for about 40 minutes, until the onions are totally soft and have taken on a deep golden color. Remove from the heat and set aside.

Meanwhile, in a medium skillet, heat the sunflower oil over medium heat to about 250°F (120°C). Drain the potatoes and pat them dry. Use a thermometer to test the oil, or drop in a piece of potato; if it sizzles on contact, the oil is ready. Add the potatoes to the hot oil and cook for about 15 minutes, or until a knife inserted into a larger piece slides in easily. Use a slotted spoon to remove the potatoes from the oil, transfer to a plate or bowl, and sprinkle them with ½ teaspoon salt.

In a large bowl, beat the eggs with the remaining 1 teaspoon salt. Add the onions and potatoes and stir to combine. Allow the mixture to stand for 3 to 5 minutes.

NOTES

Some prefer thin, round slices of potato, while others like an irregular shape. To get that, insert a knife about ½ inch (1.5 cm) into a peeled potato and then rotate and lift the knife, breaking off an irregularly shaped piece; repeat.

The choice of pan is key; it should be a 10-inch (25 cm) nonstick skillet, with its nonstick properties fully intact.

CONTINUED →

"It is a different concept from the tapa, which could even be a stew, a plate of something to go with a drink. Here you have your drink, yes, but the pintxo stands on its own."

—JESÚS IÑIGO, ÁBACO

Heat a perfectly clean, fully nonstick 10-inch (25 cm) skillet (see Notes) over high heat. (The bigger the stove burner, the more evenly the tortilla will cook.) Coat the skillet with the remaining 1 tablespoon olive oil. Add the egg-potato mixture and immediately reduce the heat to medium. Stir to even out the mixture, and then allow the egg to cook, without stirring, for 3 to 4 minutes. Move the spatula around the sides of the pan as the tortilla begins to set, slipping it under the eggs and loosening any stubborn stuck parts very gingerly, to ensure that the tortilla does not stick to the surface. The edges of the tortilla should look fully cooked, but the center should still be a bit liquid.

Place a round plate with a diameter larger than the pan upside down on top of the pan. With one hand on the plate and the other holding the pan, quickly flip the pan and plate together in one motion to invert the tortilla onto the plate.

If any of the tortilla has stuck to the pan, quickly clean the pan and coat it with a bit more oil. Return the pan to the heat and slide the tortilla back into the pan. Tuck the edges under with your spatula and cook for a minute or two more.

Slide the tortilla onto a serving plate and let rest for 5 minutes before slicing it into 8 wedges and serving.

The Big Tortilla Fiasco

❖

In 2014, the town of Vitoria-Gasteiz put on a spectacle that included the making of the world's biggest tortilla. A 15-foot pan, 1,850 pounds of eggs, nearly 2 tons of potatoes, 66 pounds of onions, and 22 pounds of salt later, the gigantic Spanish omelet became a reality. The effort was led by chef Senén González (see page 152) but became something of a scandal after the title was taken away because of a previous record achieved in Japan. The Basques claim the Japanese version was not a true Spanish tortilla because it was cooked on only one side; they tried unsuccessfully to get the *Guinness World Records* judges to revisit their decision, but locally, the event remains shrouded in notoriety.

BAR NESTOR, SAN SEBASTIÁN

✦

There are very few bars that have a wait list for their tortilla—in fact, there may be only one: Bar Nestor, in San Sebastián. For the past twenty years, one of its famous juicy, glorious egg-and-potato omelets has been set out every day at 1:00 p.m., and then another one at 8:00 p.m. And most days, within a matter of minutes, they are gone, cut into sixteen small rectangles and distributed to those who were wise enough to get their names on the list. This curious system was born of the fact that the bar has always had only three gas burners, and making more tortilla would take up too much time and space.

Nestor Morais is a bar owner made and shaped by San Sebastián's Old Town. He came to the city from Valladolid in 1970 or so, at just sixteen years of age, and put in nearly a decade behind the pintxo bar at the legendary Casa Alcalde and Beti Jai. In 1980, at the age of twenty-six, he opened Bar Nestor with his bride, Pilar Senra, by his side. Pilar churned out pintxos from the kitchen, and Nestor and his brother, Tito, manned the bar.

At first, Bar Nestor seriously multitasked, with the requisite bar full of pintxos and gin-tonics served under flashing lights into the early morning hours. Little by little, though, it streamlined its offerings, becoming what it now is: a bar with a few tables and fewer menu items. Visitors know what to expect: a fresh, simple tomato salad (the first of its kind in San Sebastián); fried and salted green Gernika peppers; and a glorious bone-in steak, charred and sprinkled liberally with flaky sea salt. (The steak has been on the menu since the night Nestor pulled out the one he'd bought for his own dinner to cook for some regulars.) And, of course, the famous tortilla.

Triángulo del Eme

THE EME TRIANGLE

This is most certainly *not* the recipe for one of Bilbao's most famous pintxos, the sandwich from Bar Eme. The secret behind the bar's beloved "triangles" lies in the sandwich bread they use, made daily in-house and impossible to duplicate, as well as the salsa Rossini, whose recipe is possibly more secret than the nuclear codes. The garlic, peppers, olive oil, and other ingredients that make up the spicy red sauce couldn't possibly be more traditional, but in the 1950s, this piquant, flavorful salsa would have been the talk of the town thanks to its exotic hint of heat, cementing Bar Eme's fame for decades to come.

To make the sandwich, the key is to find the best artisanal white bread possible. The sauce should be slathered on generously, along with the mayonnaise, and sandwiched with deli ham and lettuce. These sandwiches were once smaller, tidier affairs, cut into triangular shapes (hence the name). Nowadays the sandwich is cut into rectangles. The deli ham used at Bar Eme is cut relatively thick, so if your ham is quite thin, you may want to use more slices.

MAKES 6

2 large eggs
2 tablespoons extra-virgin olive oil
2 garlic cloves, smashed
1 jar (10.2 ounces/290 g) piquillo peppers
1 hot red Alegria Riojana pepper (see page 126)
1 tomato, chopped
2 teaspoons Worcestershire sauce
¼ teaspoon white wine vinegar
1½ cups (360 ml) water
¼ teaspoon kosher salt
½ cup (110 g) mayonnaise, preferably homemade (page 44)
2 tablespoons whole milk
6 slices white artisan sandwich bread
6 medium-thick slices deli ham
Green leaf lettuce for serving

Bring a large saucepan of water to a boil. Carefully lower the eggs into the water and cook for 12 minutes, maintaining a gentle boil. Transfer the eggs to a bowl of ice water and let cool, then drain, peel, and roughly chop.

In a sauté pan, heat the olive oil over medium-high heat. Add the garlic and sauté, turning occasionally, until golden, 3 to 5 minutes. Add the piquillo peppers with their liquid and bring to a simmer, then lower the heat to medium and cook for about 15 minutes, until the peppers lose some of their water content and begin to confit.

Add the chopped eggs, Alegria Riojana pepper, chopped tomato, Worcestershire, and vinegar to the peppers. Pour in the water, add the salt, and bring to a simmer. Lower the heat to medium and allow the sauce to cook for 15 minutes or so. Then remove from the heat and let cool slightly.

Using an immersion blender or a regular blender, blend the sauce mixture thoroughly.

In a small bowl, whisk the mayonnaise and milk together.

Spread 3 pieces of bread with the red sauce and place 2 slices of ham on each piece. Cover the ham on each piece of bread with a lettuce leaf or two. Spread the remaining 3 pieces of bread with a generous amount of the mayonnaise mixture. Place, mayonnaise side down, on top of the lettuce. (You may have extra red sauce, which can be reserved for another use.)

Cut the sandwiches in half, either horizontally into rectangles or on an angle to create triangles, and serve.

BAR EME, BILBAO

To understand Bar Eme, you must first understand its history. Established by Emeterio Arnáez in 1950, the bar was in a then out-of-the-way neighborhood, next to the city's grain exchange, the *alhóndiga*. Emeterio introduced the pintxos you will find on the current menu, from the *triángulos* to the *torres*, or towers, which are three layers of bread, sandwiched with lettuce leaves, cured anchovies, and a spicy mayonnaise-based secret sauce. The torres are very similar to the Felipada, the well-known sandwich from Bar Alameda down the street. A menu rounded out with ensaladilla rusa and different classic fried pintxos was the extent of Bar Eme's offerings in the early days. Then, the famous triangle was 7 pesetas, compared to today's price of €3.10.

Emeterio died young and his daughters took over the bar, continuing to make the famous sandwiches until they retired at the end of the 1980s. Under the daughters' care, the kitchen was totally artisanal: the bread dough was kneaded by hand and baked in a tiny oven, then the bread was sliced with a serrated knife. The bar is one of the few in town that has always offered food to go, perhaps owing to the neighborhood's blue-collar roots.

Today Emeterio's great-grandchildren are at the helm of the bar: Oscar, Koldo, Esther, and Borja Morales. The current generation broadened the menu and oversaw a 2014 renovation that left little of the former bar's wooden counters and traditional vibe. For all their concessions to modernity, however, they keep the sandwich the same, with its top-secret sauce recipe locked away in the family safe.

Pastel de Pescado

HAKE PÂTÉ

This "fish cake" was one of the emblematic pintxos at Bar Astelena (see page 175) in San Sebastián's Old Town. Poached and shredded hake is baked in a mixture of homemade tomato sauce and egg before being whipped into a creamy mound with a bit of homemade mayonnaise. Famed chef Juan Mari Arzak would snack on it after his morning market run, and he added an upscale version to the menu of his Michelin-starred restaurant, making this pintxo famous nationwide. Serve it the old-school way, on a slice of bread with some mayonnaise piped on top, or try a more modern presentation by serving it in an elegant flat spoon.

MAKES 6

Kosher salt
9 ounces (255 g) hake fillet
½ cup (120 ml) tomato sauce (see Note)
1 large egg
½ cup (110 g) mayonnaise, preferably homemade (page 44)
½ baguette, sliced on an angle into 6 pieces

SPECIAL EQUIPMENT

A pastry bag fitted with a decorative piping tip (optional)

Preheat the oven to 350°F (175°C).

In a medium pot, bring enough salted water to cover the fish to a boil. Add the fish, reduce the heat to maintain a simmer, and gently poach the fish until cooked through, 4 to 6 minutes, depending on the thickness of the fish. Remove the fish from the pot and set aside.

In a medium bowl, beat together the tomato sauce and egg. Break the cooked fish into tiny pieces, add to the tomato-egg mixture, season with a generous pinch of salt, and mix well.

Spread the mixture evenly in a loaf pan or small baking pan. Set the loaf pan in a roasting pan and place in the oven. Pour enough hot water into the roasting pan to come about halfway up the sides of the loaf pan and bake for about 30 minutes, until a toothpick inserted into the center of the pâté comes out clean. Remove from the oven, carefully remove the loaf pan from the water bath, and set aside to cool completely.

Unmold the pâté and transfer to a small bowl. Stir in ⅓ cup (73 g) of the mayonnaise, mixing well.

Mound the mixture on the pieces of baguette, distributing it evenly. Top with the remaining mayonnaise, either spooning it on in generous dollops or piping it on with a pastry bag fitted with a decorative piping tip. Serve.

NOTE

For the tomato sauce, you can use a smooth store-bought sauce or make your own (see page 209).

Pintxos Donostiarras

Pintxos Donostiarras, published in 1992, was the first book dedicated to the bars of San Sebastián and the pintxos served in them. The book, by food writer Pedro Martín, is a 347-page time capsule capturing the pintxo scene at the time in a straightforward, no-frills fashion. Each bar gets two pages, which include their name (and logo, for the savvy bars that had one), address, and three recipes. The best part is the photos of the pintxos, presented simply on a white background. There are no pretensions—several pintxos go by names like Pintxo #1, Pintxo #2, and Pintxo #3. Despite its cut-and-dried presentation (or perhaps because of it), the book was a hit across Basque Country. It was especially popular with chefs in the neighboring provinces. The book became their bible, showing them how to re-create the fabulous bar pintxos that were all the rage in San Sebastián. Martín has published a handful of other books on the pintxo, including *Donosti Pintxo a Pintxo* (1996), which also had a wide influence.

Ropa Vieja

OLD CLOTHES

Ropa vieja means "old clothes," and this dish has always been about giving scraps of meat from broths, soups, and stews a delicious second life. In most parts of Spain, and in Cuba, the dish is a generous helping of stewed meat with vegetables, and sometimes garbanzo beans. However, a pintxo of ropa vieja in San Sebastián is something quite different: an omelet studded with shredded braised meat, caramelized onions, and chopped green peppers.

This reinterpretation of the dish is thanks to the González family, who served a rich, warm broth to the farmers who supplied their bar and then mixed the meat scraps left behind with eggs in the form of a tortilla, or Spanish omelet (page 166). This take was so popular that it spread to other bars, and the ropa vieja donostiarra was born.

MAKES 18

2 tablespoons plus 1½ teaspoons sunflower or other neutral oil, plus more if needed

4 medium onions (25 ounces/700 g), finely chopped

4 sweet Italian green peppers (9 ounces/255 g), such as Cubanelle, finely chopped

1 teaspoon kosher salt

1 baguette, sliced into 18 pieces

1 cup (215 g) shredded braised beef

11 large eggs

Extra-virgin olive oil for drizzling (optional)

In a 10-inch (25 cm) nonstick skillet (see Note), heat 2 tablespoons of the sunflower oil over high heat. Add the onions and peppers and sprinkle with ½ teaspoon of the salt. Reduce the heat to medium and cook, stirring occasionally, for 30 to 40 minutes, until the onions are caramelized and a deep golden color.

Meanwhile, preheat the broiler. Arrange the slices of bread on a baking sheet and broil until just toasted on the edges; the centers should still be chewy. Remove from the broiler and let cool.

Drain off any excess oil from the caramelized vegetables, add the shredded meat, and stir to incorporate it. Remove from the heat and allow to cool.

Break the eggs into a medium bowl and whisk in the remaining ½ teaspoon salt. Add the meat-vegetable mixture and stir to combine.

Clean the skillet, set it over high heat, and add the remaining 1½ teaspoons sunflower oil. (The bigger the stove burner, the more evenly the omelet will cook.) Add the egg mixture and immediately reduce the heat to medium. Quickly stir a few times, scraping the bottom of the pan with a silicone spatula, then allow the eggs to cook, without stirring, for 5 to 7 minutes, until the edges are fully cooked but the center is still a bit liquid. During this time, move the spatula around the sides of the pan, slipping it under the omelet to ensure that it is not sticking to the skillet; very gingerly loosen any parts that have stuck with the spatula.

NOTE

The choice of pan is key here. For this quantity, it should be a 10-inch (25 cm) nonstick skillet, with its nonstick properties fully intact.

Place a round plate larger than the pan upside down over the top of the pan. With one hand on the plate and the other holding the pan, quickly flip the pan and plate together in one motion to invert the omelet onto the plate.

If any pieces of omelet have stuck to the pan, quickly clean it and coat it with a bit more oil. Return the pan to the heat and slide the omelet back into it. Tuck the edges under with your spatula and cook for 3 minutes more. Slide the omelet onto a serving plate and let rest for at least 10 minutes.

Slice the omelet into 2-inch (5 cm) squares and place each one atop a piece of bread. Stick each one with a toothpick and drizzle lightly with olive oil, if desired, then serve.

BEHIND THE BAR

BAR ASTELENA, SAN SEBASTIÁN

Alfonso González and his wife, Rita, opened Bar Astelena in 1960 in a corner of San Sebastián's Plaza de la Constitución. The couple was originally from Bilbao and Navarra, respectively, but wartime turmoil brought their families to San Sebastián, where they met. The bar was a family affair, and with just four gas burners, they worked wonders, serving traditional pintxos and, on the weekends, croquetas into the thousands.

The Gonzálezes' fastidious thriftiness extended from ropa vieja to other pintxos—their primavera was a classic, made with the trimmings from anchovies, egg yolks, and leftover mayonnaise. The famed pastel de pescado (page 172), made with hake scraps, is a nostalgic taste memory for thousands of donostiarras. Alfonso Jr. took over in the 1990s and became obsessed with experimenting in the kitchen, using a pressure cooker when the machines were still a novelty and sourcing the best puff pastry from a shop on the outskirts of the city.

In 2004, Bar Astelena was sold, but Alfonso Jr. uprooted his pintxos and his business and opened Hika Mika on Etxaide Kalea in the Centro district of San Sebastián. Hika Mika closed upon Alfonso Jr.'s passing in 2011, but his son, Ander González, has kept up the family tradition. In 1997, after working in the family's bar and studying at the Escuela de Cocina Luis Irizar, he opened his own restaurant, the now widely acclaimed Astelena. He is one of the most well-known chefs in Basque Country, thanks in part to his various successful cooking shows. In 2018, Ander opened La Jarana in the Lasala Plaza Hotel, where the family's pintxo recipes, from the hake pâté to the ropa vieja, live on.

Cruasán de Jamón Ibérico

IBERIAN HAM CROISSANT

A simple croissant, sliced while still warm and stuffed with a couple of slices of cured ham, may not seem worthy of a recipe. However, at Ganbara (see page 178), it's worthy of its very own station, where as many as eight hundred have been churned out in a single day.

Both the croissant and the ham glisten, slick and glossy with buttery fat. Paleta ibérica is jamón ibérico made from the front legs of the Iberian pig ("full-fledged" jamón ibérico is made from the back legs). It may seem like a very basic sandwich, but it's an institution and, most importantly, delicious.

MAKES 6

6 frozen parbaked or fresh miniature croissants (see Notes)
12 paper-thin slices paleta ibérica (see Notes)

If using frozen mini croissants, bake them according to the manufacturer's instructions.

If using fresh mini croissants, preheat the oven to 300°F (150°C). Warm the croissants for about 5 minutes.

Remove the croissants from the oven and, as soon as they are cool enough to handle, carefully slice them horizontally in half with a serrated knife. Drape 2 slices of paleta ibérica across the bottom of each croissant and replace the tops.

Serve immediately, while still warm.

NOTES

The quality of the croissants is key here. Use parbaked frozen croissants, if possible, and finish baking them at home, which is akin to the process used at Ganbara. If using fresh croissants, the fresher, the better. The croissants at Ganbara are made with margarine, so they have a lighter flavor profile, but butter-based croissants will work too, of course.

You can use any kind of jamón ibérico here. Ganbara uses paleta ibérica from Huelva or Extremadura. The most important thing is that it be thinly sliced and delicate. If you use larger pieces of jamón ibérico, one slice per croissant will be enough.

GANBARA, SAN SEBASTIÁN

✦

José Ignacio Martínez grew up working at his family's place, Bar Martínez (see page 78). While he was learning the business, a pretty girl, Amaia Ortuzar, working at Asador Trapos, right across Calle 31 de Agosto, caught his eye. The two married, and in 1983, José Ignacio and Amaia took over the space that had formerly been Café Elizaran on Calle San Jerónimo. Their plan was to replicate the success of Bar Martínez, and they began selling banderillas and slices of cured Spanish ham at their bar, which they named Ganbara. However, José Ignacio had inherited his father's restlessness and began to innovate, starting with the cruasán de jamón ibérico (page 177), an unheard-of use of croissants on a pintxo bar that remains the most popular choice at Ganbara today. The tartaleta de txangurro (page 206), which arose from father-daughter experimentations between José Ignacio and his eldest daughter, Nagore, is a close second.

Another of his innovations is the pile of fresh mushrooms at the end of the bar: mountains of porcini crowned by chanterelles, black trumpets, St. George's mushrooms, and whatever else is in season. When Ganbara first piled up that bounty of seasonal produce, it was an unconventional and surprising addition to the mayonnaise and marisco, but it resulted in a reputation for quality and a commitment to exquisite simplicity.

Today the couple's children play an integral part in the family business. Amaiur often mans the bar, Nagore works behind the scenes (and still makes the txangurro), and Iulene helps out at Tamboril (see page 234). Ganbara remains a classic, busy with both locals and tourists day in and day out, and the family remains at the helm, dedicated to preserving tradition.

Miniature
baking dishes

Shot
glasses

Crustacean
shells

Miniature
bowls

IF NOT BREAD, THEN...?

With the evolution of the pintxo and the crowding of bar counters, the pintxo base has become an art form in and of itself. This list of possible pintxo bases, while far from exhaustive, shows just how creative pintxo cooks have gotten with eye-catching presentations. Nowadays there are entire food and beverage catalogs devoted to zany pintxo containers. Here are some of the more popular vessels for bar pintxos.

Coffee
cups

Lollipop
holders

Bamboo
baskets

Flat-bottomed
spoons

Miniature
fry baskets

Mango con Foie y Queso

CHEESE-AND-FOIE-STUFFED MANGO

This foie-and-cheese-stuffed beggar's purse could very well be the perfect embodiment of the spirit of the pintxo. Luxurious, indulgent foie gras and cream cheese (one of the pintxo bar's secret weapons!) are blended together, wrapped in a thin slice of sautéed mango, and placed on the traditional slice of baguette.

This recipe is tastiest when made with high-quality foie gras mi-cuit, the silky-smooth "half-cooked" version of the duck liver spread. When cut with cream cheese, it becomes an irresistibly smooth, savory cream. Choose the largest mango you can find for this recipe, or your pintxos will be quite small. By just wiping the sauté pan with oil before cooking, you'll ensure that the slices of mango won't stick to the pan but avoid weighing them down with too much oil.

MAKES 6

½ baguette, sliced into 6 pieces

3 ounces (⅓ cup/85 g) light cream cheese, preferably Philadelphia

2¾ ounces (77 g) foie gras mi-cuit or bloc de foie gras (see Notes)

Kosher salt and freshly ground black pepper

1 large mango (see Notes)

1 teaspoon water, plus more as needed

1 teaspoon sugar

Olive oil

Preheat the broiler. Arrange the slices of bread on a baking sheet and broil until just toasted on the edges; the centers should still be chewy. Remove from the broiler and let cool.

Combine the cream cheese and foie gras in a food processor and process until creamy and homogeneous, scraping down the sides occasionally. Transfer to a bowl, season with salt and pepper, and set aside.

CONTINUED →

NOTES

You could also use the same amount of fresh foie gras for this recipe. Cut it into slices and sear briefly on both sides in a very hot sauté pan. Allow to cool completely before using it.

The mango should be just barely ripe and still firm. That is important for slicing it easily.

FILADELFIA

·

One of the most essential, and common, ingredients in pintxo cuisine is cream cheese. After Philadelphia brand cream cheese, or Filadelfia, as it is known in Spain, was introduced to the Spanish market in the 1970s, it was quickly, and surprisingly, picked up by the famous chefs of the Nueva Cocina Vasca, who admired its smooth, creamy texture and versatility. Juan Mari Arzak first incorporated it into an ice cream in the mid-1980s. It quickly became a staple, used to stuff peppers, mushrooms (as in the Jaizkibel, page 243), and crepes (page 213). And, of course, it has a starring role in the famous Basque cheesecake (page 288).

Peel the mango, cut it in half, and remove the pit. Using a mandoline, an electric slicer, or a very sharp knife, cut 6 large slices from the center of the fruit, thin but not paper-thin.

Transfer the remaining mango flesh to the food processor, add the water and sugar, and process until you have a smooth, thin sauce, adding a bit more water if necessary. Pass the sauce through a fine-mesh sieve into a bowl and reserve.

Wipe a large sauté pan lightly with olive oil and place over high heat. Add the mango slices and cook, turning once, until they begin to brown in spots, about 1 minute per side. Transfer to a plate, laying them flat, and allow to cool.

Spoon a generous heaping of the foie-cheese mixture onto the middle of each mango slice, dividing it evenly, and gather the edges together to form a sack. Place the little bags on the toasted bread slices.

Drizzle or swipe the mango puree over small individual plates and serve the pintxos on top.

BEHIND THE BAR

BAR ALOÑA BERRI, SAN SEBASTIÁN

José Ramón Elizondo took the helm of the family bar, Aloña, in 1960, at the age of eighteen. After studying under famed chef Luis Irizar at the Euromar Cooking School (in Zarautz), he turned down offers from leaders of the Basque culinary scene such as Juan Mari Arzak, Pedro Subijana, and other promising young chefs. Instead, in 1986 he opened his own bar, which he and his wife, Conchita Bereciartua, called Aloña Berri (*berri* means "new" in Euskara), in the newly flourishing Nuevo Gros neighborhood. They won their first award in 1991 for a sweetbread-porcini tart, making a name for themselves and their splendid pintxo counter. They were the first to use ornate fine china plates to display their pintxos, an idea that was quickly copied around the city. Both José Ramón and Conchita were in the kitchen, along with a small team that included one of their daughters, Aintzane, and Pablo Vicari, now chef de cuisine of Elkano restaurant in Getaria.

The awards continued to flow in for delicious pintxos from cod brandade to a shellfish ravioli with foie mayonnaise to the Txirrista, a "slider" of mackerel, vegetables, and foie gras. The style of Aloña Berri was groundbreaking—local products, traditional flavors, haute techniques, and plating innovation. The couple retired in March 2010, closing the bar, and José Ramón passed away in October 2020, leaving a hole in the history books of San Sebastián.

Crujiente de Manzana con Pato

DUCK WITH CRUNCHY APPLE

Duck confit in a peanutty sauce sits between golden fried apple slices in this elegant, slightly exotic pintxo from Irrintzi. If you use prepared duck confit, making this recipe is quite simple. Soaking the apples in cinnamon syrup overnight before frying requires a bit of planning ahead, but if you are pressed for time, you can soak them for as little as an hour. Otherwise, the recipe is straightforward, and the result is exquisite.

Simmering the leg bones left from the duck confit in the chicken broth fortifies the broth and makes a huge difference in this simple pintxo. One of its best features is that it can be prepared ahead of time. With just a brief reheating, it is ready to serve—and delicious.

MAKES 10

1 cup (200 g) sugar
¾ cup (180 ml) water
1 cinnamon stick
1 Golden Delicious apple, cored
2 confit duck legs (about 12 ounces/340 g total)
⅔ cup (160 ml) chicken broth
Extra-virgin olive oil for deep-frying
⅓ cup (80 g) natural creamy peanut butter
Kosher salt
1 baguette, sliced on an angle into 10 pieces

Combine the sugar, water, and cinnamon stick in a small saucepan and bring to a simmer over high heat. Remove from the heat, transfer to a shallow bowl or airtight container, and allow to cool.

Using an electric slicer or a mandoline, slice the apple horizontally into thin slices, so that the core is in the middle of the slices. You'll need a total of 20 slices for this dish. Add the apple slices to the cinnamon syrup. Allow them to soak overnight, if possible, or for 1 hour at the very minimum.

Meanwhile, remove the skin and fat from the duck legs. Tear the meat off the legs, shred it, and set aside; reserve the bones.

Combine the duck bones and chicken broth in a medium saucepan and bring to a boil over high heat, then reduce the heat to maintain a simmer and cook for 10 to 15 minutes. Strain the broth and reserve.

Pour about 1 inch (2.5 cm) of oil into a large heavy saucepan and heat over high heat until it reaches about 350°F (175°C). Test the temperature with a thermometer, or add a bit of apple to the pan; if it sizzles on contact, the oil is ready. Drain the apple slices and, working in batches to avoid crowding the pot, add them to the hot oil. Fry for about 1 minute, then turn the slices and fry for 30 seconds to 1 minute more, until golden. Remove to a wire rack set over a baking sheet or paper towels to drain. If using paper towels, flip the apple slices a few times as they cool to prevent sticking.

CONTINUED →

"Deep down, a pintxo is a bite on top of a piece of bread that you eat in two or three bites."

—MARIAN VALLEJO, IRRINTZI

Combine the shredded duck meat and broth in a saucepan and bring to a simmer over medium-high heat. Add the peanut butter and a pinch of salt and whisk until the mixture is heated through and the broth has thickened slightly. Remove from the heat.

To assemble, place a crunchy apple slice atop each baguette slice. Top with a heaping spoonful of the peanut-duck mixture and then with another crunchy apple slice. Serve immediately.

BEHIND THE BAR

IRRINTZI, BILBAO

✦

Marian Vallejo and Yoli Chicano took over the restaurant Irrintzi, in the old quarter of Bilbao, in 2000. An *irrintzi* is a loud, throaty yell traditionally used by Basque shepherds to communicate across fields and valleys, and the bar, which had been a traditional wood-covered affair complete with fishing boats under glass, definitely gets attention with its bright orange, red, and green anime illustrations.

Marian, a self-taught chef, was a major innovator from the start, preparing squid croquetas tinted black with ink, virtually unknown in the area at the time. She put out a leek carpaccio crowned with ham and octopus, and a pork and pineapple kebab perched on a glass filled with a Dijon mustard sauce—innovation after innovation. At first the people of Bilbao were shocked, and Marian found she had to continuously adapt her ambitious pintxo plans. Irrintzi also pioneered the idea of placing little paper signs among the plates of pintxos on the bar when Yoli found she couldn't keep up with explaining the pintxos one by one. After more than two decades, Marian and Yoli maintain the traditional definition of the pintxo—a couple bites of food on top of a piece of bread—albeit with a modern, rock-and-roll sensibility.

BILBAO

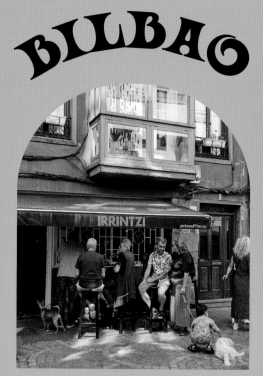

ABOVE Irrintzi, Bilbao

Bilbao is the largest city in Basque Country and the tenth largest in Spain, with 345,000 inhabitants and nearly a million in the greater metropolitan area. It has been considered the area's epicenter of industry and trade since its founding in 1300. Known affectionately as Botxo, which means "hole" in Basque, the city sits in a crater surrounded by mountains.

Its strategic position as a gateway to the north cemented Bilbao's importance, and trade, railways, and all the trappings of modern industry began to sprout up. Now it is headquarters to multinational corporations and the Frank Gehry–designed Guggenheim. Opened in 1997,

the museum marked a cultural awakening for the city, kicking off not only a wave of big-name architecture but a wave of culinary inspiration as well.

A pintxo tradition that had previously been very utilitarian began to burgeon along with the city, revitalized by an influx of visitors and their corresponding economic contributions. Chefs hungry to make a name for themselves took a cue from the elaborate productions in San Sebastián and covered their bartops with experimental creations. Each of Bilbao's neighborhoods now bursts at the seams with bars worthy of a visit, a microcosm of pintxo excellence all on its own.

ABOVE Bilbao, Bizkaia

Capricho Escombro

IBERIAN SCRAP SANDWICH

It all began with a tapa from Seville—cured ibérico ham on a soft mollete roll. Julián Galarza, the son of Cristobal Galarza, owner of the classic Pamplona bar Bodegón Sarria, thought it was so good that he wrapped it in aluminum foil and stowed it away in his carry-on. In this re-creation, a blend of Spain's best charcuterie is chopped finely and permeates the bread under the heat of the grill. In a pinch, substitute baps, hoagie rolls, bolillos, or even round dinner rolls for the molletes.

MAKES 4

3 ounces (85 g) lomo ibérico (cured pork loin), sliced ¼ inch (6 mm) thick

1¾ ounces (50 g) cured Spanish chorizo, cut into slices

1 ounce (about ¼ cup/28 g) virutas (Spanish ham shavings; see Note)

4 molletes or round dinner rolls, about 3 inches (7.5 cm) in diameter

Olive oil for brushing

Roughly chop the slices of pork loin. Transfer to a food processor and pulse a few times, until there are no large pieces. Add the chorizo and pulse a few more times. Add the ham shavings and pulse once more to combine everything.

Slice the rolls horizontally. Divide the ham mixture among them, pressing the filling between the two halves of each roll.

If using a sandwich grill or panini press, preheat it on the highest setting. Brush both sides of each sandwich with olive oil. Place the sandwiches in the grill and toast for a few minutes, until you see grill lines.

To make them on the stovetop, brush a griddle pan or sauté pan with a bit of olive oil and heat over medium-high heat until hot. Arrange the sandwiches in the pan, lay a piece of foil over them, and place a heavy skillet on top to press them. Cook until toasted on both sides, 2 to 3 minutes per side, removing the top skillet and foil to flip the sandwiches halfway through.

Cut each sandwich in half and serve warm.

NOTE

Virutas are not just scraps but pieces of meat that are too close to the bone to be sliced properly. The proximity to the bone means they pack a lot of flavor.

Sopa de Queso Idiazabal con Hongos

IDIAZABAL CHEESE SOUP WITH PORCINI

This pintxo would be just as at home on a fancy tasting menu as it is on the bartop in Bilbao's Plaza Nueva. Sautéed chopped porcini mushrooms are perched on a bed of explosively rich porcini cream that's slow-cooked for hours until thick and flavorful. A tiny soft-boiled quail egg is placed on top and then doused in a warm Idiazabal cheese "soup." You can serve the dish as is at this point—all the flavor is there. However, at Gure Toki, one of Bilbao's best pintxo bars, the lily must be gilded and the pintxos must catch your eye from the bartop, so they are garnished with edible flowers, tiny pea sprouts, and bits of freeze-dried corn. If you don't have access to these garnishes, don't let it stop you from making this delicious pintxo—you can improvise with any microgreens or colorful edible details. This pintxo is quite filling, but you'd be hard-pressed to find anyone who won't be licking their miniature bowl when they're done with it.

MAKES 8

2 tablespoons extra-virgin olive oil
1 onion, diced
Kosher salt
1 pound (454 g) porcini mushrooms
4½ cups (1.1 L) heavy cream
1¼ cups (3¾ ounces/105 g) grated smoked Idiazabal cheese
8 quail eggs
Edible flowers, pea sprouts, and freeze-dried corn for garnish (optional)

In a large sauté pan, heat 1 tablespoon of the oil over medium-high heat. Add the onion along with a pinch of salt and cook, stirring occasionally, until tender and golden, about 20 minutes.

Meanwhile, dice half the mushrooms. Once the onion is caramelized, add the diced mushrooms and 1½ cups (360 ml) of the cream. Bring to a simmer, then reduce the heat to the lowest setting and cook for 2½ hours, stirring every now and then, until the mixture is thick and not at all liquidy. Remove from the heat.

While the mushroom mixture is simmering, in a medium saucepan, combine the remaining 3 cups (720 ml) cream and the cheese and bring just to a simmer over medium heat, then reduce the heat to the lowest setting and cook for 10 minutes, stirring occasionally. Remove from the heat and pass through a fine-mesh strainer into another saucepan. Set aside.

Bring a large saucepan of water to a boil. Carefully lower the quail eggs into the water and cook for 2 minutes, maintaining a gentle boil. Drain the eggs, run under cold water to stop the cooking, and let cool.

CONTINUED →

Gently crack and peel the eggs.

Roughly chop the remaining porcini mushrooms. In a large sauté pan, heat the remaining 1 tablespoon oil over high heat until very hot. Add the mushrooms, along with a pinch of salt, and sauté for 4 to 5 minutes, until seared and tender. Remove from the heat.

When the mushroom-onion-cream mixture is ready, remove from the heat and blend to a smooth cream with an immersion blender or in a regular blender. Season to taste with salt.

To serve, reheat the Idiazabal cream over low heat, stirring occasionally, and then spoon a bit of the mushroom cream into the bottom of each of eight miniature soup bowls. Place a few pieces of sautéed mushroom on the cream and a soft-boiled quail egg on top of the mushrooms in each bowl. Pour enough of the hot Idiazabal cream over the top to cover and, if desired, garnish with a few edible flowers, some sprouts, and a bit of freeze-dried corn. Serve immediately.

"A pincho is what we snack on from a toothpick, but the pintxo has evolved. With the 'tx,' it became a new word that means it has been transformed from a mere snack to an exclusive form of culinary expression."

—JOSÉ RAMÓN ELIZONDO,
ALOÑA BERRI

GURE TOKI, BILBAO

✦

Few bars hold as many awards as Gure Toki. Siblings Iván, Yolanda, and Begoña Siles have an exquisite touch when it comes to pintxos. However, Gure Toki wasn't always on the cutting edge of Bilbao's culinary scene. Their parents, Pedro and Santiaga, opened the bar in 1982 in what was once the dining room of the famed Hotel Turrontegui, one year before a flood destroyed much of Bilbao's Old Town. They renovated and reopened after the flood, still serving classic dishes like Santiaga's famous tripe, mushrooms, sandwiches, and fried calamari and croquetas from their corner of Plaza Nueva.

When Santiaga retired in 2004, her children took the reins of the family business. Iván started working there as a waiter, but when he heard about the Bizkaia pintxo contest, he decided to enter it. Although he had never been much of a cook, he realized that he had been picking up lessons from his mother his whole life, and he began to immerse himself obsessively in cookbooks, teaching himself Nueva Cocina. He began to invent pintxos with a wow factor, like a spider crab waffle and a goxua (a traditional Basque trifle dessert) of foie gras with a cap of "cinnamon air."

Once a traditional wooden bar, Gure Toki now has a modern look after a renovation in 2013 and is also much larger than it was a decade ago, thanks to an expansion into a nearby space. Along with the Idiazabal cheese soup (page 190), the bar's pintxo of foie gras with apple and Pedro Ximénez sherry is renowned citywide. The trio is also famous for their rabas (fried calamari) and croquetas, both recipes from their mother that have been made the same way for more than thirty years. Gure Toki was named the Mejor Bar de Pintxos in the 2016 Campeonato de Euskadi and has taken various first-place awards in different competitions across Basque Country. The Idiazabal soup won first place at the Bizkaia championship the year it debuted, and in 2018, it took first place in the Idiazabal Cheese Pintxo Contest.

Tomate Relleno

STUFFED TOMATO

One of the most popular pintxos at Sorginzulo, in Bilbao's Plaza Nueva, this "stuffed tomato" is more of a tomato, guacamole, and goat cheese sandwich, breaded and fried before being dressed up as a pintxo. Once cooled, it is cut into half-moons and placed on a piece of toasted bread. A slow-cooked tomato jam adds a flavor-dense counterpoint and looks gorgeous centered atop the fried sandwich, garnished with parsley leaves and flaky sea salt. This pintxo is fantastic for entertaining, as it is served at room temperature and is always a crowd-pleaser.

MAKES 6

5 large tomatoes
1 tablespoon extra-virgin olive oil
½ cup (15 g) fresh basil leaves, finely chopped
¼ teaspoon garlic powder
Kosher salt and freshly ground white pepper
Sugar
½ baguette, sliced on an angle into 6 pieces
4 cilantro sprigs
2 avocados
Juice of 1 lime
2 tablespoons minced spring onion (or sweet onion such as Vidalia)
Cayenne pepper
6 ounces (170 g) soft-ripened goat cheese, such as Bûcheron (see Note), cut into 3 slices about ½ inch (1.5 cm) thick
2 large eggs
2 cups (130 g) panko breadcrumbs
All-purpose flour for dredging
Sunflower or other neutral oil for deep-frying
Flaky sea salt
6 fresh parsley leaves

Cut 3 of the tomatoes into a fine dice.

In a sauté pan or saucepan, heat the olive oil over medium heat. Add the diced tomatoes, basil, garlic powder, and a generous pinch each of kosher salt, white pepper, and sugar. Reduce the heat to low and cook for 45 minutes to 1 hour, or until the pan is dry. The cooking time will depend on the tomatoes' water content—you want all the water to cook out. Remove the tomato jam from the heat.

Meanwhile, preheat the broiler. Arrange the slices of bread on a baking sheet and broil until just toasted on the edges; the centers should still be chewy. Remove from the broiler and let cool.

Remove the leaves from the cilantro sprigs and finely chop them.

Halve the avocados and remove the pits. Scoop out the flesh and transfer to a small bowl. Add the lime juice, minced onion, a generous pinch of kosher salt, a pinch of cayenne, and the chopped cilantro. Using the back of a fork, mix and smash the mixture until the guacamole is mostly smooth.

Slice the remaining 2 tomatoes into ⅓- to ½-inch-thick (1 to 1.5 cm) slices; you need 6 slices for this dish.

Place a slice of goat cheese on one of the tomato slices. Spoon 2 tablespoons of guacamole onto the middle of the goat cheese. Place another tomato slice on top and press down lightly until the guacamole spreads to the edges. Repeat with the remaining tomato slices, cheese slices, and guacamole.

Beat the eggs in a shallow bowl with a splash of water. Spread the panko on a rimmed baking sheet or large plate. Spread some flour on a plate.

One at a time, dredge each tomato sandwich in flour, shaking off the excess, then dip it in the egg, allowing the excess to drip off, roll it in the breadcrumbs to coat, and set on a plate or baking sheet. Set aside until ready to fry.

Pour about 2 inches (5 cm) of the sunflower oil into a large heavy saucepan and heat over high heat until it reaches about 350°F (175°C). Use a thermometer to test the oil, or throw in a few breadcrumbs; if they sizzle on contact, the oil is ready. Working in batches to avoid crowding the pan, fry the pintxos, turning them occasionally for even cooking, until light golden brown. Remove with a slotted spoon and drain on paper towels. Let cool.

Slice the pintxos in half. Place a fried half sandwich on top of each slice of toasted bread. Top with some of the tomato jam and sprinkle with flaky sea salt. Garnish each one with a parsley leaf and serve.

BEHIND THE BAR

SORGINZULO, BILBAO

Sorgiña means "witch" in Basque, and *zulo* means "cave"—the "cave of the witches." And indeed, below the portico of Bilbao's Plaza Nueva, Sorginzulo is barely large enough for hungry guests to stand two deep. This "cave," however, shines with treasure—Sorginzulo's bar is one of the most brilliant in Bilbao. Owners Pedro Cinos and Alberto Lazkano, along with chef de cuisine Iñaki Lazkano, have kept it stocked with attractive, eye-catching (and award-winning, one might add) trays of pintxos since they took over the bar from a local restaurant group in 2012.

Sorginzulo is a bar somewhere between A Fuego Negro (see page 157) and Bar Bergara (see page 216), with an insistence on procuring delicious local products, combined with a youthful sensibility and a desire to experiment. And always, always with a gorgeously outfitted bar of pintxos nicely illuminated on a marble countertop, which partly explains their 2018 Mejor Bar de Pintxos award. Iñaki cites the famed bar Aloña Berri (see page 182) as his inspiration, and his visit there at twenty-four years old was what prompted him to submerse himself in the world of pintxos. At Sorginzulo, the pintxos fly off the bar—nearly a thousand a day on the weekends—along with their famous rabas, or fried calamari. The most popular of these include the stuffed tomato (opposite), the fried squid sandwich with black ink–tinted bread, the cod kokotxa in pil-pil sauce, and the beef cheek in puff pastry.

Huevo Trufado

TRUFFLED EGG

If you visit Bar Gaucho in Pamplona (see page 198), you're likely to see one of these pintxos on every table around the bar. The truffled egg is filling, delicious, and easy to make at home. Button mushrooms serve as the base of a thick, creamy sauce enriched with jamón ibérico. The sauce is then topped with a soft, runny egg (made in the steam oven at Gaucho, but poached eggs work nicely) and crunchy shoestring potatoes.

At Gaucho, they used to make the shoestring potatoes from scratch, until the pintxo grew so popular that they needed a full-time worker just to fry the potatoes. Feel free to follow their lead and use store-bought shoestring potatoes here. The garnish of "ham salt," which is ground fried pieces of ham, gives the dish an impressive fine-dining feel. Small parfait glasses are perfect for serving this pintxo, but any small glass bowls will do just fine.

MAKES 4

Sunflower or other neutral oil for shallow-frying

3½ ounces (100 g) serrano ham (see Note)

1 tablespoon olive oil

14 ounces (400 g) button mushrooms, cleaned and finely chopped

Kosher salt

2½ ounces (70 g) jamón ibérico, sliced

1⅔ cups (393 ml) heavy cream

¼ cup (30 g) cornstarch

4 large eggs

Truffle oil for drizzling

1 cup (40 g) fried shoestring potatoes

NOTE

You can use all jamón ibérico in the recipe if you wish, but serrano, which is less expensive, is used here to make the ham salt, since the quality of the ham is less important for that ingredient.

Pour about ½ inch (1.5 cm) of sunflower oil into a small heavy saucepan and heat over high heat until it reaches about 350°F (175°C). Add the serrano ham (it should sizzle on contact with the oil) and fry until it is golden and crispy, about 2 minutes. Drain on paper towels and let cool completely.

Pulse the fried ham in a food processor until reduced to pieces the size of flaky sea salt.

In a large sauté pan, heat the olive oil over medium-high heat. Add the mushrooms, along with a pinch of salt, and cook, stirring occasionally, until the water has cooked out of the mushrooms and they have begun to color, about 10 minutes.

Stir in the jamón ibérico, then add the cream and bring the mixture just to a boil. Reduce the heat to medium-low, add the cornstarch, and simmer, stirring occasionally, until the mixture thickens, about 15 minutes. Taste for seasoning, adding salt if necessary, remove from the heat, and set aside.

Bring a pot of water to a gentle simmer. One by one, crack the eggs into a fine-mesh sieve set over a bowl, allowing the thinner, more watery whites to run through the sieve, and carefully transfer each egg to a small bowl.

CONTINUED →

Stir the simmering water in a circular motion. Tip one egg into the center of the swirling water and, using a slotted spoon, give the water another swirl so that the egg gathers up into a neat circle. Repeat with the remaining eggs. Cook until the whites are just set but the yolks are still runny, about 2 minutes. Transfer to a plate with the slotted spoon.

To serve, divide the mushroom cream among four small parfait glasses or glass bowls. Place a poached egg on one side of the cream in each glass and drizzle with a bit of truffle oil. Arrange a quarter of the shoestring potatoes on the other side of the cream in each bowl and sprinkle it all with the ham salt. Serve immediately.

BEHIND THE BAR

BAR GAUCHO, PAMPLONA

Jesús Mari Ansa, his wife Pruden Serrano, Pruden's sister Alicia, and Alicia's husband Roberto Jiménez founded Bar Gaucho in 1987. The name is a holdover from the original owners, brothers who returned home from time abroad in Argentina and opened the bar in 1968. The two sisters and their husbands left La Solana, their restaurant in nearby Sangüesa, which had been featured in the Michelin Guide, to try their hand at cooking in the bustling capital.

At first they served simple food—tortillas, sandwiches, and banderillas. Jesús Mari attributes the beginning of the Semana del Pincho de Navarra in 1998 with inspiring them to greater heights of creativity. Since then, he and Alicia have created modern classics, including a sturgeon pintxo, in which toast is topped with smoked sturgeon and a ginger-sturgeon cream and garnished with pickled vegetables. Another is a terrine of veal cheeks crowned with a sauce made from a recipe dating back to the Middle Ages, a pintxo they made for the Festival of San Francisco Javier, Navarra's patron saint.

Jesús Mari and Alicia come from a line of self-taught cooks, which seems incredible, considering the sheer output and creativity coming from Gaucho's kitchen. Pruden can be found behind the bar, and Roberto takes care of logistics. Both couples live above the bar. They live and breathe pintxos, and they do it with a joy and excitement that hasn't faded in thirty-three years. They've also written two books: *Pintxos: Cocina en Miniatura* (2005) and *Pintxos: Pequeño Bocado, Gran Placer* (2020). Bar Gaucho is, unquestionably, one of Pamplona's best pintxo bars.

Turrón de Foie

FOIE GRAS NOUGAT

Turrón, or almond nougat, is the traditional Christmastime sweet par excellence in Spain. It signals the onset of the winter season, and no holiday table is complete without it. Foie gras mi-cuit, foie gras that has been "lightly cooked" (the literal translation of *mi-cuit*) into a terrine, is another holiday standard. In this pintxo, it is melted together with almond nougat into a silky-smooth mousse and allowed to set into golden ingot–shaped bars that just scream luxury. An itsy-bitsy pinch of curry adds a hard-to-pinpoint complexity, while buttons of yogurt, thick from being drained overnight, provide an acidic counterpoint to balance the richness of the base. Don't let the luxe ingredients stop you—this pintxo can be made ahead, and it is a total showstopper.

MAKES 10

½ cup (122 g) plain yogurt
⅓ cup (80 ml) water, plus 2 tablespoons cool water
6¾ ounces (190 g) foie gras mi-cuit or bloc de foie gras, chopped
4½ ounces (127 g) soft almond turrón (see Resources, page 302), chopped
2 teaspoons unflavored powdered gelatin
¾ teaspoon curry powder
Flaky sea salt
4 slices white bread, crusts removed
Extra-virgin olive oil
½ cup (54 g) slivered almonds, toasted
Small fresh mint leaves

SPECIAL EQUIPMENT

10 rectangular silicone molds with 3 by 1-inch (7.5 by 2.5 cm) cavities (see Note)
A pastry bag fitted with a small plain tip or a ziplock bag

Line a sieve with cheesecloth or a clean kitchen towel and set it over a bowl. Add the yogurt and allow it to drain in the refrigerator overnight.

The next day, heat the ⅓ cup (80 ml) water in a medium saucepan until you see bubbles beginning to rise from the bottom of the pan (the temperature should be 195°F/90°C). Add the foie and turrón and stir until they have melted into a homogeneous mixture with the texture of a mousse; be careful not to let the mixture get too hot, or the foie and turrón will separate. If necessary, finish blending with an immersion or regular blender until totally smooth, and transfer to a bowl.

Pour the 2 tablespoons cool water into a small bowl, sprinkle the powdered gelatin over the top, and stir well. Allow the mixture to sit for a minute, then heat it in the microwave for 20 seconds and stir to dissolve the gelatin. If the gelatin hasn't fully dissolved, heat for another 20 seconds and stir again. Whisk the gelatin into the foie mixture.

Add the curry powder to the mixture, then sprinkle in a pinch of flaky sea salt, crumbling it between your fingers, and stir well until thoroughly blended.

Place 10 rectangular silicone molds on a tray and distribute the mixture evenly among them. Chill completely in the refrigerator, 2 to 3 hours. (Once the nougat is set, you can wrap the molds well in plastic wrap and keep refrigerated for up to 3 days.)

CONTINUED →

Preheat the oven to 350°F (175°C).

Cut the slices of white bread into 3 rectangles each, to match the size of the foie gras molds. Arrange on a baking sheet, drizzle with a touch of olive oil, and toast in the oven for 3 to 4 minutes, until just beginning to color. Remove and let cool (you need 10 toasts for the pintxos; the remaining 2 toasts can be a cook's treat).

Transfer the drained yogurt to a pastry bag fitted with a small plain tip or to a ziplock bag; if using a ziplock bag, cut off one bottom corner.

Very carefully unmold the foie nougat. Place a rectangle of foie nougat on top of each toast. Pipe 4 circles of yogurt down the length of each foie rectangle. Scatter the slivered almonds down the length of each rectangle. Garnish with mint leaves and sprinkle with flaky sea salt. You can assemble these a few hours ahead and refrigerate them, or serve immediately.

BEHIND THE BAR

PERRETXICO, VITORIA

Josean Merino was already a well-known member of the Vitoria-Gasteiz dining scene when he opened PerretxiCo in 2013. His restaurant MarmitaCo had been a local favorite for decades. A businessman turned chef, he and his wife, Esti, launched PerretxiCo with the aim of making a casual pintxo bar that could be at home not only in Vitoria but also in Madrid, Barcelona, and other cities—a *tasca*, or neighborhood bar, for the twenty-first century.

They won over the tough, mostly traditional crowds in Vitoria with their modern yet undeniably delicious selection of pintxos, mixing classic ingredients with exotic international touches, served in generous portions. It didn't hurt that they picked up a few awards along the way, including Mejor Pincho Vanguardista for their Floración (a flowerpot that, when watered, magically "grows" edible vegetables) in the Concurso Nacional de Pinchos y Tapas (Valladolid) and Mejor Bar de Pinchos y Tapas de España (2011 and 2012 in Alicante). In 2019, PerretxiCo opened its first location outside Vitoria, in the Chamberí neighborhood of Madrid, and it has continued growing ever since, relying on a modern, centralized kitchen model that is becoming more and more common among restaurant groups in Spain.

PASTRY

CHAPTER SIX

PINTXOS

Puff pastry, phyllo dough, Moroccan brick (or brik) pastry (warqa), and crepes—barmen and cooks have used virtually every type of pastry in their pintxo experiments. These "pastry pintxos" waltzed onto the scene in the 1980s and '90s, breathing fresh air into the world of bread slices and toothpicks and delighting diners with their sophisticated shapes.

A boat-shaped puff pastry shell or a "purse" made of fried pastry is the perfect edible vehicle for nearly any ingredient or combination thereof. With the adoption of these different doughs comes the ability to dress up traditional foods in a modern guise. Everyday ingredients can easily be presented in dramatic fashion, as is the case with the Sweet-and-Sour Asparagus (page 222), green asparagus and shrimp that are transformed when wrapped in warqa and fried into an architectural wonder.

By the 1990s, the use of these pastry doughs at the pintxo bar had become a full-on trend—the pintxo's first swerve into the lane of haute cuisine. Pastry pintxos allowed pintxo cooks to steal a page from the playbook of Michelin-starred chefs, with minimal equipment and expertise. During the heyday of the trend, you could find pastry pintxo fillings as varied as zucchini and shrimp, the ever-popular spider crab, scallops, porcini, sweetbreads, salt cod, and more. Petit choux (pastry puffs) even had a brief moment in the spotlight, with fillings like salt cod and pisto, a ratatouille-like mixture. This style of pintxo was especially popular with budget-conscious chefs, in part because it allowed them to stretch raw materials further, bulking them up with eye-catching pastry art. Today these pintxos have a retro air, but that doesn't make them any less delicious.

Of all these pastry pintxos, the most famous and long-lasting is the Spider Crab Tartlet (page 206), a mixture of spider crab prepared "a la donostiarra," or San Sebastián–style, and stuffed in a puff pastry tart shell. It still flies off the bars today.

Tartaleta de Txangurro

SPIDER CRAB TARTLET

This tiny mouthful of a puff pastry shell filled with tender crabmeat began as a father-daughter project between Ganbara's founder, José Ignacio, and his eldest child, Nagore. It's a riff on the traditional Basque dish txangurro a la donostiarra, or San Sebastián–style spider crab. The crab is cooked and picked clean, and then the crabmeat is simmered in a mixture of caramelized vegetables, homemade tomato sauce, and fish broth, flambéed with a touch of Cognac, and scooped into mini puff pastry tart shells.

The last touch, a sprinkling of breadcrumbs and parsley and a knob of butter, should be applied right before serving. The assembled tartaleta is then placed under the broiler until it reaches melty, golden, delicious oneness. This recipe is a bit labor-intensive, but you can save time by using cooked crabmeat.

MAKES 15 TO 18

One 17.3-ounce (490 g) package
    frozen puff pastry, thawed
    (or frozen tartlet shells)
All-purpose flour for rolling
4 tablespoons (57 g) unsalted butter
Kosher salt
1 spider crab or brown crab
    (about 2¼ pounds/1 kg; see Notes)
2 tablespoons extra-virgin olive oil
1 onion, diced
1 leek, diced
1 carrot, diced
Freshly ground black pepper
½ cup (120 ml) Tomato Sauce
    (recipe follows)
¾ cup (180 ml) Fish Broth (page 156)
2 tablespoons Cognac
¼ cup (30 g) fresh breadcrumbs
¼ cup (5 g) fresh parsley leaves,
    finely chopped

SPECIAL EQUIPMENT

15 to 18 round tartlet molds, preferably
    fluted, or 1 or 2 mini-muffin tins
    (if using puff pastry)

If using puff pastry, preheat the oven to 350°F (175°C). If using frozen tartlet shells, bake them according to the package instructions and let cool.

If using puff pastry, set out fifteen to eighteen tartlet molds or one or two mini-muffin tins. Unfold the puff pastry and roll it out on a floured surface to an even thickness (see Working with Puff Pastry, page 220). Cut the pastry into pieces that are slightly bigger than your molds, so that when you line the molds, the edges of the dough hang over the sides. One at a time, drape each piece evenly over a mold and gently press it over the bottom and up the sides of the mold. Press the edges of the dough firmly against the rim of each mold and roll a rolling pin across the top of the mold to remove the excess dough, or simply slice off the excess with a sharp knife. Or, if using muffin tins, use a knife to trim the edges.

If using tartlet molds, place them on a baking sheet. Use a fork to prick the pastry in each mold or muffin cup a dozen or so times; prick the sides as well as the bottom, as you don't want the pastry to puff.

Melt 2 tablespoons of the butter and, using a pastry brush, coat each tartlet shell generously with the butter.

CONTINUED →

At Ganbara, they use centollo (European spider crab, *Maja squinado*), or buey de mar (brown crab, *Cancer pagurus*), depending on what is freshest. You can substitute meat from your own local crabs or even cooked crabmeat. You will need about ⅔ pound (300 g) crabmeat.

You can use store-bought frozen tartlet shells instead of making your own; bake them according to the package instructions.

Line each tartlet shell with a piece of parchment paper and fill with baking weights or dried beans. Bake for 10 minutes. Carefully remove the paper and weights and bake the shells for 7 to 10 minutes more, until golden brown. Remove from the oven and let cool completely.

Bring a stockpot of heavily salted water to a boil; you want at least ¼ cup (75 g) salt in the water. Add the crab to the boiling water and cook for 12 minutes. Remove from the pot and set aside to cool slightly.

When the crab is cool enough to handle, crack the shells and pick out all the meat: Holding the body in one hand, use your fingers to squeeze it on opposite ends of the head to open. Reserve any liquid inside. Using a sharp heavy knife, cut the body crosswise in half and then into quarters. Patiently pick out all the meat, using a lobster/crab pick if you have one. Crack the claws and pick out that meat, being careful to remove and discard any bits of shell. Set the crabmeat aside in a bowl.

In a large skillet, heat the olive oil over medium heat. Add the onion, leek, and carrot, along with a pinch of salt, then reduce the heat to medium-low and cook, stirring occasionally, until the vegetables are golden and very tender, about 30 minutes.

Raise the heat to medium-high, add the crabmeat and the reserved liquid from the body to the skillet, and cook, stirring, until everything is well combined and warmed through. Season with salt and pepper to taste. Add the tomato sauce and fish stock, bring to a lively simmer, and cook for about 5 minutes.

Carefully add the Cognac to the crab mixture and, with a long match or a grill lighter held near the mixture, set the Cognac on fire. Allow it to burn until the flame goes out, then simmer until the mixture has thickened somewhat, about 5 minutes. Season to taste with salt and pepper and remove from the heat.

Preheat the broiler. Spoon a rounded tablespoonful of the crab mixture into each tartlet shell, mounding it above the top. Sprinkle the tartlets generously with the breadcrumbs and parsley, then dot with the remaining 2 tablespoons butter.

Broil until the butter is melted and the tops begin to bubble and turn golden, 1 to 2 minutes. Remove from the broiler and serve immediately.

Tomate Frito

TOMATO SAUCE | TOMATE FRIJITUA

MAKES ABOUT 1½ CUPS (335 G)

2 tablespoons extra-virgin olive oil
1 spring onion (see Note, page 49), diced
1 sweet green Italian pepper, such as Cubanelle, diced
1 garlic clove, minced
Kosher salt
2 large tomatoes, chopped (juices reserved)
1 dried guindilla pepper

In a large skillet, heat the olive oil over medium heat. Add the spring onion, green pepper, and garlic, along with a pinch of salt, and sauté, stirring occasionally, until tender, 10 to 15 minutes.

Add the tomatoes, with their juices, and the dried guindilla, along with another pinch of salt, and bring to a simmer, then reduce the heat to low and cook for about 20 minutes, until the tomatoes are broken down and the sauce is slightly thickened. Remove from the heat.

Blend the sauce with an immersion blender, or transfer to a regular blender and blend until smooth. Let cool completely.

You can refrigerate the sauce in an airtight container for up to 5 days or freeze it for up to 3 months.

WHAT IS A PINTXO?

"A pintxo is a way of eating. A pintxo that you can't eat in one or two bites isn't a pintxo for me. Humbly speaking, that's my opinion."

—CARMEN BARGAÑO, TOLOÑO

THE
SHAPES
OF
PUFF
PASTRY

Puff pastry has been used in a wide range of shapes during its decades-long life span as a pintxo base—here are some of the more common ones.

TARTALETA

This is a round tart shell, which can be achieved with tartlet molds or a mini-muffin pan.

MILHOJAS

For this form, pieces of puff pastry are layered between other ingredients, like a lasagna.

VOL-AU-VENT

This tall round of puff pastry has a hollow in the center to make room for a filling.

OVAL

This is an almond-shaped or oval tartlet shell, the traditional shape for the Txalupa (page 215).

From France

❖

It's no coincidence that the pastry trend that appeared as Nueva Cocina Vasca was taking off. The chefs who created this movement got much of their inspiration from French chefs of the 1970s, such as the famed Paul Bocuse. It was an era of butter, cream, and pastries of all kinds, and the pintxos of the 1980s and '90s reflected those trends.

Crepes de Queso con Hongos

PORCINI-AND-CHEESE-STUFFED CREPES

This crepe pintxo is stuffed with a spreadable filling of garlicky porcini mushrooms blended with cream cheese. Crepe pintxos have a retro feel, and a drizzle of piquillo pepper sauce adds to the effect. You can perch the pintxo on a piece of bread, or plate it without bread and use the piquillo sauce to decorate the dish. Either way, the same crowd-pleasing flavors will shine.

MAKES 6

1 large egg

½ cup (120 ml) whole milk

1½ tablespoons unsalted butter, melted, plus butter for greasing the pan

Kosher salt

½ cup (62 g) all-purpose flour

1 tablespoon plus 2 teaspoons extra-virgin olive oil

1 garlic clove, minced

½ cup (about 3⅓ ounces/95 g) canned or jarred porcini mushrooms (see Note)

Freshly ground black pepper

6 piquillo peppers (about 4 ounces/113 g total)

5 ounces (140 g) cream cheese, at room temperature

½ baguette, sliced on an angle into 6 pieces

Combine the egg, milk, melted butter, and a pinch of salt in a small bowl. With an immersion blender or a whisk, combine well. Sift the flour into the bowl and blend or whisk until the mixture is smooth. Allow the batter to rest for at least 30 minutes at room temperature, or cover and refrigerate up to overnight.

Meanwhile, in a medium sauté pan, heat 1 tablespoon of the oil over medium-high heat. Add the garlic and cook until it begins to color. Add the mushrooms and a pinch each of salt and pepper and sauté for about 1 minute. Remove from the heat and allow to cool.

In a food processor, combine the piquillo peppers, the remaining 2 teaspoons olive oil, and a pinch of salt and process until the mixture is smooth (or use an immersion blender and a tall container to blend the sauce). Reserve, preferably in a squirt bottle.

In the food processor, blend the mushroom-garlic mixture with the cream cheese, scraping down the sides as necessary, until light and smooth. Season to taste with salt and pepper.

Heat a nonstick crepe pan over high heat and lightly grease it with butter. Pour about ¼ cup (60 ml) of the batter into the pan and swirl the pan so the batter spreads out evenly in a circle. Reduce the heat to medium and cook for a minute or two, until the edges of the crepe turn golden. Flip and cook on the other side for another minute or so. Transfer to a work surface and repeat with the remaining batter to make 2 more crepes.

NOTE

Preserved porcini mushrooms are available in jars or cans. You can prepare fresh porcini according to the recipe for the Mini Sartén (page 273) or just sauté the chopped fresh mushrooms until tender, before adding the garlic.

CONTINUED →

Cut each crepe in half. Spread one of the half crepes generously with the cream cheese–mushroom mixture. Fold it in half and spread the resulting surface with more of the cheese-mushroom mixture. Fold it over itself once more so you have a wedge-shaped piece. Repeat with the remaining crepes and filling.

Place each pintxo atop a piece of baguette. Drizzle with the piquillo pepper sauce in a zigzag pattern. These can be served at room temperature but are best when lightly rewarmed in a low oven before serving.

BEHIND THE BAR

GAZTANDEGI, BILBAO

Located in Bilbao's Indautxu neighborhood, Gaztandegi, owned and run by José Luis Ramila Vallejo, couldn't look more traditional from the outside. A green awning announces the bar's name in fat, playful Basque typography, and a lauburu, or Basque cross, crowns the stained oak exterior, giving the bar the vibe of a village watering hole. Once you're inside, though, the first clue that this bar is a bit different is the deli case of cheeses, not a common sight in your typical pintxo bar. It is there for a reason—just about every pintxo on offer at the bar gives cheese a starring role. The bar's most famous pintxos are the Idiazabal cheese mille-feuille, the fundido, and the cheese-and-mushroom crepes drizzled with bright-red piquillo sauce.

Txalupa

BOAT

The Txalupa was inspired by a creamy, béchamel-like sauce that bar owners Patxi Bergara and Blanca Ameztoy's housekeeper used to cook for them. Onions and oyster mushrooms are simmered in a thick cava-and-cream sauce before bits of fresh shrimp are folded in. The creamy mixture is spooned into small puff pastry "boats," topped with grated Swiss cheese, and broiled until golden. The heavenly mouthfuls are best served warm.

Throw good pastry practice out the window when shaping the bases—cut them with a butter knife rather than a sharp one, prick the bases and the sides full of holes, and slather generously with melted butter before baking. This will give you a more compact base with more room for the delicious filling.

MAKES 6

One 17.3-ounce (490 g) package frozen puff pastry, thawed

All-purpose flour for rolling, plus 1 tablespoon

3 tablespoons unsalted butter

½ onion, diced

9 ounces (255 g) oyster mushrooms, diced

Kosher salt

¾ cup (180 ml) cava

¾ cup (180 ml) heavy cream

5 large shrimp, peeled, deveined if desired, and diced

2 ounces (56 g) Swiss cheese, finely grated

SPECIAL EQUIPMENT

6 fluted almond-shaped tartlet molds, about 4 inches (10 cm) long (see Notes)

Preheat the oven to 350°F (175°C).

Set out 6 almond-shaped tartlet molds. Unfold the puff pastry and roll it out on a floured surface to an even thickness (see Working with Puff Pastry, page 220). Cut the pastry into pieces that are slightly bigger than your molds, so that when you line the molds, the edges of the dough hang over the sides. One at a time, drape each piece evenly over a mold and gently press it over the bottom and up the sides of the mold. Press the edges of the dough firmly against the rim of each mold and roll a rolling pin across the top of the mold to remove the excess dough, or simply slice off the excess with a sharp knife.

Use a fork to prick the pastry in each mold a dozen or so times; prick the sides as well as the bottom, as you don't want the pastry to puff.

Melt 1 tablespoon of the butter and, using a pastry brush, coat each tartlet shell generously with butter.

Line each tartlet shell with a piece of parchment paper and fill with baking weights or dried beans. Bake for 10 minutes. Carefully remove the paper and weights and bake the shells for 7 to 10 minutes more, until golden brown. Remove from the oven and let cool completely.

In a large sauté pan, melt the remaining 2 tablespoons butter over medium-high heat. Add the onion and cook until tender and just starting to color, 6 to 8 minutes. Add the mushrooms and a pinch of salt and sauté for a few minutes, until the mushrooms

If you don't have oval-shaped molds, you can use any other mini tart pans of a similar size or mini-muffin tins.

At Bar Bergara, the cava-cream mixture is rested overnight. This allows its flavors to intensify. If you want to do this (which is also a good trick if you're making these ahead of time), transfer the cooled cream mixture to an airtight container and refrigerate. Bring it to room temperature before using, and then scoop it into the pastry boats just before broiling.

let off some of their liquid. Add the cava and simmer for 12 to 15 minutes, or until the mushrooms are tender and the liquid has reduced.

Stir the 1 tablespoon flour into the mushrooms. Add the cream, bring to a simmer, and cook for 5 minutes, stirring occasionally. Add the shrimp and simmer until it is cooked through and the sauce has thickened, about 5 minutes. Taste for seasoning, adding more salt if necessary, remove from the heat, and allow to cool completely (see Notes).

Preheat the broiler.

Arrange the pastry boats on a baking sheet and distribute the filling mixture evenly among them. Sprinkle with the grated cheese. Place under the broiler and broil until golden brown, about 2 minutes (keep an eye on them so they don't burn). Serve warm.

BEHIND THE BAR
BAR BERGARA, SAN SEBASTIÁN

✦

Bar Bergara opened on April 5, 1950, a small, simple restaurant with menús del día run by Patxi Bergara and Eladia Bidegain. Their son, Patxi, grew up in the bar, and at age fourteen, he quit school to work there full-time. Eventually he took over the reins with his wife, Blanca Ameztoy, and in the early 1990s, they gave both the interior decor and the culinary offerings a makeover. They shifted from serving simple pintxos, such as blood sausage, Laughing Cow cheese triangles, and olives tossed with onions and paprika, to more elaborate ones. These new pintxos would eventually become classics in the neighborhood of Gros. Helmed by Blanca, the bar soon achieved renown, winning one of San Sebastián's premier pintxo competitions in 1992 with an innovative sweet-and-sour shellfish salad served on toasted bread.

Blanca, the artiste of the kitchen, was self-taught, having left work at the social security office to dedicate herself to cooking. The bar became one of San Sebastián's best, and Patxi and Blanca moved in the circles of pintxo royalty, even appearing at events in the United States with chef José Andrés. Today Bergara remains in the family, in the hands of the third generation, Monty Puig-Pey and Esteban Ortega, and its classics—the Txalupa, the Itxaso (monkfish with leek cream), and the anchovy omelet—are as good as ever, with Esteban's wife, Susana Erdocio, continuing the tradition of a female chef de cuisine.

Filomena

PHILOMENA

The Filomena is a tower of phyllo sheets layered with sole and green garlic–infused béchamel. When it first debuted, this combination of shrimp-and-fish-studded sauce won second place in the Semana del Pincho de Navarra. That doesn't mean it's difficult to make—the béchamel is stirred in the same pan the seafood is cooked in, and the phyllo crisps up quickly and easily. From there, it's just a matter of assembly, so you can serve these hot and enjoy.

MAKES 6

¼ cup plus 1 tablespoon (75 ml) extra-virgin olive oil

4 heads green garlic, trimmed and chopped (see Notes)

4 ounces (113 g) sole fillets (about 2), chopped

10 tiny pink shrimp, peeled and chopped

Kosher salt

⅔ cup (80 g) all-purpose flour

4 cups (960 ml) whole milk, warmed

3 sheets frozen phyllo dough, thawed (see Working with Phyllo Dough, page 220)

Olive oil for deep-frying

Parsley sprigs for garnish (optional)

In a large sauté pan, heat 1 tablespoon of the extra-virgin olive oil over medium-high heat. Add the green garlic and sauté until tender, 1 to 2 minutes. Add the fish and shrimp, along with a pinch of salt, and sauté for a minute or two longer, until the seafood is cooked through. Transfer to a plate.

Add the remaining ¼ cup (60 ml) extra-virgin olive oil to the pan and heat over medium-high heat. Add the flour, stir with a whisk, and cook, whisking, for about 1 minute. Add the warm milk little by little, whisking the entire time. Once all the milk is incorporated, add the reserved seafood mixture and a generous pinch of salt and cook, whisking frequently, until the sauce has thickened and is free of lumps, about 10 minutes total. Taste for seasoning, adding more salt if necessary, remove from the heat, and keep warm.

Cut each sheet of phyllo dough into 6 squares about 4 inches (10 cm) across.

Pour about 1 inch (2.5 cm) of olive oil into a large saucepan and heat over medium-high heat to 350°F (175°C). Use a thermometer to test the oil, or throw in a bit of phyllo; if it sizzles on contact, the oil is ready. Line a plate with paper towels.

When the oil is ready, drop in a few squares of phyllo at a time and fry until light golden brown. The phyllo will brown quickly, so keep your eyes on the pan. Transfer to the prepared plate to drain and allow to cool.

To assemble the pintxos, place a square of phyllo on a small plate. Ladle a large spoonful of the béchamel over the middle of the square. Place another phyllo square on top and add another spoonful of béchamel. Top with a final square of phyllo and garnish with a sprig of parsley. Repeat with the remaining ingredients to make 5 more pintxos.

Serve immediately.

NOTES

If you cannot find green garlic, you can substitute scallions.

The béchamel can be made up to 2 days in advance. Allow it to cool, then store in an airtight container in the refrigerator. When ready to use, reheat the béchamel on the stove over low heat, adding a little milk and whisking constantly.

Working with Puff Pastry

❖

Using frozen puff pastry falls cleanly within
the range of authenticity when making pintxos—
most bars use either frozen puff pastry or frozen
pastry shells. When working with frozen puff pastry,
let it thaw for at least 3 hours in the fridge
or 30 minutes at room temperature. Be sure it is
completely thawed before you unfold it, but it
should still be cold to the touch. If the recipe
calls for rolling out the puff pastry, do so on
a lightly floured work surface.

Working with Phyllo Dough

❖

Phyllo dough can be tricky to use. If the dough
is frozen, allow it to thaw overnight, unopened,
in the refrigerator. Then let it come to room
temperature before opening the package. Be sure
to work with dry hands. If you are using only one
sheet at a time, cover the remaining dough with
plastic wrap and place a damp towel on top. The
best way to cut phyllo dough is with kitchen shears.

BAR FITERO, PAMPLONA

✦

Bar Fitero, opened on July 6, 1956, by Cesareo Luis and Elvira Beorlegui, is parked on an enviable corner of the famous Calle Estafeta. Now under the third generation, Fitero has undergone its share of evolution. What started principally as a bar for drinking later became a marisquería, a bar-restaurant devoted to shellfish and seafood. The bar's countertop overflowed with crabs, oysters, crayfish, shrimp, and more, along with traditional pintxos like hard-boiled eggs with mayonnaise and Gildas (known in Pamplona as *pajaritos*, or little birds).

The effect of Basque separatism on the Casco Viejo of Pamplona was particularly harsh in the 1980s, and its proletariat outlook influenced the second generation of owners to shift from its decades-long highbrow seafood offerings to a trend that was gathering steam in Pamplona—pintxos. Esther Azqueta Arteta, the wife of Cesareo and Elvira's son José Mari, did her part in the kitchen to help the bar gain renown for its fritos, from croquetas to fried shrimp. The bar became known for its light, creamy béchamel, which is made with fresh cow's milk from a farm in La Ribera, in the south of Navarra. This béchamel is

the base of the Filomena (page 219), whose name is a play on both the phyllo dough it is made with and the name of the owners' great-aunt. The current generation behind the bar is Arancha Luis Azqueta, José Mari's daughter, and her husband, Javier Vinacua, although Esther still comes in every now and then to make sure the béchamel is up to par.

Esparrago Triguero Agridulce

SWEET-AND-SOUR ASPARAGUS

Warqa, or *pasta brick* (brick dough) in Spain, is very similar to phyllo and is perfect for forming edible vessels that can be fashioned into attention-grabbing shapes. This pintxo, a perennial favorite at Bar Chelsy in Pamplona, is fun to construct, and easy enough that even younger cooks can help. Rectangles of pasta brick are wrapped around raw shrimp, zucchini, and asparagus and fried just long enough to get crunchy, leaving the shrimp juicy and turning the veggies golden. The pintxo is finished with a sweet-and-sour sauce made from a reduction of pineapple juice, vinegar, and sugar.

MAKES 6

⅔ cup (170 ml) pineapple juice
2 tablespoons sugar
2 tablespoons balsamic vinegar
2 tablespoons white wine vinegar
1 tablespoon cornstarch
1 tablespoon water
Six 4 by 6-inch (10 by 15 cm) pieces warqa (aka brick dough; see Brick versus Phyllo, page 224)
6 stalks green asparagus, trimmed and cut into 2 pieces each
1 small zucchini, sliced into 12 pieces
12 extra-large shrimp, peeled, tails left on
Kosher salt
Sunflower or other neutral oil for deep-frying
2 tablespoons Balsamic Glaze (recipe follows)
6 Cape gooseberries (see Note)

Combine the pineapple juice, sugar, balsamic vinegar, and white wine vinegar in a small saucepan and bring the mixture to a boil, then reduce the heat to medium-low.

In a small bowl, mix the cornstarch and water into a slurry. Whisk the slurry into the simmering pineapple juice mixture and cook, stirring occasionally, until the sauce has reduced and thickened enough to coat the back of a wooden spoon, 10 to 12 minutes. Remove from the heat and set aside.

Lay a sheet of warqa on a work surface and arrange 2 pieces of asparagus on it like the hands of a clock pointing to 12:00, so that the tip of one of the pieces extends beyond the pastry. Place 2 slices of zucchini on top, then place 2 shrimp on top of the zucchini. Sprinkle with a pinch of salt. Wrap the pastry around the ingredients, allowing the tails of the shrimp and the asparagus spears to poke out. Pierce the pastry with a toothpick to keep it closed. Repeat with the remaining ingredients to make 5 more pintxos.

Right before serving, pour 2 inches (5 cm) of oil into a large heavy saucepan and heat over high heat until it reaches about 350°F (175°C). Use a thermometer to test the oil, or throw in a scrap of dough; if it sizzles on contact, the oil is ready.

CONTINUED →

Working in batches if necessary to avoid crowding the pan, add the bundles to the hot oil and fry, flipping once, for about 2 minutes, until golden. Use a slotted spoon to transfer the bundles to paper towels to drain.

Drizzle the balsamic glaze over serving plates. Remove the toothpicks and place a bundle on each plate. Dollop a couple of teaspoons of the reserved sweet-and-sour sauce on top of each bundle. Adorn each plate with a Cape gooseberry and serve.

Crema Balsámica

BALSAMIC GLAZE | KREMA BALTSAMIKOA

MAKES ABOUT ¼ CUP (60 ML)

1 cup (240 ml) balsamic vinegar
¼ cup (50 g) sugar

Combine the vinegar and sugar in a small saucepan and bring the mixture to a gentle boil over medium heat. Reduce the heat to medium-low and simmer, stirring occasionally, until the mixture has reduced by two-thirds to one-half, about 10 minutes. The glaze should be thick enough to coat the back of a spoon.

Remove from the heat and allow to cool before using.

Brick versus Phyllo

❖

Warqa, or *pasta brick* (brick dough), as it is called in Spain, and phyllo dough are often considered interchangeable. They are very similar, but warqa (see Resources, page 302) is a bit thicker and slightly easier to handle. It is good for creamier fillings because it absorbs less moisture than phyllo. When working with warqa, always cook it with the shiny side out. Phyllo dough is more delicate; the dough itself is essentially identical to warqa (flour, oil, salt, and water), but with one added ingredient: vinegar.

BAR CHELSY, PAMPLONA

✦

Bar Chelsy opened its doors in the Iturrama district of Pamplona in the glory days of the city's bar scene in the 1980s. In 1986, Raúl Fernández and Antonio Cristobal took over an existing bar-restaurant that had served simple lunches for the neighborhood audience since 1982. At first they retained the concept of platos combinados by day and gin-tonics by night. But a recession and stricter drinking-and-driving laws at the turn of the past century demanded that they change their focus, and in 2005 the pair began to travel, research, and then create elaborate new pintxos. It didn't take long for them to start racking

up awards, such as first place in 2011 and 2012 at the prestigious Semana del Pincho de Navarra. The bar is still utterly authentic, a 1980s time capsule with black-and-white tile floors, giant mirrors, and lacquered oak walls carved in geometric patterns. It is still headed by Raúl, and it has returned to its roots of traditional dishes in larger servings, although the pintxos on offer are those that have won Chelsy renown, like the salt cod brioche, the "energy bar" (a rectangular block of lamb, walnut, and corn cream), and, of course, the sweet-and-sour asparagus.

MIX-AND-MATCH
PASTRY PINTXOS

The raison d'être of pastry pintxos is to be creative and impress people. No matter what type of pastry you're working with, the pastries lend themselves to showy shapes and "wow" presentations. Follow this road map to make your own perfect pastry pintxos.

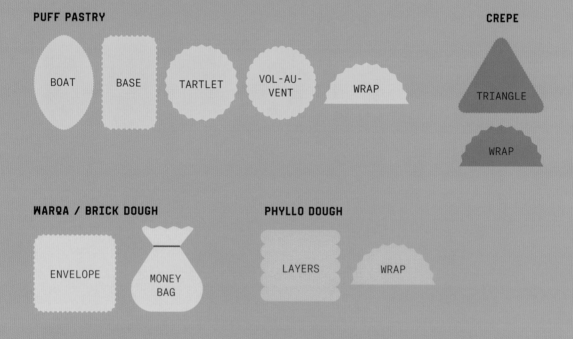

PUFF PASTRY

BOAT

BASE

TARTLET

VOL-AU-VENT

WRAP

CREPE

TRIANGLE

WRAP

WARQA / BRICK DOUGH

ENVELOPE

MONEY BAG

PHYLLO DOUGH

LAYERS

WRAP

1

Choose
Your Pastry

Txistorra

Cabbage and morcilla

Salt cod

Ham salad

Hard-boiled quail eggs and caviar

Crab salad

Duck confit sautéed with apple and Calvados

Blue cheese and cream

Foie gras sautéed with grapes and port

Tomato, basil, and zucchini

Zucchini sautéed with either
foie gras or lobster

Meat-stuffed green peppers

Tuna with caramelized onions

Crab flambé with vegetables

Sautéed mushrooms with ham

Smoked cod

Salt cod ajoarriero

GREEN PEPPER AND ONION CONFIT, BLENDED AND PASSED THROUGH A STRAINER

DOLLOP OF MAYONNAISE, WITH A BIT OF PARSLEY FOR COLOR

NUTS, SUCH AS PINE NUTS OR WALNUTS

GRATINÉED CHEESE

SAUTÉED MUSHROOMS WITH A REDUCTION OF HEAVY CREAM

CHOPPED FRESH PARSLEY

A PIECE OF SPANISH HAM, SLICED OR FRIED UNTIL CRISP

❷
Add Your Fillings

❸
Pick a Garnish

KITCHEN

CHAPTER SEVEN

PINTXOS

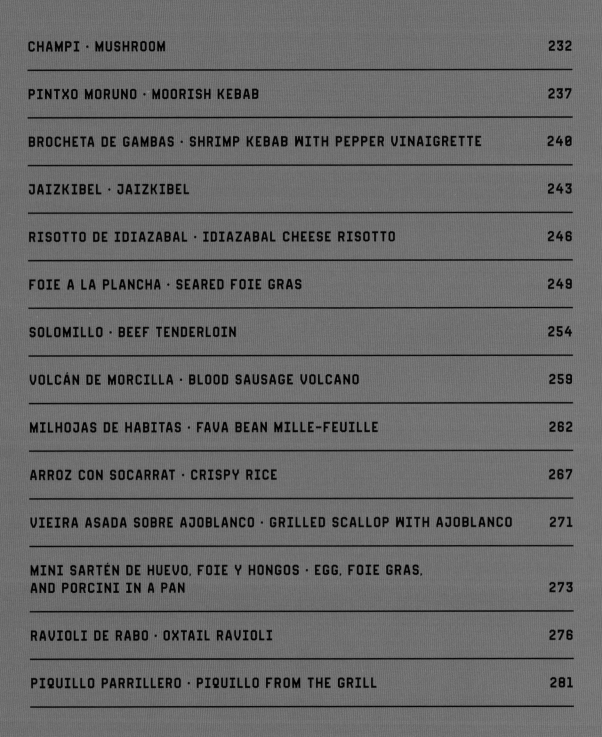

The golden age of pintxos—the initial wave of creativity in the 1980s and '90s—paved the way for a revolution at the turn of the twenty-first century, represented by a new type of pintxo: the kitchen pintxo.

The term *kitchen pintxo* doesn't truly exist within the confines of an actual pintxo bar. The pintxos in this chapter would usually be called hot pintxos (pintxos calientes). However, for the purposes of better categorizing the different trends during the pintxo's history, I've separated these pintxos from more traditional hot pintxos, such as croquetas and puff pastry pintxos, which predate the invention of these miniature dishes. Kitchen pintxos are small versions of complex main dishes, and at their fullest realization, they become works of fine-dining art.

The famous mushrooms from Tamboril (page 232) and the spiced lamb kebab (page 237), along with a few other pintxos in this chapter, date back to the last century. But you'll find that most of the recipes here didn't appear until the early 2000s, when there was a real turning point in the world of pintxos. This was when the idea of transforming an entrée into a pintxo or using haute cuisine techniques for miniature formats really took off. Pioneering bar La Cuchara de San Telmo was a revelation in itself, with a bartop bare of pintxos but with a groundbreaking chalkboard menu of pintxo-sized versions of *platos de cuchara*, or braises, stews, and other traditional dishes. If it hadn't been La Cuchara, though, it would have been another hungry young chef—the road had already been paved for pintxos to take an evolutionary step forward. Luxurious ingredients and elaborate techniques were already on the scene. The tradition of pintxo eating was a well-rooted social norm in San Sebastián. The first kitchen pintxos are now classics found in nearly every bar: seared foie gras (page 249) and risotto (page 246).

Champi

MUSHROOM

Classic simplicity is the hallmark of Basque cuisine. This mushroom pintxo is one of the few hot pintxos created in the twentieth century, and the secret of its success is surely in its simple, hearty nature. White button mushrooms are transformed when simmered in a wine-rich broth with garlic, chile, and olive oil. This pintxo is served two mushrooms tall, stacked on a piece of baguette perched in a bowl of the steaming brothy cooking liquid. The most important part of this pintxo is choosing the freshest mushrooms available.

MAKES 6

⅔ cup (160 ml) extra-virgin olive oil
5 garlic cloves, peeled
1 dried guindilla pepper, torn into pieces
½ small bunch parsley
12 button mushrooms, stems removed and reserved
1 teaspoon kosher salt, plus more if needed
¾ cup (180 ml) white wine
1 cup (240 ml) water
½ baguette, sliced into 6 pieces

Combine ½ cup (120 ml) of the olive oil and 4 of the garlic cloves in a medium pot and heat over medium heat. Add the guindilla pepper pieces and parsley, stir, and cook until the garlic takes on a bit of golden color.

Add the mushroom caps and stems to the pot and sprinkle with the salt. Cook, stirring occasionally, until the mushrooms begin to let off liquid, 3 to 4 minutes. Add the white wine and cook, stirring, for about 1 minute, until it reduces a bit. Add the water and bring the mixture to a boil.

Mince the remaining garlic clove and add it to the pot. Drizzle with the remaining olive oil and stir well. Taste the liquid and add salt if necessary. Reduce the heat to maintain a simmer and cook until the mushrooms are tender, about 15 minutes.

Thread a mushroom cap, a stem, and another mushroom cap on a long toothpick. Pierce a piece of bread with the bottom of the toothpick and lay the pintxo in a miniature serving bowl. Repeat for the remaining pintxos. Ladle ⅓ cup (80 ml) or so of the cooking liquid into the bottom of each bowl and serve.

TAMBORIL, SAN SEBASTIÁN

✦

In the 1940s, Manuel Martínez, Juliana Gil, and their five children moved to San Sebastián from Haro, the capital of La Rioja, unaware that their nuclear family unit would go on to form an integral part of a culinary era. Manuel and Juliana opened Bar Martínez (see page 78), but their children went on to each have their own respected bars in San Sebastián's Old Town. In 1954, Luis Martínez, along with his wife, Pilar (known as Pili), bought Bar Tamboril, a cornerstone of the Plaza de la Constitución (two of the other establishments run by the children included Ganbara and the now-defunct Urbano). Luis manned the kitchen when they opened, but he died tragically young, leaving Pili with three children at home and pregnant with twins. Her oldest, Tibu, later took charge of the bar, and was subsequently joined by the identical (and equally quirky) twins, Miguel and Jesús.

The twins became a legend in San Sebastián, thanks to their gift of gab and a favorite joke: "One of us is the boss and the other the son of the owner. Who can tell the difference?" Tambo, as the bar is affectionately known, is now in the hands of cousins from Ganbara (see page 178). When they took it over after the twins retired in 2019, they kept it much the same, simply stripping and revarnishing the intricate wooden bar that occupies most of the minuscule establishment. The most famous pintxos are still on the menu—the Pipas (gamba a la gabardina, page 130), and, of course, the cousins' famous mushrooms, a recipe that originated with their Riojan grandmother.

ANATOMY OF A PLATED PINTXO

Hot pintxos are by no means formulaic—they are as varied as Spanish and Basque cuisines in general. However, broadly speaking, kitchen pintxos often have components in common, and knowing what they are makes it easier to get creative.

2
The Protein

The heart of the kitchen pintxo, the protein can range from shrimp to octopus to hake to beef cheek. It is typically no larger than a few bites.

1
The Base

Almost without fail, the protein, or the star of the pintxo, rests on a base, for both visuals and for practicality—a base prevents it from sliding around the plate— as well as for flavor. A common base is a vegetable puree, most typically potato, but vegetables such as red peppers or even cabbage can also be spotted here. Savory streusel-type crumbs are occasionally seen in the more creative pintxo kitchens, perhaps even tinted with squid ink, as in the Piquillo Parrillero (page 281).

3
The Garnish

A kitchen pintxo nearly always has some sort of finishing sauce or sprinkle. Among the most common garnishes or finishing touches are parsley oil and flaky sea salt. Other sauces, such as demi-glace or mayonnaise, are also used.

Pintxo Moruno

MOORISH KEBAB

Moruno means "Moorish," so it's no surprise that this pintxo hails from the south of Spain, where heady spices regularly find their way into dishes, thanks to a long history of influence from nearby Africa. For this pintxo, hearty lamb meat is marinated in a secret mix of spices (the one in this recipe is a close approximation) before being skewered and grilled. You can also make the recipe with chicken or even pork, a common substitution across Spain, where pork is king. Be generous with the marinade sauce and lemon juice when finishing the kebabs.

MAKES 6

3 teaspoons cumin
2 teaspoons spicy paprika
2 teaspoons table salt
1½ teaspoons freshly ground black pepper
1 teaspoon ground turmeric
1 garlic clove, minced
½ onion, minced
6 cilantro sprigs
6 parsley sprigs
2 lemons, halved
⅔ cup (160 ml) olive oil, plus more for the grill grates
12 ounces (340 g) boneless lamb leg with most of the fat removed, cut into 1-inch (2.5 cm) pieces (about 36)

SPECIAL EQUIPMENT
6 metal skewers, about 10 inches (25 cm) long

In a small bowl, whisk together the cumin, spicy paprika, salt, pepper, and turmeric. Remove 2 teaspoons of the spice mix and set aside.

Combine the spice mix, garlic, onion, cilantro, and parsley in a food processor and process to a puree. Squeeze the juice from 1 lemon and add the juice and olive oil to the processor; process to blend. Transfer ⅓ cup (80 ml) of the mixture to a small bowl and set aside. Transfer the remaining mixture to a bowl or ziplock bag, add the lamb, and turn to coat. Cover the bowl or seal the bag and let the lamb marinate in the refrigerator for at least a few hours or, preferably, overnight.

Prepare a medium-high fire in a grill and oil the grates (see Variation). Thread 6 pieces of the lamb on each of six long metal skewers. Grill the lamb over direct heat, turning often, until browned and beginning to char, 3 to 4 minutes.

Transfer the skewers to a platter and sprinkle evenly with the reserved spice mix. Transfer the reserved marinade mixture to a plate and dip each kebab in it, turning to coat, and squeezing on a bit more lemon juice before serving.

VARIATION

If you don't have a grill, you can prepare the kebabs on the stovetop. Heat a griddle or large sauté pan over high heat until hot. Place the kebabs on (or in) the pan, without crowding. Cook for about 2 minutes, brushing with the reserved marinade mixture, until lightly charred. Turn, sprinkle evenly with the reserved spices, and cook for another 2 minutes, or until charred on both sides. Brush again with the marinade mixture and squeeze on a bit of lemon juice.

CAFÉ IRUÑA, BILBAO

✦

Café Iruña's history begins in 1903, on the saint's day of San Fermín, July 7, when it was opened by Severo Unzué Donamaría, a businessman from Navarra. The interior, by architect Joaquín Rucoba, was spectacularly ornate, lively with Andalucían tiles, intricate woodwork, and artists' frescoes. The café-bar quickly became the center of Bilbao's artistic, political, and literary culture, frequented by prestigious writers and poets like Pío Baroja and Miguel de Unamuno for the *tertulia*, the afternoon meeting over coffee and alcohol, where everything from politics to poetry was debated with fervor. During times of scarcity, it was even a point for sales of contraband tobacco and other items.

However, by the late 1970s, the café had fallen into decline and was expected to shut down until Iñaki Aseguinolaza Azkargorta, a developer from

Gipuzkoa, and his wife, Alicia Garmendia, swooped in to save it in 1981; they were later joined by their son, Gaizka Aseguinolaza. The pintxo moruno at Café Iruña played a big part in its newfound life as a pintxo destination, when, in the late 1990s, Ahmed Belkhir installed a pintxo pop-up before pop-ups really existed in a small corner of the century-old café. Ahmed stood for years behind a charcoal grill, a fan blowing the smoke in the direction of a makeshift extractor, while he grilled his famous kebabs of lamb marinated in a secret sauce, a family recipe dating back to the 1960s from the family bar Melilla y Fez.

THE PINTXO
SCRIBES

Although pintxos have been far more thoroughly enjoyed than written about, there are a handful of journalists and authors who have spent a major chunk of their word count talking about pintxos, their creators, and the bars of the Basque capitals. Pedro Martín (see page 173) was the first, with *Pintxos Donostiarras*, which was the bible for many chefs across Basque Country in the 1990s. This was later followed by multiple books gathering the pintxos of San Sebastián into one place, a groundbreaking publishing effort. Peio García is another who has been a defender of the pintxo from day one. He has written four books on the topic, including *Donosti y Sus Pinchos*, which focuses on more elaborate pintxos than Martín's book, with more explanation.

García also organized one of the first pintxo contests, d'Pintxos (officially the Feria Congreso Mundial de la Cocina en Miniatura). Mikel Corcuera, who died in 2022, wrote about both Basque cuisine and the pintxo scene and was widely revered for his philosophical words on pintxos and the riches of Basque cuisine. It wouldn't be a stretch to call him the chronicler of the evolution of Basque cuisine during the last half of the twentieth century. His work appeared mostly in regional newspapers. Josema

Azpeitia is currently the most active proponent of the Basque dining scene. His magazine and his website, ondojan.com ("good eating" in Euskara), feature news about local dining in Basque Country and restaurant reviews. He is the author of *La Senda del Pintxo* (*The Pintxo Trail*), which highlights local pintxos and the bars they come from. He has written several other books about pintxos as well as innumerable words about Basque cuisine and has won prestigious awards for his efforts.

Brocheta de Gambas

SHRIMP KEBAB WITH PEPPER VINAIGRETTE

Goiz Argi, the bar that made the ganba brotxeta famous, is on San Sebastián's crowded Fermín Calbetón street. Their bacon-and-shrimp kebab recipe is top secret, but this is a delicious approximation. The surf-and-turf combination of smoky bacon and charred shrimp is divine, especially when drizzled with an acidic vinaigrette.

To make these kebabs at home, you'll need a griddle or a large heavy skillet. They also taste fantastic grilled outdoors. The pepper vinaigrette is best made in advance, the farther ahead the better, up to a day before.

MAKES 6

1 sweet Italian green pepper, such as Cubanelle
½ red bell pepper
1 carrot
½ spring onion (see Note, page 49)
½ cup (120 ml) apple cider vinegar
Kosher salt
1 cup plus 1 tablespoon (255 ml) extra-virgin olive oil
18 small shrimp, peeled and deveined
6 bacon slices, halved crosswise
½ baguette, sliced on an angle into 6 pieces

In a food processor, combine the peppers, carrot, and onion and pulse until finely chopped. (Alternatively, mince by hand.) Transfer to a bowl, add the vinegar and a pinch of salt, and let soak for at least 10 minutes or up to overnight.

Slowly whisk 1 cup (240 ml) of the olive oil into the vegetable mixture. Set aside.

Pierce a shrimp from tail to head with a wooden skewer, then thread on a piece of folded bacon, followed by another shrimp, another piece of bacon, and a final shrimp. Repeat to make 5 more skewers. Season with salt.

On a griddle or in a large heavy skillet, heat the remaining 1 tablespoon olive oil over high heat. When it is very hot, add the kebabs to the pan and sear for about 1 minute, until the shrimp start to take on a golden color. Flip the kebabs and cook for about 30 seconds more. Transfer the kebabs to a plate.

Arrange the slices of bread in the hot pan in a single layer and toast lightly on the bottom side. Transfer to a platter.

Place the kebabs on top of the toasted bread, ladle a bit of the vinaigrette over each one, and serve.

Forks, Knives, and Pintxos:
The Controversy

❖

When hot pintxos served straight from the kitchen first began to appear in bars, they challenged the very definition of what a pintxo is, bringing an onslaught of critics and controversy. In most cases, the principal argument against the kitchen pintxo was its deviation from tradition. Purists believed that a true pintxo should never be more than a couple of bites and should never, under any circumstances, require a fork or knife. Their protests weren't fierce enough to stifle the popularity of these new creations, but the critics clung to their ideas by referring to this type of pintxo as *cocina en miniatura*, or "miniature cuisine," separating them, at least in terms of nomenclature, from traditional pintxos.

Jaizkibel

JAIZKIBEL

The Jaizkibel is one of the only pintxos at Gran Sol that has never won an award—the Muñoz brothers deem it too simple to enter into contests. However, the pintxo has been flying off the bar at the famed Hondarribia establishment since the very beginning. Why? This towering mountain (named after the nearby mountain range that peaks at 1,795 feet/547 m) is easy to love.

Cremini or button mushroom caps are stuffed with a cream cheese mixture studded with jamón ibérico, then fried in an egg batter until warm and gooey inside. To serve, they are blanketed in an extra-garlicky mayonnaise cream and drizzled with parsley oil and a caramel sauce. A slice of baguette is practically mandatory to sop up the delicious, abundant herb oil, sauce, and juices. This pintxo is best served immediately, although you can prepare everything up to the moment of frying ahead of time.

MAKES 8

2 cups (440 g) mayonnaise, store-bought or homemade (page 44)
2 garlic cloves, minced
3 tablespoons heavy cream
Kosher salt
½ cup (100 g) sugar
1 cup (240 ml) warm water
7 slices jamón ibérico
9 ounces (255 g) cream cheese
8 large cremini or button mushrooms
Sunflower or olive oil for deep-frying
2 large eggs
All-purpose flour for dredging
Parsley Oil (page 82) for drizzling

NOTE

At Gran Sol, they peel the cremini mushrooms, but you can leave the exterior skin on to fine effect.

Combine the mayonnaise, garlic, 2 tablespoons of the cream, and a pinch of salt in a food processor and process for a minute or two, until smooth. (Alternatively, combine in a tall narrow container and blend with an immersion blender.) Set aside.

To make the caramel sauce, put the sugar in a small sauté pan, add about one-quarter of the warm water, or enough to just barely cover the sugar, and set the pan over high heat. Cook, without stirring (although you can swirl the pan to ensure more even cooking), until the mixture begins to turn a golden color, about 5 minutes. Add the remaining water and cook for about 5 minutes more, or until the caramel has thickened but is not at the thread or soft ball stage (i.e., below 220°F/104°C).

Remove the caramel from the heat and carefully stir in the remaining 1 tablespoon cream. Set aside.

Pass the garlic mayonnaise through a fine-mesh sieve and discard the solids. Set aside.

Finely chop 4 of the ham slices. Cut the remaining 3 slices into 3 pieces each.

Put the cream cheese in a small bowl, add the chopped ham and a pinch of salt, and stir until the mixture is smooth and creamy and the ham is evenly distributed. Taste for seasoning and set aside.

CONTINUED →

Remove the stems from the mushrooms and, if using creminis, shave off the outer skin with a peeler (see Note). Stuff the mushroom caps with the cheese mixture, dividing it evenly among the mushrooms.

Pour about 2 inches (5 cm) of sunflower oil into a large heavy saucepan and heat over high heat until it reaches about 350°F (175°C). Use a thermometer to test the oil, or throw in a bit of flour; if it sizzles on contact, the oil is ready.

Beat the eggs with a splash of water in a bowl. Spread flour on a plate or in a shallow bowl.

Working in batches to avoid crowding the pan, pass the mushrooms through the flour, coating them completely and shaking off the excess, then dredge in the egg, coating them completely and letting the excess drip off, and add to the pan. Fry the mushrooms, turning them occasionally for even cooking, until light golden brown, 3 to 5 minutes. Remove with a slotted spoon and drain on paper towels. Sprinkle immediately with salt.

Add the remaining pieces of ham to the hot oil and fry until the fat renders a bit, 20 to 30 seconds. Drain on paper towels. (You just need 8 pieces for the pintxos; the least beautiful piece can be for snacking.)

Place a mushroom, cheese side up, on a small serving plate. Top it with some garlic mayonnaise, covering it halfway or entirely. Generously drizzle parsley oil around the mushroom and drizzle a zigzag of caramel across the top. Arrange a piece of the ham atop the mushroom. Repeat with the remaining ingredients to make 8 pintxos. Serve immediately.

"This is a pintxo: a bit of food in small portions, two or three bites, that is often eaten standing up. I would also add that it is quality cooking. A pintxo with a glass of wine? Nowhere in the world but here can you get such a luxury."

—PATXI BERGARA, BAR BERGARA

BAR GRAN SOL, HONDARRIBIA

✦

Today Gran Sol is a family affair. In 1968, José Bixente Muñoz and María Antonia Esnal took over a bar, with the name Gran Sol, from a local fisherman who was throwing in the towel. They began to offer classic pintxos and small plates at a time when these were virtually nonexistent in the small seaside town of Hondarribia, and their banderillas and tortilla de patatas met with great success. Their children, Mikel, Bixente, and Nekane, helped out from a very early age. Bixente went on to study cooking, working under Martín Berasategui and other top chefs in the area. When he returned to Gran Sol around 1999, it was to work behind the stoves, and he soon revolutionized the bar's offerings, focusing more on pintxos delivered hot from the kitchen and on entering (and winning) local pintxo contests. Relentlessly creative, Bixente had a special talent for crafting pintxos that tell a story, not only awakening the diner's taste buds but also sparking a larger conversation, a thoughtful reaction. He gathered inspiration from faraway travels, but also from things as simple as the broth his grandmother made on cold winter mornings.

Gran Sol appeared in an article in the *New York Times* in 2010 that cited Hondarribia as the site of a dining explosion, thanks to a handful of stellar pintxo bars and restaurants. Without a doubt, Bixente has been one of the most creative and important contributors to the world of the pintxo in the twenty-first century. Not a year has gone by that Gran Sol hasn't won some award, even coming in second at the national pintxo and tapa championship in Valladolid. It is the only bar to date to win the most prestigious Euskadi pintxo championship three times. Nowadays, Gran Sol is run by Mikel and Nekane, and in 2021 they opened a franchise in the Shibuya neighborhood of Tokyo.

Risotto de Idiazabal

IDIAZABAL CHEESE RISOTTO

What could very well be the most famous risotto outside of Italy began at La Cuchara de San Telmo (see page 251) and found its path to stardom in the kitchen of Borda Berri. This risotto has a trick, however—instead of rice, it uses oval-shaped orzo pasta, which is easier to cook and can be prepared in advance.

This cheesy, creamy crowd-pleaser combines three different types of Idiazabal cheese, leveraging the creaminess of the younger version, the smoky flavor of the ahumado, and the sharp tang of the longer-cured reserva. If you don't have access to all three, the risotto can still be made to great effect with even just one type. Much less fussy than its Italian cousin, this risotto will become one of your favorite hot pintxos. Don't skip the parsley oil— it adds a dash of color and a slash of bright green flavor to cut through the intensity of the cheese.

MAKES 6

2 tablespoons extra-virgin olive oil
1 garlic clove, sliced
1¼ cups (210 g) orzo
¼ cup (60 ml) white wine
1¼ cups plus ⅓ cup (380 ml) vegetable broth
Kosher salt
One 3-ounce (85 g) piece curado reserva Idiazabal cheese (with rind; see Note)
One 2¼-ounce (65 g) piece ahumado curado Idiazabal cheese (with rind)
One 2¼-ounce (65 g) piece ahumado joven Idiazabal cheese (with rind)
¾ cup (180 ml) heavy cream
Parsley Oil (page 82) for drizzling

In a medium saucepan, combine the olive oil and garlic and heat over medium-high heat until the garlic turns a light golden brown. Remove the garlic with a slotted spoon and discard.

Add the orzo to the pan and cook, stirring, until some of the orzo begins to color. Add the white wine, bring to a simmer, and cook until the alcohol has burned off and the wine has been absorbed. Add 1¼ cups (300 ml) of the vegetable broth, along with a pinch of salt, reduce the heat to maintain a simmer, and cook until the orzo is al dente, 6 to 8 minutes, stirring often to prevent sticking. There should be little to no broth remaining. Remove from the heat and let cool.

Grate the cheeses, reserving the rinds. Set aside.

Combine the cream, the remaining ⅓ cup (80 ml) vegetable broth, ¼ teaspoon salt, and the cheese rinds in a saucepan and bring to a boil over medium-high heat. Remove from the heat and set aside to infuse for at least 15 minutes.

Strain the cream mixture to remove the rinds and return it to the saucepan over medium-low heat. Add the grated cheeses and cook, stirring, until the cheese has melted and the sauce has thickened.

CONTINUED →

Add the sauce to the pan of orzo and cook over medium heat, stirring, for a few minutes, until heated through. Taste for seasoning and add salt if necessary. Remove from the heat and allow to rest for 5 minutes before serving.

Divide the pasta among six small plates. Drizzle with parsley oil and serve.

BEHIND THE BAR

BORDA BERRI, SAN SEBASTIÁN

✦

Isidro Castrillo was ready to retire after a lifetime at Borda Berri, the bar he had taken over from his father, who had opened it after the Spanish Civil War. He found two willing (and able) bodies in Iñaki Gulín and Marc Clua. These two skilled chefs left La Cuchara de San Telmo (see page 251), where Iñaki was a partner, to open the new Borda Berri in 2007. Their vision was to use Borda Berri as a stepping stone to a full-blown restaurant, but the pintxo bar was so successful that to this day Marc is still at the helm of the tiny L-shaped kitchen (Iñaki left in 2017), serving more than three hundred pintxos at a service on the busiest days.

A chalkboard on the wall lists a selection of about a dozen pintxos, whose names get erased as the dishes run out. The pintxo selection reads more like the menu at an upscale contemporary restaurant: spider crab ravioli, tuna with coconut and curry, slow-roasted duck breast, and, of course, the risotto and the famous kebab. These are, however, pintxos—served up on tiny plates, quite efficiently, by Lucía Hueso and the rest of the bar staff. The difference between a place like Borda Berri and La Cuchara de San Telmo is that here the kitchen staff are cooks and chefs who have trained in French haute cuisine–influenced kitchens. They know how to make a demi-glace and a sharp, flavorful vinaigrette, and they continue to employ their haute cuisine skills, changing nothing but the number of grams (or ounces) per plate. And the seasons dictate the menu, something that Marc, a Catalan, says he learned from the Basques.

Foie a la Plancha

SEARED FOIE GRAS

You might not think a luxury ingredient like seared fresh foie gras would belong on a pintxo. However, Alex Montiel at La Cuchara bucked tradition by offering this pintxo of seared foie (for a measly €3 per pintxo!), and it immediately became a classic. With such a simple recipe, the basics are super important. Be sure to splurge on the best foie gras you can get. And don't skip the step of allowing it to come to room temperature before cooking. Many restaurants sear foie gras in a blazing-hot pan, but in this recipe, you'll follow La Cuchara's lead and work with medium-high heat, cooking the foie a bit more gently.

The seared foie gras is served with a basic apple compote, born of the space restrictions of a pintxo-sized kitchen, and a cider reduction. Basque cider is the best option, but you can sub another cider in a pinch.

MAKES 4

4 slices fresh foie gras (see Notes), about ¾ inch (2 cm) thick and 2½ ounces (70 g) each
¼ cup (60 ml) cider, preferably Basque
¼ cup (50 g) sugar
2 apples, preferably Reinette, Russet, or Golden Delicious, cored and cut into quarters
Kosher salt and freshly ground black pepper
Guérande gray salt for garnish (see Resources, page 302)
Ground Szechuan pepper for garnish (optional)

Bring the foie gras to room temperature, still wrapped or covered (this will probably take about an hour).

Meanwhile, to make the cider reduction, combine the cider and sugar in a small saucepan and bring to a boil, stirring to dissolve the sugar. Lower the heat and simmer until the cider has reduced to a slightly thick, syrupy consistency, 5 to 7 minutes. Remove from the heat and set aside.

Put the apple pieces in a small saucepan set over medium-high heat and drizzle with 2 tablespoons water. Put the lid on the pan, reduce the heat to the lowest setting, and cook the apples in their own juices, stirring occasionally, until tender and broken down, about 15 minutes. Remove from the heat.

Transfer the apples to a food processor and process to a puree. Pass the puree through a fine-mesh sieve into a small bowl and set aside.

CONTINUED →

Season the slices of foie with kosher salt and pepper.

Heat a large sauté pan over medium-high heat until hot. Gently lay the slices of foie in the pan and cook until the surface is a deep golden brown, 1½ to 3 minutes. Flip the foie and cook until golden brown on the second side. Transfer to a plate and allow to rest for a minute or two.

Place a spoonful of apple puree in the middle of each plate and place a slice of foie gras on top. Sprinkle with gray salt and a bit of Szechuan pepper, if desired. Drizzle the cider reduction over the foie and the plates. Serve immediately.

BEHIND THE BAR

LA CUCHARA DE SAN TELMO, SAN SEBASTIÁN

On the Day of Santo Tomás, December 21, in 1999, La Cuchara de San Telmo opened its doors, with just Alex Montiel, Iñaki Gulín, a single bartender, and the goal of doing something simple. Alex had arrived from Barcelona in 1995, looking for a change. He began working under Martín Berasategui and opened Bodegón Alejandro, but he soon became eager to start his own project, far away from the fancy trappings of avant-garde cuisine.

He and Iñaki decided from the start that there would be no slices of bread with assorted toppings on their pintxo bartop. They had the (then) crazy idea of cooking the dishes they wanted, plating them in pintxo format, and sending out every last thing freshly made from the kitchen. At first, and in part because of La Cuchara's tucked-away location, people would poke their heads in, see the empty bartop, and turn around. But little by little, those who stayed found they were blown away. Iñaki and Alex stayed so busy they couldn't even take a vacation for the next three years (Iñaki eventually left to start Borda Berri in 2007; see page 248).

With its hearty dishes like braised oxtail, La Cuchara de San Telmo closed the gap between going out for pintxos and going out to eat, thereby singlehandedly, and almost accidentally, creating a whole new world. Many of the modern classics now seen everywhere around town—the seared foie gras, the charred octopus—originated in their tiniest of kitchens. Their pintxos are so popular and in such demand that Alex has trouble making room on the menu for new items. But the guiding force behind La Cuchara remains simplicity and flavor.

FANCY
KITCHEN
PiNTXOS

The pintxo's transformation into haute cuisine is a natural evolution, considering both the pintxo and Spain's modern culinary movement were born in San Sebastián. The Nueva Cocina Vasca culinary wave began in the 1970s, when chefs Juan Mari Arzak and Pedro Subijana united a group of Basque chefs determined to place Basque cuisine on the world stage. This in turn gave way to the birth of molecular cuisine and greats like Ferrán Adriá, king of Nueva Cocina Española. Here are a few of the dazzling pintxos that came onto the scene in the 2000s, complicated to make at home but a feast for the eyes.

"Bob Limón"

ZERUKO (SEE PAGE 100), SAN SEBASTIÁN, 2010 An egg, a sausage, and a bit of toast. At first glance, this pintxo resembles a plate of breakfast, a trompe-l'œil that disguises one of the world's most elaborate dessert pintxos. But what looks like a sunny-side-up egg is a passion fruit spherification perched on a cloud of lemon mousse. And a link of what resembles the local txistorra sausage is actually a homemade raspberry gummy.

"Street Food"

ÁBACO, PAMPLONA, 2014 A spectacular bánh mi rectangle dotted with fragrant mayonnaises and marinated red tuna, Street Food is a showstopping pintxo. It won first place in La Semana del Pincho de Navarra in 2015, third in Basque Country, and third in all of Spain.

ÁBACO / PAMPLONA, NAVARRA

Chef Jesús Íñigo and his pastry chef wife, Nerea Sistiaga, met as stagiaires in the famous Basque restaurant Arzak. In 2008, they opened Ábaco in the Contemporary Art Center in Huarte, and won La Semana del Pincho four times and the Campeonato de Pintxos de Euskal Herria twice.

"El Silencio"

BAR ERKIAGA, VITORIA, 2013
El Silencio is a "toast" of cured hake stacked with confit scallops, a mix of strawberries and tomatoes, and a bit of stewed octopus. The name was born when Josune Menéndez's hard-to-please family tried it and could only moan with pleasure. The pintxo won both the top prize and the audience prize at La Semana del Pintxo, Vitoria's pintxo competition.

"La Hoguera"

ZERUKO, SAN SEBASTIÁN, 2007 La Hoguera always made heads turn, trailing smoke from its earthenware casserole dish. The pintxo has three components: a slice of smoked salt cod on a clothespin, a piece of toast with parsley mousseline, and a test tube full of liquefied, bubbly green salad, made with techniques like spherification and an effervescent texturizer.

BAR ERKIAGA / VITORIA, ÁLAVA

Josune Menéndez and her partner Jesús "Txus" Palomo man the bar at this unassuming spot on Calle Herrería in the medieval part of Vitoria's old town. Josune has created multiple award-winning pintxos from the bar's tiny kitchen. She was learning the trade next to her mother from the age of seven years old, watching her cook traditional dishes for Bar Erkiaga's loyal clientele. Since then, Josune has won multiple awards, from the best pintxo in Álava to a finalist mention in the Euskal Herria pintxo competition.

Solomillo

BEEF TENDERLOIN

This simple yet delicious bite is the pintxo-sized version of the famed Basque txuleta. Bite-size pieces of steak, charred on the outside and red in the middle, are served atop slices of baguette and crowned with sautéed green peppers and crunchy sea salt. The secret to this pintxo is using high-quality aged beef and making sure not to take it past rare.

MAKES 6

2 sweet Italian green peppers, such as Cubanelle
1 tablespoon extra-virgin olive oil
One 10-ounce (280 g) piece aged beef tenderloin, cut into 6 pieces
Kosher salt
½ baguette, sliced on an angle into 6 pieces
Flaky sea salt

Preheat the oven to 400°F (200°C).

Arrange the peppers on a small baking sheet and roast, turning once, until the skin is charred and the peppers collapse, about 30 minutes. Remove from the heat and let cool.

Remove the cores and seeds from the peppers (leave the skin on) and cut the peppers into strips. Set aside.

Heat a large sauté pan over high heat. Add the olive oil, and when it is very hot, add the pieces of tenderloin to the pan, leaving space between them. Sprinkle with kosher salt and cook for about 1 minute. Flip the pieces and cook for 30 seconds to 1 minute on the other side. You want the exterior to be browned and crisp but the interior to still be bright red. Transfer to a plate.

Wipe the sauté pan clean and return it to the heat. Add the peppers and a pinch of kosher salt and stir until they are hot.

Place each piece of meat on a slice of bread. Arrange a few pepper strips in a pile in the middle of each piece. Sprinkle with flaky sea salt and serve immediately.

GANDARIAS, SAN SEBASTIÁN

When a couple of brothers moved to the big city from the paradisiacal village of Ataun and opened a simple bar, Juantxo, in the Old Town of San Sebastián in the 1970s, their sandwiches, the bocadillos del Juantxo, quickly became the stuff of legend. In 2003, the brothers, Felipe and José Mari Agirre, decided to take over one of the city's emblematic locations: Gandarias, formerly Casa Domingo. At first they imagined making it into another successful sandwich spot. Some advice from one of their purveyors, however, convinced them to fill an empty niche in the neighborhood: a restaurant that focused on good raw materials and stayed open from noon to night. Gandarias was possibly the first bar in San Sebastián to serve high-quality steak in pintxo format.

Nowadays Gandarias is in the hands of José Mari and his wife, Gregori Iturrioz, along with Oihane, their daughter (one of her brothers still holds down the fort at Juantxo). They focus squarely on tradition, reviving dishes that were nearly forgotten even by locals, and the result is a restaurant that is always busy. The menu is home to several local favorites, including kebabs (from kidney to scallop) and a creamy risotto. In 2018, they opened Xibaritak, a gourmet food store, also located on the Calle 31 de Agosto.

ABOVE San Sebastián

Volcán de Morcilla

BLOOD SAUSAGE VOLCANO

One of San Sebastián's most famous and beloved pintxos, the blood sausage volcano at Hidalgo 56 is a rich combination of blood sausage, pipérade, and raisins, topped with a still-runny egg yolk. The blood sausage takes on a volcano-like shape when formed in a ramekin with sloping sides, and after the first bite, the egg yolk runs down the sides of the pintxo, pooling like magma into the apple compote that garnishes the plate.

This pintxo is simple to prepare ahead of time and can be finished quickly and easily in the microwave after adding the egg yolks. It's won over many a professed morcilla hater, so don't be put off by the blood sausage. The milder Burgos version, which contains rice, melds beautifully with the peppers and raisins.

MAKES 6

2 apples, preferably Reinette, Russet, or Golden Delicious, peeled, cored, and coarsely chopped
½ cup (120 ml) water
1 tablespoon unsalted butter
1 rosemary branch
1 to 2 tablespoons extra-virgin olive oil
½ onion, diced
1 garlic clove, minced
Kosher salt
½ red bell pepper, diced
1 sweet Italian green pepper, such as Cubanelle, diced
1⅓ pounds (600 g) Burgos blood sausage (see page 260), casings removed
¼ cup (30 g) raisins
6 large eggs
Flaky sea salt

SPECIAL EQUIPMENT
6 ramekins, preferably with slanted sides

In a medium saucepan, combine the apples, water, butter, and rosemary and bring to a boil over high heat. Reduce the heat to medium, cover, and cook at a simmer until the apples are tender, about 10 minutes. Remove from the heat and remove and discard the rosemary.

Puree the apples in a food processor or directly in the pot using an immersion blender. Set the puree aside.

In a large skillet, heat 1 tablespoon olive oil over medium-high heat. Add the onion and garlic, along with a pinch of kosher salt, reduce the heat to medium, and cook, stirring, until the onion begins to caramelize, about 15 minutes.

Add the red and green peppers, a pinch of kosher salt, and, if the mixture looks dry, another tablespoon or so of olive oil. Cook, stirring, until the onion is caramelized and the peppers are tender, 15 to 20 minutes.

Raise the heat to medium-high and crumble the blood sausage into the skillet. Cook, breaking up the sausage with a spoon and stirring, until it is thoroughly cooked, about 5 minutes. Add the raisins, stir, and remove from the heat.

Separate the eggs, taking care not to break the yolks, and set the yolks aside. Reserve the whites for another use or discard them.

CONTINUED →

Divide the morcilla mixture among six ramekins, preferably with slanted sides, pressing it gently into the ramekins. Invert each ramekin onto a small plate, as if you were making sandcastles, and lift off the ramekins. Make a small indentation in the top of each "volcano" and carefully place an egg yolk in each indentation.

Swipe a spoonful of apple puree along one side of each plate and heat the plates in the microwave for 20 seconds. Sprinkle the egg yolks with flaky sea salt and serve.

ODOLKIA / BLOOD SAUSAGE / MORCILLA

·

There are two types of blood sausage commonly served in Basque Country—morcilla de Burgos and what Basques call morcilla de verduras, or just morcilla, which the rest of Spain knows as morcilla de Beasain. This sausage's texture is similar to that of superfine ground meat mixed with caramelized vegetables, while morcilla de Burgos is a rice-studded blood sausage also found elsewhere in Spain. Preferences as to which type is best are highly personal, but the rice-studded version is a better beginner's sausage. Morcilla is usually served simply boiled or sliced and fried.

WHAT IS A PINTXO?

"A pintxo is an informal way to enjoy good food and see the creativity that comes out of a kitchen. Something that can surprise you, excite you, in a bite."

—SENÉN GONZÁLEZ, SAGARTOKI

HIDALGO 56, SAN SEBASTIÁN

Although it wasn't until 2005 that Hidalgo 56 opened its doors in the Gros neighborhood of San Sebastián, the bar's history goes back much further. Hidalgo 56 gets its name from Juan Mari Hidalgo's parents' bar, which opened in 1956 on the corner of Calle Bermingham and Calle San Francisco, long before Gros experienced the renaissance it later had. It was a glorious establishment, with a thirty-foot-long bartop crowded with earthenware dishes and pintxos.

Juan Mari was working in the family business by the age of thirteen, working the bar and kitchen after school and soccer practice. He eventually became a self-taught chef, developing the first menu of hot pintxos in the city and earning a Michelin star in 1994 for the food he served in the twelve-table dining room. He passed through other local kitchens before meeting his wife, Nubia Regalado, and deciding to take the plunge with his own pintxo bar, Hidalgo 56. From a tiny kitchen off the hallway that connects the dining room with the bar, Juan Mari would prepare fifteen to twenty different pintxos every day in what he and Nubia called a *gastrotasca*—a neighborhood bar where one can eat especially well. Juan Mari and Nubia retired in 2022, but their son, Sergio Humada, carries on the culinary legacy at his own restaurant, Txitxardin.

Milhojas de Habitas

FAVA BEAN MILLE-FEUILLE

A pintxo composed of one of Araba's most lauded legumes, the fava bean, was perhaps destined to become a legend. A nod to the locals' nickname for the beans, babazorro, favas are the star of this pintxo, sitting atop a ratatouille-style vegetable stew known as pisto. A few strips of smoked Atlantic mackerel (see page 284), a preserved fish that's not easy to find outside Spain, adorn the top, but you can substitute any preserved smoked fatty fish. This surf-and-turf combination, which is perched atop a folded and fried strip of rice paper, is best assembled just before serving, as the rice paper will get soggy otherwise.

MAKES 8

Kosher salt

2 pounds (450 g) fava beans in the pod, shelled (about 1 cup)

Olive oil for deep-frying

8 sheets rice paper, preferably square ones

2 tablespoons extra-virgin olive oil

1 spring onion (see Note, page 49), finely diced

1 red bell pepper, cored and finely diced

1 sweet green Italian pepper, such as Cubanelle, cored and finely diced

1 small zucchini, finely diced

1 tomato, finely diced

8 fillets smoked preserved mackerel (see Notes), cut in half

4 fillets unsmoked preserved mackerel (see Notes), cut in half

Bring a pot of salted water to a boil. Add the fava beans and boil them for 3 minutes, then drain in a colander and run under cold water to stop the cooking; drain again.

Peel the beans, pinching to squeeze them out of their skins and into a bowl. Set aside.

Pour 2 inches (5 cm) of olive oil into a large heavy saucepan and heat over high heat until it reaches about 350°F (175°C). Use a thermometer to test the oil, or drop in a bit of rice paper; if it sizzles on contact, the oil is ready.

Meanwhile, break each sheet of rice paper into a rectangle about 4 by 5 inches (10 by 12 cm) by folding over the sides and removing any excess; if your sheets are round, fold each one over itself four times to remove the rounded edges.

Fill a shallow dish larger than the rice papers with warm water. Working with one rice paper sheet at a time, dip it into the warm water for a few seconds, then remove, fold it lengthwise in half, and pat dry. Fry in the hot oil for about 30 seconds, flipping it halfway through. Transfer to a paper towel–lined plate, standing it upright to drain.

CONTINUED →

NOTES

Removing the fava bean skins
results in a brighter green
appearance and a more refined
taste.

Have extra rice papers on hand
in case any of them break or don't
turn out beautifully.

If you can't find both smoked and
regular canned mackerel, you can
use all of one kind or substitute
another canned fatty fish.

To make the pisto, in a large sauté pan, heat the extra-virgin olive oil over medium heat. Add the onion and cook, stirring, for about 5 minutes, until it begins to turn translucent. Add both peppers and a pinch of salt, reduce the heat to low, cover, and cook for about 15 minutes, until the vegetables begin to caramelize.

Raise the heat to medium, add the zucchini, cover, and cook for about 15 minutes, until tender. Add the tomato and cook for 15 minutes more, until the mixture is homogeneous, uncovering the pan for the last 5 minutes to evaporate some of the liquid. Taste and add more salt if needed. Remove the pisto from the heat.

Place a rice paper toast on each of eight small plates and divide the vegetable pisto among the toasts. Top each with a scattering of the fava beans. Arrange 2 pieces of smoked mackerel on opposite edges of each toast. Place a piece of the unsmoked mackerel in the middle of each toast and serve.

BERDELA / ATLANTIC MACKEREL / VERDEL

•

Verdel is one of the Spanish names for Atlantic mackerel (*Scomber scombrus*); it is also known as *caballa* and *sarda*. You can differentiate it from Pacific mackerel by the lack of marks on its belly and the greenish tone of its skin. Atlantic mackerel is fatty, with nearly twice as many B vitamins and omega-3s as salmon. Its season is from mid-February to May, and it's one of Basque Country's most important catches. The Day of Verdel is celebrated every spring in Mutriku, outside Bilbao. Conservas Nardín makes the delicate smoked version that Toloño uses in its pintxo.

TOLOÑO, VITORIA

✦

Toloño has been one of the most important pintxo bars outside of San Sebastián for more than twenty-five years. After moving to Vitoria-Gasteiz from Gipuzkoa in 1995, Enrique Fuentes, Carmen Bargaño, and their son, Mikel, took over Toloño, one of the capital's most famous establishments, which dates back to the 1910s and '20s. Working in the kitchen, Carmen maintained the line of simple pintxos, from Gildas to tortillas and the classic hard-boiled egg, that Toloño had previously had on offer.

In the early 2000s, Enrique was able to quit his day job and join Carmen in the kitchen, and they began to enter their pintxos in the local contest in Vitoria, winning for their stewed tripe served in a classic earthenware casserole. They went on to win the first-ever Campeonato de Pintxos de Euskal Herria in 2006 with their milhojas de habitas. Toloño became known for its small, exquisite bites—a far cry from the rest of the city's large, unrefined pintxos meant to fill the drinker's stomach.

In 2011, they took over the former printer's space next door, tripling the bar's square footage but still serving a menu made up solely of pintxos. Enrique's easy, jocular air and Carmen's glamorous gregariousness have definitely been part

of Toloño's successful formula. And, of course, there's the food—Carmen still cleans pounds and pounds of anchovies in spring and fall to cure them as vinegary boquerones. Several of their pintxos are the stuff of legend, like the irlandés de perretxiko, a pintxo of St. George's mushrooms plated to look like an Irish coffee; a glossy red peperoncino stuffed with tuna and capers; and porcini risotto. Enrique and Carmen have since retired, an event so monumental it was celebrated at one of the annual pintxo competitions. The business now lies in the hands of their children, Mikel and Sonia.

Arroz con Socarrat

CRISPY RICE

This deconstructed take on classic paella features sautéed shrimp served atop savory rice, flavorful thanks to the elaborate broth. The dish is crowned with a medallion of socarrat, the crispy layer of caramelized rice found on the bottom of the paella pan. The final garnish is a few dots of aioli.

MAKES 6

One whole head garlic, plus 5 garlic cloves, 4 left whole, 1 minced
4 tablespoons plus 1 teaspoon (65 ml) extra-virgin olive oil
Kosher salt
2 chicken wings
1 chicken thigh
A piece of beef marrowbone (about 6 ounces/170 g)
1 yellow or Spanish onion, quartered
1 carrot, chopped
½ leek, chopped and rinsed well
½ tomato, cut in half
6 button mushrooms, stems removed and halved
¼ cup (60 ml) tomato puree
⅓ cup (80 ml) brandy
1 teaspoon pimentón dulce (sweet)
1 dried choricero pepper (see Notes) or other dried mild red chile
8 cups (960 ml) fish broth, homemade (page 156) or store-bought
6 extra-large shrimp, preferably head-on, or langoustines, peeled and heads removed, shells and heads from 4 of the shrimp (or langoustines) reserved
1 large egg yolk
1 teaspoon fresh lemon juice
¾ cup (180 ml) sunflower or other neutral oil
½ spring onion (see Notes, page 49), diced
2 small squid, cleaned and finely chopped
¼ cup (60 ml) Tomato Sauce (page 209)
Pinch of saffron threads
1⅓ cups (240 g) Bomba or other short-grain rice

Preheat the oven to 400°F (200°C).

Slice off the top of the garlic head. Place the head on a piece of aluminum foil, drizzle with 2 teaspoons of the olive oil, and sprinkle with a pinch of salt. Wrap the garlic tightly in the foil and roast for 40 minutes, or until the cloves are golden and feel soft when pressed. Remove from the oven and allow to cool.

Meanwhile, place the chicken wings, thigh, and beef bone on a baking sheet. Roast for 20 minutes, or until the wings are golden. Remove from the oven and transfer to a stockpot.

Add the yellow onion, carrot, leek, tomato, mushrooms, the 4 whole garlic cloves, tomato puree, brandy, pimentón, and choricero pepper to the pot, then add the fish broth. Bring just to a boil over high heat, skim off any foam that has risen to the surface, and reduce the heat to maintain a low simmer. Cook the broth for about 2 hours, skimming off the foam as necessary.

Meanwhile, 20 minutes before the broth is done, heat 2 teaspoons of the olive oil in a sauté pan over high heat. Add the reserved shrimp heads and shells and sauté, turning once, for about 1 minute on each side, until seared. Add the seared shells and heads to the broth and simmer for about 15 minutes longer. Remove from the heat and allow to cool.

Strain the fish broth through a fine-mesh sieve into a bowl or other container; discard the solids.

Squeeze the pulp from the roasted garlic bulb into a tall cylindrical container. Add the egg yolk, lemon juice, a pinch of salt, and the sunflower oil. Insert an immersion blender into the container so it touches the bottom and, without moving it, blend on the lowest setting to emulsify the mixture. Once the aioli is almost totally emulsified, move the blender slowly up and down to incorporate the remaining oil. (Alternatively, use a conventional blender: Combine the roasted garlic, egg yolk, lemon juice, and salt in the blender and, with the blender running, slowly stream in the oil through the hole in the lid.) Set aside, refrigerating in an airtight container if you won't be using the aioli within an hour or so.

CONTINUED →

If you're unable to find dried choricero peppers, you can substitute 2 tablespoons jarred choricero puree, which can be found in specialty markets or ordered online (see Resources, page 302). It is often labeled "pulpa de pimiento choricero" or "carne de pimiento choricero."

You can make the rice ahead by cooking it only halfway through; reserve the remaining broth. Then, just before serving, transfer the rice to a pot and cook over low heat, gradually adding the remaining broth as directed in the recipe, until the rice is done.

What makes this dish so special is the complex broth enhanced with brandy, tomato, and pimentón. To save time when making this pintxo, you can instead fortify a store-bought chicken broth with these ingredients.

In a large sauté pan, heat 1 tablespoon of the olive oil over medium-high heat. Add the spring onion and cook until tender and translucent, about 3 minutes. Add the squid and minced garlic and sauté for 2 to 3 minutes, until the squid begins to color. Add the tomato sauce, saffron, and a pinch of salt and cook for another 2 to 3 minutes.

Add the rice to the pan and cook briefly, stirring to mix. Pour in 3 cups (720 ml) of the reserved broth and cook, stirring occasionally, until the rice has absorbed the broth. Continue cooking, adding more broth ½ cup (120 ml) at a time and stirring to prevent the rice from sticking, until the rice is al dente but there is still enough liquid remaining to give it a brothy consistency, 20 to 25 minutes (the total amount of broth will be around 4½ cups/1 L). Remove from the heat.

Heat 1 tablespoon of the olive oil on a griddle or in a large sauté pan over medium-high heat. When the oil is hot, add a tablespoon of the rice and flatten it carefully with the back of a spoon into a thin layer about 2 inches (5 cm) in diameter. Repeat to make another one or two "medallions" of rice, without crowding the pan, and cook until the rice has formed a crust on the bottom, about 2 minutes. Turn the medallions and cook for 2 minutes more, or until golden brown on both sides. Transfer to a plate and repeat this process until you have 6 socarrat medallions.

In another large sauté pan, heat the remaining 1 tablespoon olive oil over high heat. Working in batches if necessary to avoid crowding, add the shrimp to the pan, sprinkle with salt, and sear for a minute or two on each side. Remove from the heat.

Spoon a serving of rice onto each of six small plates or bowls. Prop a crispy socarrat medallion against one side of the rice on each plate. Place a shrimp on the other side of the rice and dollop or pipe small circles of aioli around the rice. Serve immediately.

CHORICERO PEPPERS

•

Choricero peppers are a Spanish cook's secret weapon, adding a deep, smoky-sweet note to sauces, stews, and numerous other dishes. The peppers have been dried, concentrating their flavor, so that when they are reconstituted, an intensely flavored layer of flesh lies waiting to be scraped from the skin.

NARRU, SAN SEBASTIÁN

✦

Narru opened in 2007 in an unremarkable location in the Gros neighborhood, before the quarter had experienced its culinary and touristic boom in the mid-2010s. Chef Iñigo Peña chose the moniker of his first restaurant in homage to his great-grandfather, a jai alai player turned restaurateur. As is to be expected from a graduate of the city's top restaurants (Arzak, Mugaritz, Martín Berasategui), Narru was a standout spot for pintxos from the start. The basement level of the bar held a restaurant whose menu was designed to attract locals, achieving that sought-after trinity of fantastic raw material, subtle technique, and affordability. In 2011, Iñigo moved Narru to the Hotel Niza, where it enjoyed the same setup—a pintxo bar upstairs (with gorgeous sea views of La Concha Bay) and a dining room downstairs (larger and more vibe-y than before). Narru flourished in the hotel, a boutique spot owned by family of famed Basque sculptor Eduardo Chillida.

   Iñigo's culinary philosophy has always sat well with the donostiarras—great product is a given, seasonality determines the menu, and overly modern techniques are eschewed in favor of classic ones that allow the flavor of the ingredients to shine through. In 2020, Iñigo made a final move to the ground floor of Arbaso Hotel, in the colonnades in front of the Buen Pastor Cathedral, cementing his spot in the city's culinary culture with a prime, always-packed location.

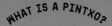

WHAT IS A PINTXO?

"Supposedly a pintxo is something
you eat with your hands in two bites,
but the poteo part is important, going
from one spot to another, eating and
drinking along the way."

—IÑIGO PEÑA, NARRU

Vieira Asada Sobre Ajoblanco

GRILLED SCALLOP WITH AJOBLANCO

An unexpected combination of sweet scallop, creamy almond ajoblanco, and a lovely bitter coffee vinaigrette, this pintxo is an homage to chef Pablo Loureiro's Galician roots and a constant on the chalkboard of Casa Urola, on San Sebastián's Fermín Calbetón street.

Ajoblanco, which serves as a base for the scallops, is a staple of southern Spain, a cool and creamy white soup redolent of garlic, almonds, and olive oil. Here the garnish of almonds, pistachios, toasted nori, and a drizzle of espresso vinaigrette gives the pintxo a star quality, yet the preparation is not as complicated as it may seem and is fantastic even prepared in a home kitchen. It is a prime example of a fine dining–level dish, with its luxe ingredients and careful technique, democratized in small-bite size. While this pintxo does have many components, all of them can be prepared ahead of time, leaving the scallops to be seared and the pintxos assembled just before serving.

MAKES 6

1 garlic clove

1 cup plus 1 tablespoon (255 ml) sunflower or other neutral oil

2 sweet onions, such as Vidalia, cut into julienne

1 sweet Italian green pepper, such as Cubanelle, cut into julienne

Kosher salt

3½ tablespoons olive oil

1 slice rustic white bread

1 cup (100 g) raw almonds

Sherry vinegar

1 cup (240 ml) water

1 tablespoon espresso, brewed

Freshly ground white pepper

6 large sea scallops

¼ cup (25 g) shelled pistachios, toasted and chopped

¼ cup (25 g) slivered almonds, toasted

Toasted nori with sesame for garnish

Bring a small pot of water to a boil. Drop the garlic clove into the water and blanch for 1 minute, then remove it and rinse it under cool water. Repeat twice more, then pat dry and reserve.

In a large skillet, heat 2 tablespoons of the sunflower oil over medium-high heat. Add the onions, green pepper, and a pinch of salt, reduce the heat to medium, and cook, stirring occasionally, for 30 to 40 minutes, until the vegetables are caramelized and deep golden. Remove from the heat.

Meanwhile, in a medium skillet, heat 1 tablespoon of the olive oil over high heat. Add the slice of bread and cook, turning once, until golden on both sides. Remove from the heat.

Preheat the oven to 350°F (175°C).

For the ajoblanco, combine the raw almonds, blanched garlic, fried bread, a drizzle of sherry vinegar, the water, and ¾ cup (180 ml) of the sunflower oil in a food processor or blender and process until a very smooth cream forms. Add 1 tablespoon olive oil and process until incorporated. Pass the mixture through a fine-mesh sieve into a bowl and reserve.

In a small bowl, whisk together the espresso and the remaining 3 tablespoons of the sunflower oil. Season with salt and white pepper.

CONTINUED →

Season the scallops with salt and white pepper. In a large sauté pan, heat the remaining 1½ tablespoons olive oil over high heat until hot. Add the scallops and sear for about 2 minutes, until golden, then turn and cook for another minute.

Transfer the scallops to a baking sheet, sprinkle them with a bit more white pepper, and slide them into the oven to finish cooking, about 2 minutes (you want them to still be juicy).

Place some of the warm onion-pepper mixture in the bottom of each of six small bowls. Top each with a scallop. Ladle a generous amount of ajoblanco around each scallop, drizzle with the espresso vinaigrette, and sprinkle with toasted pistachios, toasted almonds, and flaked pieces of nori. Serve immediately.

CASA UROLA, SAN SEBASTIÁN

The bar-restaurant Urola, named for the geographical region that encompasses the coast from neighboring Orio to Zumaia, opened its doors in 1956, serving the people of San Sebastián from its central Old Town location for years. One day, a young cook named Pablo Loureiro and budding lawyer Begoña Arenas had their first dinner date at one of its tables. Decades later, in 2012, this same couple, married by that time, and with extensive kitchen experience under Pablo's belt, took over Urola. Coming from the restaurant Branka, a fine-dining spot adjacent to the Real Club de Tenis, Pablo initially focused more on the restaurant, but it didn't take long for the couple to realize that their location would demand equal attention to pintxos.

One of Urola's trademarks is its seasonal pintxos, which feature everything from ephemeral spring vegetables to seasonal seafood. Pablo's creative process can vary, with some pintxos taking just a day to conceive and others that take years before they finally feel "right." His main criteria is that his kitchen be able to prepare the pintxo day in and day out at the same level, even during busy weekend services. The upstairs restaurant, one of the best in the city, makes it possible for the pintxo bar to serve seasonal products in regular rotation, which in 2012 was virtually unheard of. It also means the ingredients used are top quality, the same ones that appear on the white tablecloths upstairs. Pablo won the prestigious Premio Euskadi de Gastronomía award as best restaurateur in 2019.

Mini Sartén de Huevo, Foie y Hongos

EGG, FOIE GRAS, AND PORCINI IN A PAN

This pintxo starts off simply enough—a bed of potato puree crowned with an egg yolk is placed under the broiler until the egg is slightly cooked. The still-runny yolk is then topped with two luxurious ingredients—porcini mushrooms and foie gras—and when you eat it, the yolk breaks and creates a gorgeously silky sauce. For the generous chunk of foie, you can use high-quality foie mi-cuit or bloc de foie gras. A drizzle of a red wine caramel and a sprinkling of chopped chives finish off this showstopper. Served in a miniature saucepan, the pintxo is incredibly rich and would make a great entrée for a multicourse meal.

MAKES 6

Kosher salt

4 medium potatoes, preferably Kennebec, Yukon Gold, or Monalisa

⅓ cup (80 ml) extra-virgin olive oil

1 garlic clove, sliced

1 rosemary branch

1 thyme sprig

1 pound 3 ounces (540 g) porcini mushrooms, chopped (see Note)

1 cup (200 g) plus ¼ teaspoon sugar

1 cup (240 ml) red wine

¾ cup (180 ml) whole milk, warmed

2 tablespoons unsalted butter

Freshly ground black pepper

4 ounces (113 g) foie gras mi-cuit or bloc de foie gras

6 large egg yolks

Flaky sea salt for garnish

Chopped fresh chives for garnish

SPECIAL EQUIPMENT

6 ovenproof miniature saucepans or 10-ounce (300 ml) ramekins

Bring a pot of water to a boil and add a generous pinch of salt. Add the potatoes and cook for 30 to 40 minutes, until they are tender and a knife inserted into the middle of one slides in easily. Drain and allow to cool.

In a large sauté pan, heat the olive oil over high heat and add the garlic, rosemary, and thyme. When they start to sizzle and the garlic has started to color lightly, remove the rosemary, add the mushrooms, ¼ teaspoon salt, and the ¼ teaspoon sugar, and reduce the heat to low—the oil should be just simmering. Cook, stirring occasionally, for 20 to 30 minutes, until the mushrooms are beginning to brown.

Meanwhile, combine the red wine and the remaining 1 cup (200 g) sugar in a small saucepan and bring to a boil over high heat. Lower the heat to medium so the liquid is simmering actively, and simmer until the mixture has reduced to the consistency of a syrup, 20 to 22 minutes. Remove from the heat.

Peel the boiled potatoes. Transfer half of them to a food processor or a tall narrow container, if you're using an immersion blender, add the warm milk, and process until all the milk is incorporated and the mixture is smooth. Add the remaining potatoes and process until incorporated and smooth, then add the butter, ¾ teaspoon salt, and a pinch of pepper and blend again. Taste for seasoning and keep warm.

Preheat the broiler. Slice the foie gras into 6 thin circles or half circles, depending on the shape of your foie.

Arrange six ovenproof miniature saucepans or 10-ounce (300 ml) ramekins on a broiler pan or baking sheet. Scoop

You can use frozen porcini mushrooms in this recipe (which is what La Viña del Ensanche does when they don't have fresh ones!). Just add the mushrooms straight from the freezer to the pan of olive oil.

a couple heaping spoonfuls of the potato puree into each vessel. Tuck a spoonful of mushrooms into the center of each portion of potatoes and slide an egg yolk onto the mushrooms.

Place the pans under the broiler for 1 to 2 minutes, until the egg yolks are warmed through and beginning to set. Remove from the heat.

Place a piece of foie next to each yolk and sprinkle with flaky sea salt. Drizzle with the red wine caramel and sprinkle generously with chives. Serve immediately.

BEHIND THE BAR
LA VIÑA DEL ENSANCHE, BILBAO

Bars don't get much more classic than La Viña del Ensanche. It all began when Bautista, Emilio, and Ramiro Gonzalez, three brothers from Léon, moved to Bilbao after a five-year stint as waiters in Cuba. Together they opened a food shop on Calle Diputación, but after a fight, the business landed solely in the hands of Bautista. In 1927, he turned the store into a bar that served ham and wine, including mistela, a fortified wine made by adding alcohol to unfermented grape must.

In those days, the bar's location was practically in the countryside, and a nearby farmhouse with a handsome plantation of vines was the inspiration for its name. Bautista married a Navarran woman, Flora, and she began to work in the kitchen while he ran the bar. There is a record from 1958 of the bar selling seven thousand legs of jamón ibérico that year (seventy-three on Christmas Eve alone!)—the bar was a leader in sales of jamón for all of Spain.

In 1965, Bautista rented out La Viña del Ensanche so he could pursue a career in construction. When Bautista passed away, his son José Ramón inherited the bar, which was going through a rough patch, and he decided to begin running it in 1980. José Ramón took the bar back to its roots, *poco y bueno* ("quality over quantity"), focusing on ham and conservas, canned seafood, and vegetables. In 1993, Juan, Mónica, and Elena, the third generation, took over, adding hot pintxos to the menu. Spanish ham remains the specialty—their pan con tomate is a spectacular light toast spread with tomatoey salmorejo and topped with exquisite ham. The bar still uses Joselito ham, widely recognized as one of the world's best, as they have since the very beginning. The interior of the bar is nearly the same as it was over a half century ago, and the clients who return day after day are also much unchanged. However, this generation has expanded the business, opening both a restaurant-slash-workshop area with an open kitchen and a corner delicatessen, a return to their roots.

Ravioli de Rabo

OXTAIL RAVIOLI

Soft wonton wrappers envelop tender stewed meat and sautéed vegetables for a take on ravioli. The savory bite is set atop a silky-smooth cream made of roasted garlic and béchamel, before being enveloped in the rich braising liquid.

Oxtail, or rabo, is in the same camp as short ribs, beef cheek, and other sinewy, gelatinous cuts of beef—it must be braised or stewed and coaxed into softness. In this dish, the oxtail is braised, as is traditional in Spanish cuisine, but it is also enriched with aromatic herbs. Much of the dish can be prepared in advance, making it a great option for dinner parties—the bites are small enough to serve a few to a plate as part of a sit-down meal. This recipe makes a good number of ravioli, but any that you do not use immediately will freeze perfectly.

MAKES ABOUT 24

2 carrots
2 leeks
2 onions
¼ cup plus 3 tablespoons (110 ml) olive oil
One whole head garlic, plus 2 cloves, peeled
3 thyme sprigs
1 bay leaf
5 parsley sprigs
1 rosemary branch
Kosher salt
1 small oxtail (about 2 pounds/900 g), cut into pieces
Freshly ground black pepper
1½ cups (360 ml) red wine
4 cups (960 ml) beef broth
2¼ cups (540 ml) whole milk, warmed
4 tablespoons (56 g) unsalted butter
2 tablespoons all-purpose flour
1 tablespoon cornstarch
2 tablespoons cold water
1 small red bell pepper, finely diced
2 tablespoons heavy cream
24 wonton wrappers
Toasted sesame seeds (optional)
Parsley Oil (page 82) for drizzling (optional)

Preheat the oven to 275°F (135°C).

Roughly chop 1 carrot, 1½ leeks, and 1½ onions.

In a large Dutch oven or other heavy ovenproof pot (large enough to hold the pieces of oxtail without crowding), heat 2 tablespoons of the olive oil over medium-high heat. Add the chopped vegetables, the 2 garlic cloves, the thyme, bay leaf, parsley, rosemary, and a pinch of salt and cook until the vegetables are golden and tender, 15 to 20 minutes.

Meanwhile, in a large sauté pan, heat 1 tablespoon of the olive oil over high heat. Season the oxtails with salt and pepper on each side, add to the pan, and cook, turning as necessary, until browned all over, 2 to 3 minutes per side. Transfer the oxtails to the pot of vegetables.

Lower the heat beneath the sauté pan to medium, add the red wine, and stir, scraping up any browned bits from the bottom of the pan, then simmer for a few minutes.

Add the reduced wine to the pot of vegetables and oxtails, along with the beef broth, raise the heat to high, and bring to a boil. Lower the heat and simmer for 5 to 10 minutes to reduce the liquid a bit.

CONTINUED →

WHAT IS A PINTXO?

"For me, a pintxo is something that I can grab off a bar without asking, eat in a couple of bites, have a beer or wine along with it, and then leave."

—PAUL ARRILLAGA, ZAZPI

Cover the pot, transfer to the oven, and cook for 3 to 4 hours, until the oxtails are tender and falling off the bone. Remove from the oven and let cool. Raise the oven temperature to 350°F (175°C). Remove the oxtails from the liquid and set aside in a bowl. Strain the braising liquid into a saucepan and skim off the fat (you should have about 2 cups/480 ml).

Pick the oxtail meat from the bones, removing and discarding all the bones and cartilage, and set aside.

To make the garlic cream, cut the top off the garlic head to expose the cloves. Drizzle with 2 tablespoons of the olive oil and wrap tightly in aluminum foil. Roast for 40 minutes, or until the cloves have turned golden brown. Remove from the oven and let cool enough that you can handle it. Squeeze the pulp of the roasted garlic into a bowl and discard the skins. Add 1 tablespoon of the warm milk and whisk until smooth.

In a medium saucepan, melt the butter over medium-high heat. Stir in the flour and cook, stirring, until the mixture colors a bit. Gradually add the remaining milk, whisking constantly, and then simmer until the béchamel thickens. Remove from the heat and let cool a bit.

Add the roasted garlic mixture to the béchamel and mix well with a whisk or immersion blender. Season with salt and pepper to taste.

In a small cup, mix the cornstarch with the water to form a slurry. Warm the reserved braising liquid, whisk in the slurry, and simmer for about 5 minutes, until the liquid has thickened. Remove from the heat and set aside.

Finely chop the remaining carrot, ½ leek, and ½ onion. In a large sauté pan, heat the remaining 2 tablespoons olive oil over medium-high heat. Add the carrot, leek, onion, and red bell pepper, along with a pinch of salt, and sauté until translucent and tender.

Add the reserved oxtail meat and 1 cup (240 ml) of the reserved braising liquid to the pan and bring to a simmer. Add the cream, bring to a simmer, and cook for about 5 minutes to thicken the sauce. Taste for seasoning and adjust if necessary. Transfer the oxtail mixture to a small baking pan, cover, and let cool completely in the refrigerator.

Bring a large pot of water to a boil. Working in batches, add the wonton wrappers to the boiling water and cook for about 1 minute. Remove with a slotted spoon and lay the cooked wrappers out on a clean work surface.

Place a generous spoonful of the oxtail mixture in one corner of a wonton wrapper. Fold the corner over the mixture and roll the wonton over once so that the corner is now on the bottom. Fold the two sides over and roll up, burrito-style, into a packet. Repeat with the remaining wrappers and filling.

When ready to serve, arrange the ravioli on a plate or in a bowl, and microwave on high for about 30 seconds. Alternatively, arrange the ravioli in a steamer basket or in a perforated double-boiler insert and steam, covered, over boiling water for 3 minutes. (Any ravioli you will not be serving now can be frozen; see Notes.)

Meanwhile, rewarm the remaining braising liquid.

To serve, place a heaping spoonful of the garlic cream in each small serving bowl. Place a ravioli atop the garlic cream. Spoon a generous amount of the braising liquid over the ravioli. Sprinkle with sesame seeds and drizzle with parsley oil, if desired. Serve immediately.

BEHIND THE BAR
Zazpi, San Sebastián

Paul Arrillaga and his partner, Maite Múgica, opened their doors on Calle San Marcial in the Centro neighborhood of San Sebastián in 2014. It didn't take long for Zazpi to go from a small team of five to eighteen employees to become one of the best pintxo bars in the city.

Paul began his cooking career in 2005, working in prestigious kitchens across the city, including Mirador de Ulia and Bokado, and under Michelin-starred chef Oscar García in Mallorca. When he opened his own place, he knew exactly what kind of food he wanted to serve: homey, traditional dishes executed with technical perfection and a sophisticated touch. Zazpi's chalkboards featured a mouthwatering list of hot pintxos: oxtail ravioli, salt cod served in tripe stew (a crowd favorite!), pig's ear stewed to perfection, and an oxtail–foie gras dish, to name just a few. The bar was named winner of the Gipuzkoa pintxo championship two years in a row, in 2016 and 2017, and took third place in the prestigious Basque Country–wide championship in 2017.

In 2021, Paul and Maite left their location in the Centro and moved into the culinary space of the Museo San Telmo in San Sebastián's Parte Vieja. Although the new Zazpi is more of a traditional restaurant, some of the modern pintxo classics are still on the menu.

Piquillo Parrillero

PIQUILLO FROM THE GRILL

Stuffed piquillo peppers have graced pintxo bars since the early days, filled with the likes of meat, tuna salad, or salt cod with béchamel. None, however, are quite like this version from Xarma, a distillation of the very essence of the piquillo into a gorgeous plated pintxo. Whole piquillos are stuffed with a puree of confited piquillos thickened with a little xanthan gum.

Piquillo peppers are most often sold roasted and jarred (or canned). The inspiration for the plating of this pintxo comes from the traditional roasting process—the pepper sits on crunchy black "ashes," an almond meal crumble tinted with squid ink, next to lumps of "coal," which are chunks of yuca also tinted with squid ink. At Xarma, they stuff fresh piquillos. However, these are quite difficult to source—even in Spain, they are available for only a brief window in the warmer months. This recipe uses large canned or jarred piquillos, and the pintxo still tastes amazing.

MAKES 8

1 cup (240 ml) sunflower oil

6 garlic cloves, peeled

1 pound 2 ounces (510 g) jarred or canned piquillo peppers (about 20; see Notes)

1½ teaspoons water

Kosher salt

Pinch of sugar

½ teaspoon xanthan gum (see Resources, page 302)

1 tablespoon plus ⅔ teaspoon squid ink

3½ ounces (100 g) yuca, peeled and chopped into 1-inch (2.5 cm) pieces

¾ cup (93 g) all-purpose flour

¾ cup (93 g) almond meal

5 tablespoons (70 g) unsalted butter, chilled

2½ ounces (70 g) cooked beets, chopped (about ½ cup)

Flaky sea salt

SPECIAL EQUIPMENT

A pastry bag fitted with a large plain tip or a ziplock bag

In a large sauté pan, combine the sunflower oil and garlic and heat over medium-high heat until the garlic turns a golden color. Remove it with a slotted spoon and discard.

Add the peppers to the pan, reduce the heat to medium, and cook slowly for 10 minutes. Reduce the heat so that the oil is just barely bubbling, flip the peppers, and cook for about 5 minutes more, or until they begin to soften. Remove from the heat.

Remove 8 of the peppers and reserve them for stuffing. In a food processor or in a tall narrow container using an immersion blender, puree the remaining peppers with the water, a pinch of kosher salt, the sugar, and 2 tablespoons of the cooking oil for a few minutes, until the mixture is emulsified and smooth. Pass the mixture through a fine-mesh sieve or a strainer into a bowl. Taste and adjust the seasoning.

Add the xanthan gum to the pepper puree and process or blend well. The puree should be creamy but with some body. Transfer the puree to a pastry bag fitted with a large plain tip or a ziplock bag (if using a ziplock bag, snip off one of the bottom corners just before piping out the puree). Set aside.

CONTINUED →

Any neutral oil can be used in place of the sunflower oil.

If you have access to fresh piquillos, you can use them here. Toss the peppers with olive oil and spread out on a foil-lined baking sheet. Roast in a 400°F (200°C) oven for about 5 minutes, turning them halfway through. Remove from the oven and carefully fold the foil over the peppers. Set aside to steam for about 10 minutes, then carefully open the foil. Peel the peppers, leaving the stems on. They are ready to stuff.

The recipe yields about 1½ cups (180 g) of beet "soil," which means you will have more than you need. It can be used for other dishes or frozen for later use.

In a small saucepan, bring 1 cup (240 ml) water and 1 tablespoon of the squid ink to a boil. Add the yuca, reduce the heat to maintain a simmer, and cook for 18 to 20 minutes, until the yuca is tender. Be sure to watch the yuca toward the end of cooking, as it can stick to the pan; add a bit of water if the yuca is sticking and not yet cooked through. When the yuca is fully cooked, remove from the heat and set aside.

Preheat the oven to 350°F (175°C). Line a baking sheet with parchment paper or a silicone baking mat.

In the food processor, pulse the flour, almond meal, and butter together. Add the beets and the remaining ⅔ teaspoon squid ink and pulse until the mixture is evenly tinted black and homogeneous.

Spread the squid ink dough out on the prepared pan and bake for 30 minutes, or until the middle looks cooked through. Remove from the oven and allow the dough to cool completely.

Break the baked dough into pieces and pulse in the food processor until it looks like loose soil.

Preheat the broiler.

Using the pastry bag or ziplock bag, fill the piquillo peppers with the pepper puree. Place the peppers on a baking sheet along with 16 pieces of yuca "coal." Slide the baking sheet under the broiler and broil until the peppers are heated through.

Spread a bit of the "soil" over eight small plates. Place the peppers on top and arrange 2 pieces of the yuca "coal" next to each pepper. Sprinkle the peppers with flaky sea salt and serve.

Xarma Cook & Culture, San Sebastián

✦

Before Xarma was a hip pintxo bar a block away from Zurriola Beach, it was a somewhat staid fine-dining restaurant tucked away at the back of the Antiguo neighborhood. Aizpea Oihaneder and Xavier Díez met behind the stoves at Arzak in 1996, two young cooks on their way up in the culinary world. They fell for each other, and from that point on, they continued their training together at other top restaurants across Europe. In 2008, they returned to San Sebastián to open the first Xarma, where they crystallized their experience in haute cuisine, combining it with their passion for local products and a youthful style.

They had a nearly ten-year run at the first Xarma, cooking together every day—through their separation, various recessions, and San Sebastián's changing landscape. Then, in 2017, they found the perfect location for their next venture—a former smoking club on one of the best blocks in the vivacious, bustling neighborhood of Gros. They closed Xarma restaurant and opened Xarma Cook & Culture, letting their hair down and incorporating their passion for pop culture and rock-and-roll into their cooking. The entrance opens onto a street-level bar, with good music, vibe-y lighting, and a pintxo-lined counter featuring their modern twists on old favorites, including the piquillo parrillero and the Gilda maki, a deconstructed Gilda turned sushi. Downstairs is a cool, clubby restaurant with an open kitchen, where the menu also displays their deep culinary knowledge but in a more informal, distilled way.

DESSERT

CHAPTER EIGHT

PINTXOS

Pintxos started as an aperitif to a full meal, a savory bite to whet the appetite. They were never meant to be sweet, so it's no wonder that the very definition of what constitutes a pintxo slipped into ambiguity when dessert pintxos entered the scene. The cheesecake from La Viña (page 288) has arguably become the world's most famous dessert pintxo, yet the idea of designating nothing more than a slice of cheesecake on a plate as a pintxo would make San Sebastián's earlier generations of pintxo pioneers roll over in their graves.

Sweet pintxos are a relatively recent phenomenon, dating back to the turn of the twenty-first century. But the dessert pintxo was a natural by-product of the creation of savory kitchen pintxos. When "miniature cuisine" and bite-size entrées entered the scene, diners gained the ability to create a tasting menu of tiny bites by hopping from bar to bar the entire night, without ever sitting down at a restaurant. It stands to reason, then, that some of the first sweet pintxos on record were served at La Cuchara de San Telmo (see page 251), the innovative bar behind the popularization of the kitchen pintxo. Not long after La Cuchara opened in 1999, the owners saw that after downing foie gras, pig's ear, and octopus, people wanted to finish with something sweet. Their first offering was a chocolate ganache with confit oranges, and it kicked off a wave of dessert pintxos across the city, mostly at the more avant-garde pintxo bars like A Fuego Negro (see page 157) and Atari (see page 297). A Fuego Negro opened in 2006 with a pineapple brioche pintxo, served with coconut ice cream and rosemary essence. One of Atari's classic sweet pintxos, around since the beginning, is the Limón Cuadrado (page 294).

To understand dessert pintxos, it is essential to view them as the ultimate evolution of a food that slowly became a form of dining. To enjoy them, however, is far, far easier. A night of small bites (or a party) is perfectly ended with a thin slice of rich cheesecake or a sweet, crunchy Torrija (page 293). The Mini Polo (page 299) is an example of a more experimental sweet pintxo, meant to wow as well as finish a meal.

Tarta de Queso

LA VIÑA CHEESECAKE

In recent years, the popularity of this cheesecake has become something of a phenomenon. With more than 200,000 tags on Instagram to date and a shocking array of variations, #BasqueBurntCheesecake has gone viral from its perch on San Sebastián's Calle 31 de Agosto. So, what's all the fuss about? The cheesecake is a Basque adaptation of traditional cheesecake, falling somewhere between a New York cheesecake and a flan. What might be seen as the cake's flaws become its virtues: Cooked at too high a temperature, the parts of the cake in contact with the pan brown into a natural crust and the top caramelizes in places, and all the while, the interior remains jiggly and loose. Basque cheesecake, in all its rough simplicity, is a product of the small, crowded pintxo bar kitchen where it was born. You can garnish the cake, of course, but the most authentic way to serve it is in thin slices on small dessert plates.

SERVES 12

1¾ cups (350 g) sugar
2¼ pounds (1 kg) cream cheese, at room temperature
¼ teaspoon kosher salt
5 large eggs
2 cups (480 ml) heavy cream
¼ cup (30 g) all-purpose flour

Preheat the oven to 400°F (200°C). Grease a 10-inch (25 cm) springform pan and line it with parchment paper, leaving a 2- to 3-inch (5 to 7.5 cm) overhang. (You can cut a circle to fit the base and then cut a band of paper to fit around the sides, but the more rustic method is to press an entire sheet of parchment into the pan, pleating the paper where it begins to crease.)

In a large bowl using a handheld mixer, or in the bowl of a stand mixer fitted with the paddle attachment, cream the sugar and cream cheese until smooth. (This can be done by hand as well—beat with a wooden spoon for about 5 minutes.) Beat in the salt and mix well. Add the eggs one by one, mixing until fully incorporated after each addition. Whisk or mix in the cream. Sift the flour over the top of the mixture (remove the mixer bowl from the stand, if using) and fold it in gently.

Pour the batter into the prepared pan and bake for 45 to 50 minutes, or until browned and almost burnt-looking on top; the center should still be very jiggly. Ovens vary, so keep your eye on the cheesecake beginning at the 30-minute mark. Remove from the oven and allow to cool.

When ready to serve, remove the springform ring and gently tug away the parchment paper from the sides. The cake can sit out overnight with no problem, but it should be refrigerated after a day. Cut into thin slices and serve.

LA VIÑA, SAN SEBASTIÁN

✦

La Viña, founded by Eladio Rivera, his brother Antonio, and their wives, Carmen Jiménez and Conchi Hernáez, respectively, opened its doors in 1959. In the early days, wine was the big seller at La Viña—money was tight everywhere, and the txikiteros (pub crawlers) were the regulars, making their drinking rounds before lunch and dinner. The bar and restaurant served the most traditional of dishes, like fish soup, hake, and salt cod. In 1987, Antonio and Conchi left the business in the hands of Eladio, Carmen, and their son, Santi, who was by that time working in the bar. Santi was also a passionate self-taught cook, and on the days the restaurant was closed, he would head into the empty kitchen and do all kinds of tests, spurred by advice from his chef friends and the occasional cooking course. He brought a 100 percent donostiarra sensibility—having been born and raised in the old part of the city and spent his life soaking up local culinary tradition—that formed the base on which La Viña's new phase was built.

One of his recipe tests became La Viña's cheesecake; Santi places it around 1988, although he says it wasn't a fixture on the menu until 1990. He attributes its success to its simplicity, along with—what else?—the internet. By 1997, Eladio and Carmen had retired and left the bar in Santi's hands. His original creations are the pintxos you'll still find on the bar at La Viña, from the cheesecake to the anchovy-and-cheese-stuffed cone, a pintxo that won the coveted Premio a la Originalidad prize in the 1999 Gipuzkoa pintxo contest.

THE FINAL FRONTIER
OF THE PINTXO

Dessert pintxos were made possible when pintxos became miniature versions of entrées instead of more of an afterthought to accompany a drink or a prelude to a meal. Their evolution took pintxos where pintxos had never been before—sweet tooth territory. They have been the object of ridicule by pintxo purists, but also a vehicle for innovation for the most open-minded pintxo chefs, like Edorta Lamo, Joxean Calvo, Marc Clua, Alex Montiel, and Iñaki Gulín. Their fantastical creations helped lend legitimacy to this expression of the pintxo, but there is still plenty of room for a developing collection of sweet pintxos.

Torrija

CARAMELIZED CUSTARD BREAD

Torrija is a sweeter, richer Spanish take on French toast. This recipe is for the version that has come to dominate bars and restaurants in Basque Country, made with rich, buttery brioche soaked in a bath of flavor-infused full-fat milk and cream.

The big, blocky slices of bread make for a beautiful presentation. Once soaked, the slices are cooked in a hot pan, seared on all four sides, and sometimes finished with a layer of sugar caramelized with a kitchen torch (see Note). The result is a crispy exterior that hides a warm, creamy interior. This pintxo is perfect served with a scoop of ice cream alongside.

MAKES 6

1 cup (240 ml) heavy cream
1 cup (240 ml) whole milk
¾ cup plus 2 tablespoons (175 g) sugar
1 cinnamon stick
½ loaf brioche or white bread (about 7 ounces/200 g), a few days old
6 tablespoons (85 g) unsalted butter

In a medium saucepan, combine the cream, milk, ½ cup (100 g) of the sugar, and the cinnamon stick and heat over medium-high heat, stirring to dissolve the sugar, until steaming. Remove from the heat and let cool to room temperature.

Strain the milk mixture through a sieve into a bowl; discard the cinnamon stick.

Cut the bread into 6 rectangular bars, about 4 inches (10 cm) long, 2 inches (5 cm) high, and 2 inches (5 cm) wide (the exact length may be determined by the size of the loaf). Place the bread pieces on a rimmed baking sheet, pour the milk mixture evenly over them, and let soak for about 10 minutes.

In a large sauté pan, combine 2 tablespoons of the butter and the 2 tablespoons sugar and heat over medium-high heat until the butter has melted. While that mixture is heating, remove 2 pieces of bread from the milk mixture and set on a layer of paper towels to drain.

Add the 2 pieces of bread to the pan and cook for 1 minute before flipping them 90 degrees. Cook for a minute on that side, then flip 90 degrees again. The sugar and butter mixture should be beginning to caramelize. Flip again and, after another minute, flip over to the last side and cook for about 30 seconds. Swirl the pan around to distribute the caramelized sugar-butter mixture and flip the bread pieces once more, so the most presentable side is down. Cook for 1 minute. Very gently remove the bread with a spatula and set on a serving plate, with the best side up.

Repeat with the remaining bread in batches of two, using 2 tablespoons of the remaining butter and 2 tablespoons of the remaining sugar for each batch. Serve immediately.

NOTE

To finish the bread with a kitchen torch: Working in batches as directed, melt only the butter in the pan, no sugar. Cook the bread as directed, then remove from the pan, sprinkle the three visible sides of the bread with sugar, and run the flame of a kitchen torch back and forth over it until the sugar melts and then caramelizes, similar to crème brûlée. The caramelized sugar will cool into a crunchy coating.

Limón Cuadrado

LEMON SQUARED

Limoia Ber Bi, as it appears on the menu at Atari (see page 297), is a study in textures and contrasts. A lemon curd sits atop a crunchy, buttery crumble, crowned by an ice cream made with a base of the same lemon cream, packing a super-citrusy punch. Don't be put off by the number of steps and components—they come together quite easily, and all of them can be made ahead of time.

Garnish the pintxo with grated lime zest, as they do at Atari. Atari also happens to make one of the city's best gin-tonics, Spanish-style: served in a fishbowl glass, with huge ice cubes, a generous pour of gin, and a glass bottle of Schweppes—the ideal pairing for this lovely, bright dessert.

MAKES 6

1 cup (240 ml) fresh lemon juice (from 4 to 5 lemons)
1¾ cups (350 g) granulated sugar
6 large eggs, beaten
12 tablespoons (1½ sticks/170 g) unsalted butter, diced and chilled, plus 7 tablespoons (100 g), diced and chilled separately
1⅓ cups (166 g) all-purpose flour
2 cups (480 ml) heavy cream
½ cup (60 g) confectioners' sugar
1 teaspoon xanthan gum (see Resources, page 302)
Grated lime zest for garnish

SPECIAL EQUIPMENT

Ice cream maker

> **NOTE**
>
> You will probably have extra ice cream and crumble. The two go great together as a snack.

In a medium saucepan, whisk together the lemon juice and 1¼ cups (250 g) of the granulated sugar. Place the pan over high heat and cook, stirring, until the sugar is dissolved. Gradually add the eggs, whisking continuously. When you see the first bubble, indicating that the mixture will come to a boil soon, reduce the heat to low and cook, stirring with a silicone spatula all the while, until the mixture begins to thicken.

Whisk in the 12 tablespoons (170 g) butter little by little. Cook, whisking, until the mixture thickens enough to coat the back of a spoon, 5 to 8 minutes. Remove from the heat.

Strain the mixture through a fine-mesh sieve into a bowl or other container. Cover immediately with plastic wrap pressed directly against the surface. Refrigerate until completely chilled. (It can be refrigerated, tightly covered, for up to 1 week.)

Preheat the oven to 400°F (200°C). Line a baking sheet with parchment paper or a silicone baking mat.

Combine the flour and the remaining ½ cup (100 g) granulated sugar in a food processor. Add the remaining 7 tablespoons (100 g) butter and pulse until it is fully incorporated and the mixture begins to come together.

Spread the mixture out evenly on the prepared baking sheet. Bake until lightly golden around the edges, 10 to 15 minutes, stirring once halfway through. Remove from the oven and let cool completely.

CONTINUED →

Break up the mixture into crumbs and small pieces. (The crumble can be made up to 5 days ahead and stored in an airtight container at room temperature.)

In a large bowl using a handheld mixer, or in the bowl of a stand mixer fitted with the whisk attachment, whip the cream to soft peaks. Fold in the confectioners' sugar.

Transfer 1⅔ cups (410 g) of the lemon mixture to a medium bowl. Stir in the xanthan gum until well incorporated. Fold this into the sweetened whipped cream, mixing well.

Pour the ice cream mixture into an ice cream maker and freeze according to the manufacturer's instructions. Transfer to a freezer container and freeze until ready to serve. (The ice cream can be frozen for up to 1 week.)

To plate, put some of the crumble in the base of six miniature bowls. Add some of the remaining lemon mixture and top each with a scoop of the ice cream. Garnish with grated lime zest and serve.

WHAT IS A PINTXO?

"The purists say it's two bites, and that it has to have a support such as a piece of bread or a toothpick. But everything evolves."

—PABLO LOUREIRO, CASA UROLA

ATARI GASTROLEKU, SAN SEBASTIÁN

✦

Atari Gastroleku opened in February 2010 on what could quite possibly be the best location in the Old Town of San Sebastián: right in the shadows of the Basílica de Santa María del Coro at the corner of Calle 31 de Agosto and Calle Mayor. Atari was a bar the likes of which San Sebastián had never seen, with touches of tradition—in the familiar wood, chalkboard menus, and life-size black-and-white photos of country folk that greet you in the bathroom—given a modern air with things like soft lighting and pleasing music to match the time of day. This new twist on a pintxo bar was the idea of Asier Arriola and his business partner, Anders Denne, the latter having moved to San Sebastián from Sweden around the year 2000.

Asier had grown up in his family's bar and restaurant (which also served as a barbershop!) in Mendaro. His career has long been linked to tourism—at one point in the late 1990s, he even opened a museum dedicated to artisan crafts, Museo Laia, in Zumaia. A love and appreciation for the local culture drove Atari's vision in its early days, summed up in its slogan, *No existe modernidad sin una buena tradición* ("Modernity cannot exist without tradition").

The renovation of the space, formerly a beloved *marisquería* (seafood spot) and before that a restaurant that was founded in the 1920s, coincided with that of the basilica, and many of the wooden beams in Atari were originally part of Santa María del Coro. Atari innovated in so many ways—serving vegetarian pintxos, for example, and using microgreens and colorful produce in cold pintxos; the partners even attempted to open a barbershop within the bar (it never came to be, due to zoning restrictions). The bar was an immediate success, and Asier and Anders eventually formed Gastroleku, a dining group that grew to include other similar concepts: Sirimiri, the little brother of Atari; Txalupa, a clubbier version with a basement restaurant; and other locations, including a cider house and a nightclub. The idea of a restaurant group that used centralized kitchens for production was also quite innovative for San Sebastián, and now the partners have also expanded into the hotel business, opening a hotel right above Atari in 2022.

Mini Polo

MINI ICE POP

The cuteness factor of this pintxo is off the charts. *Polos*, or ice pops, are the ubiquitous premium industrial frozen dessert offering in Spain, and this pintxo riffs on their familiar shape with a totally gourmet and artisan twist. A tiny ice pop mold is filled with a mixture of cream and Idiazabal cheese that has been melted into a smooth cream and folded, semifreddo-style, into whipped cream. The frozen pops are bathed in white chocolate and sprinkled with dried raspberries—a delicious, showstopping dessert.

MAKES 8

1 cup (240 ml) heavy cream

5 ounces (140 g) Idiazabal cheese, grated

7 ounces (200 g) white chocolate, chopped

2 tablespoons cocoa butter drops (see Note)

2 tablespoons roughly chopped freeze-dried raspberries

Black olive powder (optional)

SPECIAL EQUIPMENT

8 mini silicone ice pop molds with wooden sticks

NOTE

The cocoa butter drops used in this recipe are to be used at 10 to 15 percent of the weight of the white chocolate. If using a different type of cocoa butter or a cocoa butter powder, follow the manufacturer's instructions regarding proportions.

Prepare a hot-water bath by setting a heatproof bowl over a saucepan of simmering water, or use a double boiler. Add ½ cup (120 ml) of the cream and the cheese to the bowl or the top of the double boiler and stir gently, being careful not to let them scorch, until the mixture is smooth and creamy, a minute or two. Remove from the heat and allow to cool completely.

In a large bowl using a handheld mixer, or in the bowl of a stand mixer fitted with the whisk attachment, beat the remaining ½ cup (120 ml) cream to stiff peaks. Carefully fold the whipped cream into the cooled cheese mixture.

Place the sticks in the ice pop mold and fill just to the top with the cream mixture. Transfer to the freezer and freeze until completely solid, at least 12 hours or up to overnight.

Melt the white chocolate in a heatproof bowl set over a saucepan of simmering water or in the top of a double boiler, stirring occasionally. Alternatively, you can heat the chocolate in the microwave in 15-second bursts, stirring after each burst, until most of the chocolate is melted.

When the white chocolate is almost completely melted, remove from the heat, stir in the cocoa butter drops, and let stand, stirring occasionally, until the cocoa butter has melted; the mixture will look slightly grainy. Return to the hot-water bath once or twice if necessary to melt the cocoa butter drops fully. Then stir the mixture well; the chocolate should look smooth and not at all grainy, and the temperature should be around 87°F (29.5°C).

CONTINUED →

"Most important is that a pintxo taste good, that it have one main ingredient and a couple that accompany it, and that altogether it is delicious."

—JORGE MARTÍNEZ, SABURDI

Unmold the frozen cheese pops. One by one, coat them in the melted white chocolate, rotating to coat all sides, and then, before the chocolate has fully set, decorate with a sprinkling of raspberry pieces and, if using, a dash of olive powder, and set on a baking sheet. Transfer to the refrigerator and let set completely.

The coated pops can be refrigerated for up to 6 hours before serving. You can also make them further ahead and keep them frozen until you are ready to use them. Allow them to defrost overnight in the refrigerator to prevent condensation from forming on the pops.

BEHIND THE BAR

SABURDI, VITORIA

Jorge Martínez de Aramayona and Óscar Abajo took over Saburdi in 1998, leaving jobs at nearby pintxo bar Usokari to set out on their own. From the beginning, Saburdi had one of Vitoria's most illustrious bartops, filled with a visually striking array of cold pintxos, complemented by a selection of hot pintxos that was one of the city's most exciting, consistently winning awards for taste and creativity. The Mini Polo pintxo was created for the X Semana del Pintxo de Álava 2012, the region's tenth annual pintxo competition. One of the cooks at Saburdi proposed a pintxo featuring Idiazabal, and the idea of the ice cream pop was born. It took third place in the contest, but, tellingly, it is still served at the bar today. In April 2020, the partners renovated the bar, leaving the traditional wood and stone walls but transforming it from a dimly lit tunnel of a bar into a light-filled place to eat. The regulars and the award-winning pintxos, however, haven't changed a bit.

ABOVE La Espiga, San Sebastián

Resources

DELICIAS DE ESPAÑA

tiendadelicias.com

DESPAÑA

despanabrandfoods.com

EURO FOOD DEPOT

eurofooddepot.com

- Warqa (brick dough)

SPANISH TABLE

spanishtable.com

LITTLE SPAIN

littlespain.com/shop

MARIANA FOODS

marianafoods.us

HOT PAELLA

hotpaella.com

LA TIENDA

tienda.com

- Soft almond turrón
- Membrillo

DOS OLIVOS MARKETS

dosolivosmarkets.com

- Alegria Riojana peppers

LA COCINA DE SENÉN

lacocinadesenen.com

LA ESPAÑOLA MEATS

laespanolameats.com

- Jarred choricero puree

GOURMET FOOD STORE

gourmetfoodstore.com

- Bloc de foie
- Duck confit

AMAZON

amazon.com

- Cocoa butter drops
- Guérande gray salt
- Xanthan gum

MADE IN SPAIN

madeinspain.store

Further Reading

Asociación de Hostelería de Hondarribia.
Pintxos 2019. Ulzama (2019).

Azpeitia Salvador, J. *Famous Pintxos of Donostia–
San Sebastián*. Ttarttalo Argitaletxea (2016).

Azpeitia Salvador, J. *La Senda del Pintxo*, 2nd ed.
Zum Edizioak (2014).

Elizondo, J. R. *Aloña: Solo Pintxos* (2007).

Fernandez Beobide, J. J., L. Horcajo Calixto, and C. Blasco
Olaetxea. *Comercios Donostiarras 1813–2013:
Historias de Cafés y Cafeterías,* vol. 4 (2013).

Garcia Amiano, P. *A Donostia de Pinchos*, 3rd ed. (2000).

Garcia Amiano, P. *Donosti y Sus Pinchos*.
R&B Ediciones (1995).

Garcia Amiano, P. *La Alta Cocina Vasca en Miniatura* (2003).

Martín Villa, Pedro. *Donosti Pintxo a Pintxo*.
Ttarttalo Argitaletxea (1996).

Martín Villa, Pedro. *Pintxos Donostiarras*. Lur Argitaletxea
(1992).

Serrano, A., and J. M. Ansa. *Pintxos: Bocados de Placer*.
Alai Argitaletxea (2019).

acknowledgments

THIS BOOK IS, IN AND OF ITSELF, an acknowledgment and a heartfelt symbol of gratitude for all the people who have been a part of this culinary tradition. Good, hardworking people make up its core, and the way they consistently value family, tradition, and culture over everything else is what makes the Basques so special. I am thankful to be a part of it.

At the top of this list is the team that helped bring this book to life: Artisan, for giving me a second go-round; Judy Pray, for her patience with me through a pandemic and the birth of my new baby; Simon Bajada, for his amazing photography and his company; Sonia Tapia, for the food styling and for offering up her wonderful Frontón for our photo session; and Ana Villar, for doing the best job propping! I couldn't have done it without you.

A very special thanks to Josema Azpeitia—there are very few people as knowledgeable and as passionate as he is about pintxos and Basque cuisine. *Eskerrik asko*, Josema, for your constant insights, your connections, and for being so selfless. I highly recommend all of his books, which capture the living memory of Donostia's culinary scene (and have been translated into several languages).

It is nearly impossible to name everyone, but thank you to all who sat with me for interviews, opened doors, shared their wisdom—and fed me pintxos (some of you for more than a decade, for which I am especially grateful): Manu from Txepetxa; Humberto and Ramón at Antonio Bar; Pablo and Begoña at Casa Urola; Ander González at Astelena; Edorta Lamo; the legends Patxi and Blanca from Bergara, and Monty and Esteban as well; Mikel at Bar Martínez;

Enrique, Carmen, Sonia, and Mikel of Toloño; Asier of Atari; Alex from La Cuchara de San Telmo; Jesús (and Txema, Luma, and Koro) at La Espiga; Yosune Menéndez and Txus from Erkiaga; Nestor, Esther, and family at Bar Eme; José María at Baste; Mikel and Joserra of Café Bar Bilbao; Iván Siles and family at Gure Toki; the Ganbara family; Marian and Yoli at Irrintzi; Jésus Mari, Pruden, Alicia, and Roberto at Bar Gaucho; Josean of PerretxiCo; Arancha and Javier at Bar Fitero; Gaizka of Café Iruña; Maren Iturburu of Iturriza; Iñaki at Sorginzulo; Raul of Bar Chelsy; Chris, aka Garbancita; Mikel from Gran Sol; Marc and Lucía of Borda Berri; Santi at La Viña; Javi from Urkabe; Paco and Gorka at Paco Bueno; Joseba from Ezkurra; Juan Mari and Nubia from Hidalgo 56; Jesús and Nerea at Ábaco; Aizpea and Xabi of Xarma; Oihane of Gandarias; Iñigo Peña of Narru; Mitxel Ezquiaga; José Carlos Capel; Xabier Agulló; Peio Garcia; Paul at Zazpi; Juan Gonzalez, Mónica, and Elena from La Viña del Ensanche; Nagore at Casa Vallés; Vano at El Tulipán del Oro; Senén of Sagartoki; Clara, Carlos, and Maite from Hostería del Temple; Aitziber Pollos; Joxean Calvo; Mónica and Luis of El Globo; Iñigo of El Rincón de Luis Mari; Alberto at Bar Charly; Miguel from Bodega Donostiarra; the Santamaría family; Osane Redondo; Pablo Vicari; Tote González de Heredia; Rubén González; Pepe Barrena; Jon Mikel Fiestras; Iban Lopetegi Beltran and Agustín Lopetegi Albeniz; Juan Manuel Garmendia; the Instituto del Pintxo; the Cofradía Vasca de Gastronomía; Nacho Calvo; Piluka Unzu; and the Asociación de Hostelería de Navarra.

On a more personal note, I have to thank my family and friends, without whom life would lose all meaning: Mom, Dad, Katharine, Bryan, Danny, and Grandmaw, I love y'all! Maite, thanks again for your Euskara expertise and lasting friendship. Thanks to Xabier de la Maza, Ane Fano, Aitor Buendia, Lesli, Randy, Chesko, and Majo for going the extra mile so many times. Thanks to Celia Tejada for being an endless source of fun and inspiration, and for housing me through part of this process at the incredible Molino Tejada. Thanks to my friends who witnessed the last three years, for keeping me sane, tasting pintxos, and answering random queries at even more random hours: Naike, Eider, Katerina, Leire, Teresa, Alex, Camille, Cait, Xabier, Nacho, Dani, Sergio, Julian, Katie, Gorka, Ion, Federica, Iñigo, Beñat, Brittany, Todd, Dan, and David. And to my friends who saw it from afar but were still there for me: Stef, Bekah, Emily, Jen, Katie, Louise, Kirby, Hannah, and Kari Beth. Thanks to God for all of you and for this simply amazing life.

Last but most definitely not least, to Buckley and Lima . . . all of this is for you, my baby girls.

Index

About the Author

MARTI BUCKLEY is the author of *Basque Country* (Artisan, 2018), winner of the IACP International category and of Best Publication from the Academía Vasca de Gastronomía. She is passionate about all things Spain, France, and Basque Country, and her work has appeared in *Food & Wine*, *Travel + Leisure*, *The Telegraph*, *National Geographic*, and *Wine Enthusiast*, among other publications. She coauthored the *Wallpaper* City Guide Bilbao/San Sebastián*. She lives with her two daughters in San Sebastián, Spain, which she has called home since 2010.

Marti believes that sharing good food and drink can change the world, something she learned when she first lived in Spain in 2005 that then became a way of life when she cooked professionally under chef Frank Stitt. She continues to do her part as cofounder of the International Society for the Preservation & Enjoyment of Vermouth, as well as through regular appearances on television and radio. Her blog, travelcookeat.com, is where she writes about food and drink in Spain. Follow her on Instagram at @martibuckley.